ROADSTER GUIDE TO AMERICA'S
CLASSIC CAR MUSEUMS & ATTRACTIONS

Also by Michael Milne
Philadelphia Liberty Trail: Trace the Path of America's Heritage
(written with Larissa Milne)

Roadster Guide to America's Classic Car Museums & Attractions

FIRST EDITION

MICHAEL MILNE

CHANGES IN LONGITUDE PRESS
WWW.CHANGESINLONGITUDE.COM

ISBN 978-0-9975333-0-9

For Larissa, my navigator on road trips and in life,
and
my parents, for loaning me the car keys.

CONTENTS

Introduction

Note: This book focuses on car and truck museums that are open to the public with regular operating hours. Private collections are not included. Museums that are members of the National Association of Automobile Museums are noted with NAAM in their listing. Further information about this group is available at www.naam.museum.

Throughout the book you'll find "Side Trips" that are automotive related attractions of interest. There are also selected "Pit Stops" to grab a bite to eat, all that driving makes me hungry!

Admission Fees

Museum prices change and are often offered in several different categories. For convenience, the following price ranges indicate what a typical adult ticket costs. Note that many museums offer free pricing for young children and discounts for students, seniors, veterans and AAA members.

Regular Adult Admission

Free
$ $1-9
$$ $10-19
$$$ $20-29
$$$$ $30+

Every attempt is made to keep the information up to date. If you find something that's changed, or an attraction that you feel should be included in the next edition, please contact me at

Michael@ChangesInLongitude.com.

INTRODUCTION

I love cars of all eras and constantly seek out museums and attractions that showcase them wherever I travel. But I couldn't find a current, in-depth guide to them. I already write about car museums and road trips for the *Philadelphia Inquirer, Hemmings Motor News,* and other publications, so I created this guide.

Along with my (very patient) wife Larissa, I spent two years criss-crossing the United States on an epic road trip, seeking out the best collections that are also open to the public. The result is this comprehensive guide that presents over 225 auto-themed museums and sights from all across America, featuring every era and field of automotive history.

The destinations covered here range from full-throttle collections, like the NASCAR Hall of Fame and the Henry Ford Museum, to hidden treasures like the Pontiac-Oakland Museum in Illinois and the National Sprint Car Hall of Fame in Iowa.

The guide also includes sights like the Dale Trail in "The Intimidator's" North Carolina hometown, as well as "car-iosities" such as Cadillac Ranch in Texas and Carhenge in Nebraska … which are as wonderfully quirky as they sound.

Whatever your specialty, be it Model Ts, elegant roadsters of the 1920s, the "tail fin" era, muscle cars, or racecars, fans of classic and vintage cars will find all their favorites here. Bring this book along on your next road trip to discover fascinating car museums and attractions across America.

Now it's time to hit the road!

Michael Milne

1

NEW ENGLAND

As the birthplace of America's Industrial Revolution, it's not surprising that New England boasts a strong automotive history. The Duryea brothers, Frank and Charles, are credited with creating the first successful gasoline-powered car in America in Springfield, Massachusetts in 1893. The **Wood Museum of Springfield History** pays tribute to them.

Another set of brothers, twins Francis and Freelan Stanley, inventors of the Stanley Steamer, are honored at the **Stanley Museum** in Kingfield, Maine. In Maine and Massachusetts several auto museums are open seasonally, making them timely destinations for summer travelers.

A trip to Vermont showcases the **Hemmings Vehicle Display** in Bennington, home of *Hemmings Motor News,* the "Bible of the Collector Car Hobby."

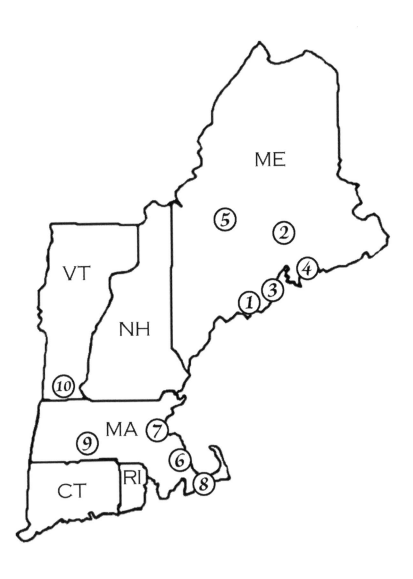

NEW ENGLAND

MAINE

    1) Boothbay Railway Village

    2) Cole Land Transportation Museum

    3) Owls Head Transportation Museum

    4) Seal Cove Auto Museum

    5) Stanley Museum

MASSACHUSETTS

    6) Heritage Museums and Gardens

    7) Larz Anderson Auto Museum

    8) Toad Hall Classic Sports Car Museum

    9) Wood Museum of Springfield History

VERMONT

    10) Hemmings Vehicle Display

MAINE

Boothbay Railway Village
Boothbay, ME

Despite its name, there are more than 60 vintage cars from 1902 through 1962 on display at the Boothbay Railway Village. The museum's goal is to preserve and demonstrate railroad history, vintage automobiles and rural life in Maine between 1850 and 1950.

One of the coolest-looking cars is a **1935 Swallow SS-1 Tourer**. This sporty British vehicle looks like it's going 80 mph when it's sitting still. Of the 78 built, this is one of only seven survivors. As sleek as the Swallow is, it may be better known for its name change: The next year it became a Jaguar, a marque that blazed a trail in British automotive history. After admiring the automobiles, walk around the recreated historical village and ride on a steam-powered train.

Number of vehicles: 60+

Highlights: 1910 Brush Runabout; 1929 Packard Custom 8 Limousine (with built-in intercom to communicate with the chauffeur); 1930 Franklin 147 Dietrich Speedster; 1940 Cadillac Limousine owned by Thomas Edison's widow; Cushman Truckster Hot Dog Wagon.

Location: 586 Wiscasset Road, Route 27, Boothbay, ME 04537

Admission: $

Hours: Open seasonally from Memorial Day through the third Sunday in October; daily, 10 a.m. to 5 p.m.

Phone: (207) 633-4727   **Web:** www.RailwayVillage.org

COLE LAND TRANSPORTATION MUSEUM
Bangor, ME

The Cole Land Transportation Museum presents a wide range of options for going mobile in Maine. Given the northern clime, snowplows are well represented, as are tractors and farm equipment, motorcycles and bicycles, horse-drawn carriages, sleds, and Ahrens-Fox and Mack fire engines. The collection includes a series of vintage Maine license plates from 1905 to the 1950s and racing chariots, along with a **1970 black Cadillac hearse, 1949 Chrysler New Yorker, 1960 Ford Fairlane, 1972 Chrysler Imperial** (museum founder Galen Cole's personal car) and a **King Midget** (tiny car). Long wooden benches throughout the museum were salvaged from the grand old Bangor train station. In keeping with the railway theme, visitors can stroll through an original caboose from the Maine Central Railroad. NAAM member.

Number of vehicles: 150+

Highlights: 1923 Packard Roadster; 1979 Olds 98, a former governor's car with 5.7-liter diesel engine; traveling dentist chair.

Location: 405 Perry Road, Bangor, ME 04401

Admission: $

Hours: Open seasonally May 1 through November 11; daily, 9 a.m. to 5 p.m.

Phone: (207) 990-3600

Web: www.ColeMuseum.org

Michael Schumacher's Ferrari F2002.
(Photo credit Owls Head Transportation Museum)

For car buffs who also like vintage aircraft, this is the place to go. More than 50 automobiles from the late 19th century through 1980 are on display, along with another 100 aircraft, motorcycles, bicycles and carriages.

With its focus on Maine, the museum features several **Stanley Steamers** built by Maine natives (and twins) Francis and Freelan Stanley. Seek out the **1923 Cretors Popcorn Wagon;** the red-and-white awning looks as if it was plucked straight from a carnival. It's based on a **1922 Ford Model T** and was used to roast and sell popcorn to tourists.

The collection also includes early aircraft, such as a 1917 Curtiss JN-4D Jenny, bicycles, engines and motorcycles. Among the latter are a **1919 Harley-Davidson Model J** and a **1931 Henderson.** Check their website for car shows throughout the spring, summer and fall. NAAM member.

Number of vehicles: 50+ (plus 100 aircraft, motorcycles, bicycles, carriages and more)

Highlights: 1958 BMW Isetta 300 ("The Rolling Egg"); 1898 Leon Bollee Tri-Car; 1914 Rolls-Royce Limousine; 1926 Ford Snowmobile.

Location: 117 Museum Street, Owls Head, ME 04854. Two miles off of U.S. Route 1, about 85 miles north of Portland.

Admission: $$ **Hours:** Daily, 10 a.m. to 5 p.m.

Phone: (207) 594-4418   **Web:** OwlsHead.org

Seal Cove Auto Museum
Mount Desert Island, ME

The Seal Cove Auto Museum highlights autos and motorcycles from the Brass Era (1895-1917). It was an exciting and experimental time in New England, when anyone with a mechanical bent could repair – or even build – an automobile.

The gleaming assemblage is based upon the collection of auto enthusiast Richard Paine and includes such rarities as a **1904 Searchmont,** a **1915 F.R.P.** (one of only nine produced) and a Maine-built **1900 Skene.** The **1908 Stanley Steamer Model K Semi-Racer** may be the most valuable Stanley in the world: It's one of only three survivors of 25 that were built and the only one that's still in its original condition.

A scavenger hunt for kids keeps them engaged during a visit. A wide range of events throughout the spring, summer and fall include the opportunity to ride in one of the vintage cars and fun end-of-season Halloween activities. NAAM member.

Number of vehicles: 50+

Highlights: Four Stanley Steamers, including a rare 1908 Model K Semi-Racer and a 1914 Mountain Wagon; 1904 Ford Model A; 1911 American Victoria Underslung.

Location: 1414 Tremont Road, Seal Cove, ME 04674. Three hours' drive north of Portland and convenient for visitors to nearby Acadia National Park.

Admission: $ **Hours:** Open seasonally May 1 through October 31; daily, 10 a.m. to 5 p.m.

Phone: (207) 244-9242   **Web:** www.SealCoveAutoMuseum.org

STANLEY MUSEUM
Kingfield, ME

This museum celebrates the work of two local boys made good – twins Francis and Freelan Stanley, the inventors of the revolutionary car known as the Stanley Steamer. Located in the 1903 Stanley School (named after the creative brothers), the building was almost razed in the 1970s. In its day the Stanley set several land speed records, completing a mile in 28.2 seconds in 1906. That's the equivalent of 127 miles per hour! Three Stanleys from 1905, 1910 and 1916 are usually on display.

Francis died in a car crash during a drive in the country at age 69, while Freeland went on to develop the Stanley Hotel in Estes Park, Colorado. (See separate listing.) Horror fans know it as the setting for the terrifying novel *The Shining*, written by fellow state-of-Mainer Stephen King. The Stanley Twins' sister, Chansonetta, was a renowned photographer and much of her work recording local everyday life is also on display. An annual consignment auction includes Stanley Steamers and hard-to-find parts.

Number of vehicles: 3

Highlights: Stanley Steamers; violins built by the brothers and their nephew Carlton; vintage photography equipment.

Location: 40 School Street, Kingfield, ME 04947. Kingfield is about a two-hour drive north of Portland.

Admission: $

Hours: June through October: Tuesday to Sunday, 1 p.m. to 4 p.m.; November through May: Tuesday to Friday, 1 p.m. to 4 p.m. or by appointment.

Phone: (207) 265-2729

Web: www.StanleyMuseum.org

Note: If you're planning an overnight stay to visit the museum, consider the Three Stanley Avenue Bed & Breakfast. It's the former home of Bayard Stanley, the youngest brother of the car-building twins. For more information go to www.StanleyAvenue.com.

MASSACHUSETTS

HERITAGE MUSEUMS & GARDENS
Sandwich, MA

This large attraction includes sweeping gardens, galleries showcasing American folk art, a vintage carousel and, somewhat incongruously, a display of collectible automobiles. In keeping with the museum's New England setting, the automotive collection is housed in a replica of a Shaker Round Barn.

The car collection ranges in age from the early days of the industry to about 1960. While it is smaller than some car museums, the focus is on keeping the cars in pristine condition.

Number of vehicles: 20+

Highlights: 1909 White Steam Car that was in the fleet of President William Howard Taft; 1922 Rolls-Royce made in Springfield, MA; actor Gary Cooper's 1930 Duesenberg; 1930 Cadillac V-16 Convertible Coupe. There are monthly behind-the-scenes tours to view more vehicles in the collection.

Location: 67 Grove Street, Sandwich, MA 02563. (Located at the base of Cape Cod, known as the "Upper Cape," just north of Route 6.)

Admission: $$

Hours: Mid-April through mid-October; daily, 10 a.m. to 5 p.m. *Note:* The opening and closing dates vary, so check the website for further details.

Phone: (508) 888-3300   **Web:** HeritageMuseumsAndGardens.org/Exhibitions/Automobile-Gallery

LARZ ANDERSON AUTO MUSEUM
Brookline, MA

Larz Anderson first started collecting cars more than 85 years ago. Appropriately enough, the museum is housed in a former carriage house that belonged to Larz and his wife, Isabel. In 1927 the Andersons began a tradition of welcoming the public into the carriage house on Sundays to view their growing collection. The sights included their first purchase, an **1899 Winton Phaeton,** that is still on display. Today visitors can come six days a week to see 18 mostly Brass Era vehicles, 14 of which were originally owned by the Andersons. A **1905 English Electromobile** demonstrates how in motoring's early days, it wasn't a forgone conclusion that gasoline-powered engines would become dominant. An ungainly-looking **1924 Renault Torpedo** was Larz Anderson's car of choice when he drove himself.

   A **1926 Lincoln Seven** reveals why "suicide doors" were invented: to prevent passengers from catching their expensive clothing on exposed door hinges. In that vein, women's fashions of the era are displayed on artfully arranged mannequins. NAAM member.

Number of vehicles: 16

Highlights: 1901 Winton Bullet, the first production racecar for sale to the public; 1905 Electromobile; 1903 Gardner-Serpollet, the only one of these rare French steam-powered vehicles in America.

Location: 15 Newton Street, Brookline, MA 02445. It's about 30 minutes southwest of downtown Boston.

Admission: $$ **Hours:** Tuesday through Sunday, 10 a.m. to 4 p.m.

Phone: (617) 522-6547   **Web:** www.LarzAnderson.org

TOAD HALL CLASSIC SPORTS CAR MUSEUM
Hyannis Port, MA

All the vehicles at Toad Hall are red, so it's not surprising that the focus here is on sports cars. The bulk of them are British, with a few Japanese and European marques added to the mix. Plan on seeing a dozen Lotuses; half-a-dozen MGs, Triumphs and Jaguars; and a slew of cars from Austin Healey, TVR, Datsun, Ferrari, Mazda, Morgan, AC, Sunbeam, Mini, Porsche and other makers.

The MG collection ranges from a **1951 MG TD Midget** to a **1974 MG Midget MK IV.** A **1964 Datsun 1500** demonstrates the influence of British car designers on post-war Japanese automakers. More recent vintages include a **2000 Lotus Exige 190 Coupe.** One of six sold in America, it's the only red one, so naturally it ended up here.

The museum is affiliated with the Simmons Homestead Inn, a circa-1800 bed-and-breakfast once owned by a sea captain. The autos belong to Bill Putman, who is known as the "Innkeeper of Sorts" at the B&B. The inn's official car is a **1967 Bentley Salon Type T** that is used to pick up guests from the local airport – incentive enough to stay there.

Number of vehicles: 50+

Highlights: 1953 Jaguar XK-120 FH Coupe; 1958 MGA Roadster; 1960 Lotus Elite.

Location: 288 Scudder Avenue, Hyannis Port, MA 02647

Admission: $

Hours: Daily, 11 a.m. to 5 p.m.

Phone: (508) 778-4934   **Web:** www.ToadHallCars.com

The 1899 Knox three-wheeler on the right was steered by a tiller.

This comprehensive local history museum hosts a compact but important collection of early American automobiles and motorcycles. Early car companies associated with Springfield were Duryea, Stevens-Duryea, Knox and Atlas. This automotive pedigree made Springfield a natural choice for Rolls-Royce to open their American plant in the 1920s to meet growing demand.

An exhibit is devoted to Frank Duryea, who with his brother Charles is credited with producing the first successful gasoline-powered automobile in America; he drove the pioneering vehicle on the streets of Springfield back in 1893. An **1893 Duryea** replica is on display, along with a **1903 Stevens-Duryea Model L Stanhope**, the oldest in existence. The locally built **1928 Rolls-**

Royce Phantom I is a one-owner car; M. Allen Swift purchased it new and kept it until he stopped driving 77 years later.

The gallery also includes more than two dozen motorcycles that were once housed in the Indian Motorcycle Museum, which closed its doors in 2006. Springfield-built Indian motorcycles on display include a rare **1945 Indian Chief with Commercial Sidecar Box** and a **1951 Indian Chief with Sidecar**. Indian also made a brief foray into car production; their **1928 Indian X4 Experimental Roadster** on display is one of only four that they built. The Smith & Wesson Gallery of Firearms History highlights arms manufacturing in Springfield dating to the American Revolution. NAAM member.

Number of vehicles: 12+

Highlights: 1899 Knox three-wheeler; 1925 Rolls-Royce Silver Ghost Piccadilly Roadster (owned by the co-founder of Friendly's Ice Cream).

Location: 21 Edwards Street, Springfield, MA 01103

Admission: $$ Includes admission to: Wood Museum of Springfield History, Springfield Science Museum, George Walter Vincent Smith Art Museum and the Michelle & Donald D'Amour Museum of Fine Arts.

Hours: Tuesday through Saturday, 10 a.m. to 5 p.m.; Sunday, 11 a.m. to 5 p.m.

Phone: (800) 625-7738

Web: www.SpringfieldMuseums.org/the_museums/springfield_history

VERMONT

Vintage oil cans highlight the petroliana collection at Hemmings.

Hemmings Motor News is widely considered "the Bible of the Collector Car Hobby." Founded by Ernest Hemmings in Iowa in 1954, it moved to Bennington after a Vermont businessman purchased it. Today a collection of 25 cars and trucks is on display in the same building as the Hemming world headquarters, where they also publish several other auto-themed magazines.

What makes the collection unique are the restored pickup trucks that have been used over the decades to deliver Hemmings publications to newsstands. The **1936 Dodge Panel Delivery Truck** has won several awards. The **1937 Hudson Terraplane**

Delivery Sedan is a rare vehicle that may be the last survivor of these streamlined Art Moderne beauties in delivery mode.

Vintage motor oil cans, license plates and various auto memorabilia are also on display. At the old-time Sunoco station out front, attendants will even clean your windows and check your oil; a reminder of why these used to be called "service" stations. You also have to like a place where the restrooms are marked DIESEL and ETHYL.

Number of vehicles: 25

Highlights: 1908 Maxwell LC Runabout in unrestored condition; 1934 Brewster Town Car; 1934 Dodge Panel Truck, which competed in the 2005 Great Race.

Location: 222 Main Street, Bennington, VT 05201. (In the southwest corner of Vermont, 35 miles northeast of Albany, NY, and 50 miles east of the **Saratoga Automobile Museum** in Saratoga Springs, NY.)

Admission: Free

Hours: May: Saturday and Sunday, 10 a.m. to 3 p.m.; June 1 thru October 31: daily, 10 a.m. to 3 p.m. November 1 through April 30: closed, with tours by appointment only and subject to availability. Closed: Memorial Day, Independence Day and Labor Day. The Sunoco Station and gift shop are open year-round.

Phone: (802) 447-9580

Web: www.Hemmings.com/aboutus/tour

Hemmings is located in Vermont, which is not the state that first comes to mind when you think about automobile production. However, in the nearby **Bennington Museum** you'll see among its local artifacts what was considered a prestigious car in its day, a **1924 Martin Wasp Touring Car.** Produced in Vermont by Karl Martin, this is the last of the 16 Wasps that were built. The Martin family's automotive legacy lives on in an unexpected way – Martin's father Truman purchased America's first car insurance policy in 1898. This regional art and history museum also features a section devoted to famous folk artist Grandma Moses.

Bennington Museum, 75 Main Street, Bennington, VT 05201 (802) 447-1571

www.BenningtonMuseum.org.

(**Note:** Closed in January.)

2

MID-ATLANTIC

The Mid-Atlantic boasts a proud automotive history, much of it centered around upstate New York and southeastern Pennsylvania. The town of Fleetwood, Pennsylvania gave its name to a classic Cadillac model. The 1909 Fleetwood Auto Bodies factory there still stands. Nearby, the **Boyertown Museum of Historic Vehicles** focus on locally built autos.

Truck lovers are not left out at the **Mack Trucks Historical Museum** in Allentown, Pennsylvania. The central part of the state is nirvana for Tucker seekers; five can be seen in one day at the **Antique Automobile Club of America** in Hershey and the **William E. Swigart Jr. Auto Museum** in Huntingdon.

Offerings in upstate New York range from the **Buffalo Transportation Pierce-Arrow Museum** in Buffalo, the hometown of the "Car of the Presidents," to the **Northeast Classic Car Museum** in Norwich, which features Syracuse-built Franklins.

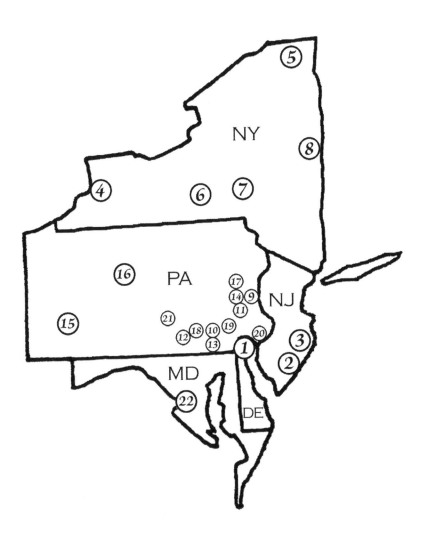

MID-ATLANTIC

DELAWARE

   1) Marshall Steam Museum

NEW JERSEY

   2) Studebaker dealership

   3) Vintage Automobile Museum of New Jersey

NEW YORK

   4) Buffalo Transportation Pierce-Arrow Museum

   5) Champlain Valley Transportation Museum

   6) International Motor Racing Research Center

   7) Northeast Classic Car Museum

   8) Saratoga Automobile Museum

PENNSYLVANIA

   9) America on Wheels
     Mack Trucks Historical Museum

   10) Antique Automobile Club of America Museum
      Museum of Bus Transportation

11) Boyertown Museum of Historic Vehicles

12) Carlisle Nationals

13) Eastern Museum of Motor Racing

14) Fleetwood

15) Frick Car and Carriage Museum

16) Grice Clearfield Community Museum

17) Jerry's Classic Cars and Collectibles Museum

18) Rolls-Royce Foundation and Museum

19) Seiverling Car and Pedal Car Museum

20) Simeone Foundation Automotive Museum

21) William E. Swigart, Jr. Auto Museum

WASHINGTON, DC

22) Smithsonian National Museum of American History

DELAWARE

Marshall Steam Museum
Yorklyn, DE

*The only surviving 15-passenger
1915 Stanley Mountain Wagon 820.*

The Marshall Steam Museum is one component of the Auburn Heights Preserve, a state park dedicated to Delaware's industrial history. The 1897 mansion on the property was owned by T. Clarence Marshall, a former car dealer for the Stanley Motor Carriage Company, builder of the famous Stanley Steamers. In 1940 Marshall started collecting the vehicles he once sold, and was joined by his son, Tom, in this endeavor.

The museum has the heady aroma of kerosene, which is required as a pilot fuel to generate the steam. A **1901 Mobile** is the oldest car in the collection. While not built by the Stanley Brothers, it was based on their designs. Among the impressive Stanley Steamers is a **1915 Stanley Mountain Wagon Model 820.** This 15-passenger behemoth was the largest Stanley ever built. Steam cars were not only strong hill climbers, but were also relatively fast. Tom calls them "the Corvettes of their day." The **1908 Stanley Semi-Racer Model K** reached 75 mph! Among the non-Stanley steam-powered automobiles is a **1909 White Model O** made in Cleveland.

A Stanley engine is also on display. The surprisingly small piece of equipment can be hand-cranked by visitors to see how the innovative power plant worked. Combustion engine vehicles (which the Stanleys referred to as "internal explosion") include a gloriously turned-out **1937 Packard Twelve Model 1508** that has always been in the Marshall family.

Visitors are taken for rides in the Stanleys on special "Steamin' Days." If you plan your trip for late September, be sure to catch the nearby Hagley Museum Car Show, with more than 500 cars on display.

For more information, go to: www.Hagley.org/event/hagley-car-show-home

Number of vehicles: 15+

Highlights: World's largest collection of operating steam cars, including over a dozen Stanley Steamers; 1916 Rauch & Lang Electric Car (it was driven from the backseat, with a tiller no less, so it can be considered the original "backseat driver").

Location: 3000 Creek Road, Yorklyn, DE 19736. (It's 12 miles northwest of downtown Wilmington.)

Admission: $ **Hours:** As a volunteer organization, the Marshall Steam Museum has very limited operating hours. Call to make an appointment, or look for open-to-the-public dates on their website. The first Sunday of the month from June through November, plus the Saturday after Thanksgiving, are "Steamin' Days," when visitors can take a ride in one of the steam-propelled vehicles.

There are also Open House Tour Days from April through November. Registration is required at least two days in advance. For questions, contact them via e-mail at: admin@auburnheights.org.

Phone: (302) 239-2385   **Web:** AuburnHeights.org

NEW JERSEY

Vintage Automobile Museum of New Jersey
Point Pleasant, NJ

*The compact Vintage Automobile Museum
fits in a wide range of cars.*

If you're heading to the Jersey Shore, it's hard to pass up the only car museum in the Garden State – particularly with its backstory of triumph over adversity. After years of planning and fundraising, the museum opened in September 2012; a month later they were wiped out by Hurricane Sandy. The group behind the museum, which includes the Vintage Automobile Club of Ocean County, persevered and reopened in a year.

The building is about the size of a mechanic's garage, housing about a dozen vehicles. The walls are lined with shelves stacked with car models and vintage automobilia, including old fan belts, oil cans and radiator hoses. It's that kind of a place.

There is one permanent vehicle in the rotating collection: a **1912 Mercer Type 35R Raceabout**, a New Jersey-made automobile that is as native to the Garden State as Bruce Springsteen. Mercers were built by the Roebling family, the same people responsible for the Brooklyn Bridge and other iconic structures. Other than the Mercer, the collection is changed four times a year, which encourages repeat visits. Past exhibits have been devoted to hot rods, orphan cars (makes that are no longer produced), muscle cars, and more. Car shows are also held throughout the year. The guides are all volunteers and vintage-car aficionados who have wonderful stories to share about automobile collecting. NAAM member.

Number of vehicles: 12

Highlight: 1912 Mercer Type 35R Raceabout

Location: 1800 Bay Avenue, Building 13, Point Pleasant, NJ 08742. (Turn left at the Johnson Brothers Boat Works and drive to the end of the road, where the museum shares a building with the New Jersey Museum of Boating.)

Admission: Free

Hours: Wednesday, Thursday, Friday, noon to 4 p.m.; Saturday, 10 a.m. to 4 p.m.; Sunday, noon to 4 p.m. Museum is staffed by volunteers, so hours may vary. Make sure to call ahead.

Phone: (732) 899-0012

Web: www.VintageAutoMuseum.org

Side Trip: Old Studebaker Dealership

On the East Black Horse Pike, four miles west of Atlantic City, a 1920s Mediterranean-styled building is the last remnant of a former high-end development that popped up back when Atlantic City was a thriving resort town. I just happened to be driving by when I saw the terra-cotta Studebaker signs that festoon the exterior, hinting at its former life as the **Mathis Studebaker Dealership**. It's a miracle this building has survived.

Location: North side of Route 322/40 at Toulon Avenue, Pleasantville, NJ

NEW YORK

BUFFALO TRANSPORTATION PIERCE-ARROW MUSEUM
Buffalo, NY

*The helmeted archer hood ornament
was an icon of the "Car of the Presidents."*

Buffalo boasts a long automotive tradition. It was the home of the "Car of the Presidents," the legendary Pierce-Arrow. In its heyday, this was the most prestigious auto built in America and the car of choice for occupants of the White House. Many of history's most famous car engines were also built in the Buffalo area; in fact, a plant in nearby Tonawanda still produces Corvette engines. The museum highlights many Buffalo-built vehicles, including a **1902 Buffalo Electric Stanhope** (with three separate speeds for reverse); **1909 Thomas Flyer 6-40 Flyabout; 1918 Pierce-Arrow 7-Passenger**

Touring Car; **1919 Pierce-Arrow Intercity Bus,** which moved people in comfort with air shock absorbers; **1922 Automatic Electric,** which was only built for about a year; and a very rare **1948 Playboy.** Only 97 of these kiddie-carnival sized cars were built before the company went belly-up.

The museum is unique among its peers for having a newly constructed service station designed by Frank Lloyd Wright under its roof. Due to its position on Lake Erie, in the 1920s Buffalo was one of the wealthiest cities in the country and Wright designed homes for several area benefactors. His 1927 plans for a filling station in downtown Buffalo weren't realized until 2013, when it was built inside the museum, complete with the second-floor customer's "observation room."

The museum also hosts the Women's Transportation Hall of Fame, which honors such luminaries as Alice Ramsey, who in 1901 was the first woman to drive coast-to-coast across the United States. With mannequins in period garb posing by the cars and vintage auto advertising on the walls, the museum really transports visitors back in time. The building once housed a Mack Truck dealership and showroom and is also a repository for Pierce-Arrow memorabilia and documents. NAAM member.

Number of vehicles: 30+

Highlights: 1902 Buffalo Electric Stanhope; 1903 Pierce Stanhope; 1919 Pierce-Arrow Bus.

Location: 263 Michigan Avenue, Buffalo, NY 14203

Admission: $$ **Hours:** April through December: Thursday through Sunday, 11 a.m. to 4 p.m.; January through March: Saturday and Sunday, 11 a.m. to 4 p.m.

Phone: (716) 853-0084   **Web:** www.Pierce-Arrow.com

Side Trips: Packard Motor Car Buildings

Noted architect Albert Kahn left his mark on Detroit with the design of many buildings, including Ford's massive River Rouge plant, the General Motors building, the Packard plant that now lies infamously in ruins, and hundreds of other structures. His firm's work is also seen beyond the Motor City. Three buildings he designed for Packard are still in use in Buffalo, Dayton, and Philadelphia.

A former Packard showroom in Buffalo is located at 1325 Main Street, with the Packard name still visible etched along the top of the building. In Philadelphia, you can sleep in a renovated Packard showroom and storage facility at the Packard Motor Car apartment building at 317 N. Broad Street. **America's Packard Museum** (see separate listing) in Dayton, Ohio, occupies a fully restored Packard dealership at 420 S. Ludlow Street. Each of these is a wonderful architectural legacy of the once mighty Packard brand.

CHAMPLAIN VALLEY TRANSPORTATION MUSEUM & KIDS' STATION
Plattsburgh, NY

What started out as a car museum, with historical artifacts of the Plattsburgh and northern New York State area, now also covers other forms of transportation, with a train, die-cast model cars, boats, tractors, bicycles, sleighs, airplanes, fire trucks, and more on display.

The museum highlights two locally designed autos, the **1914 Lozier Type 77 5-Passenger Touring** and **1915 Lozier Type 82 7-Passenger Touring**. In its day, the Lozier name was up there with Cadillac's reputation for quality. Although Lozier started in Plattsburgh, the company soon expanded its manufacturing operations to Detroit, where the two cars in the museum were built. Other Lozier products on view are three bicycles (one from

1878 and two from 1890), a boat manufactured in Plattsburgh, and two marine engines.

There's also an incredible collection of over 1,000 miniature vehicles, including cars, trucks, ships, farm tractors, and fire trucks. In addition, two model railroad layouts depict the Plattsburgh area. NAAM member.

Number of vehicles: 30+

Highlights: 1947 Crosley Coupe; 1960 BMW Isetta (one- cylinder microcar).

Location: 8 Museum Way, Plattsburgh, NY 12903. Plattsburgh is in far upstate New York, only 20 miles from the Canadian border.

Admission: $ **Hours:** Tuesday through Saturday, 10 a.m. to 2 p.m. (*Note:* The building is an unheated former Air Force hangar, so sometimes there are winter shutdowns. Make sure to call ahead.) Drop-in visitors are given guided tours on a first-come, first-served basis; you can also call ahead to schedule one.

Phone: (518) 566-7575

Web: www.CVTMuseum.wix.com/cvt-museum

INTERNATIONAL MOTOR RACING RESEARCH CENTER
Watkins Glen, NY

Picture a library with racing cars and auto memorabilia parked among the stacks of books, and you'll have a good idea of the International Motor Racing Research Center. It's located in the historic racing village of Watkins Glen, a world-famous racing destination since 1948, when road races first barreled through the streets of this upstate New York hamlet. The Center's mission is to preserve, archive and share the history of all forms of motorsports worldwide.

Approximately 2,500 rare reference books, hundreds of magazine and newspaper titles, racing programs, historic scrapbooks, posters, videos, trophies, and other items relating to motor racing line the shelves. You don't have to be a hardcore academic to visit this library, though; casual car fans are also welcomed and the friendly staff will go out of their way to answer your questions. A monthly series of free lectures by racing historians is also offered.

Although this isn't a museum, you will find a car or two in the library, sometimes related to the theme of the monthly lecture. In the past there have been McLaren and BRM Formula One cars, a Penske Dodge NASCAR Stock car, a 1973 Indianapolis 500 Eagle, and a 1950 Ferrari 166 MM Barchetta.

Location: 610 S. Decatur Street, Watkins Glen, NY 14891. (In the Finger Lakes region of upstate New York, about 80 miles southwest of Syracuse.) Combine a visit here with the **Northeast Classic Car Museum** in Norwich, which is about two hours east.

Admission: Free

Hours: Monday through Friday, 9 a.m. to 5 p.m. Saturday, 9 a.m. to 5 p.m. or by appointment

Phone: (607) 535-9044   **Web:** www.RacingArchives.org

Northeast Classic Car Museum
Norwich, NY

Because the museum is located in upstate New York, there is a special exhibit of cars built in the Empire State, with a strong focus on Franklins built in nearby Syracuse. There are 28 on display, running the gamut from a **1903 Franklin** to a **1934 Franklin** that was the last to leave the factory.

In addition to the Franklin exhibit, there are comprehensive displays including the Staley Collection; American Beauties; Auburn Cord Duesenberg: The Legends; the Post-War Collection; and As Found in Barns. The last one is particularly interesting and a bit unusual for a car museum. Here you'll see old cars in their unrestored state, just as they were found after hiding out in someone's barn or garage for decades. The collection is almost exclusively American-made and many are one-of-a-kind.

To keep non-car buffs occupied, mannequins dressed in period vintage clothing stand beside many of the autos. You can take your photo behind the wheel of a **1928 Ford Model T** or a **1933 Franklin Olympic**. There are also vintage gas pumps, a small exhibit of World War I and World War II aircraft engines, and a stripped Franklin chassis that shows the original wood construction used in early automobiles. NAAM member.

Number of vehicles: 160+

Highlights: 1910 Waverley Electric; 1929 Duesenberg Model J Holbrook limousine, the only survivor of a pair that were produced.

Location: 24 Rexford Street (State Route 23), Norwich, NY 13815. (In upstate New York, about a two-hour drive west of the capital, Albany. Sports fans should note that it's only an hour from the National Baseball Hall of Fame in Cooperstown.)

Admission: $$ **Hours:** Daily, 9 a.m. to 5 p.m.

Phone: (607) 334-2886

Web: www.ClassicCarMuseum.org

SARATOGA AUTOMOBILE MUSEUM
Saratoga Springs, NY

The museum occupies a unique setting in the 1934 Saratoga Bottling plant amidst the 2,500-acre Saratoga Spa State Park, where it offers a mix of ongoing and specially curated temporary exhibits. Permanent exhibits include "East of Detroit," which highlights New York's early role in the automotive industry, with over 100 manufacturers in the Empire State; "Racing in New York State," harkening back to 1896, when the first auto race took place here (drivers averaged 10 MPH); and the New York State Stock Car Hall of Fame, which displays decades of cars that revved their engines in the state. Try one of the driving simulators that enforce the dangers of distracted or impaired driving.

Special events include the popular "Cars & Coffee" road rallies that meander through the scenic Saratoga County countryside. During the peak summer tourist season there are activities almost every weekend; check the website for details. There are also many car-related, hands-on activities for children. NAAM member.

Number of vehicles: 30

Highlights: 1910 Maxwell built in Tarrytown, NY; 1931 Pierce Arrow from Buffalo, NY; 1935 Maserati known as "Poison Lil" that won at the Seneca Cup in Watkins Glen.

Location: 110 Avenue of the Pines, Saratoga Springs, NY 12866. (About 50 miles east is the **Hemmings Vehicle Display** in Bennington, VT.)

Admission: $ **Hours:** Tuesday through Sunday, 10 a.m. to 5 p.m.; open Mondays in August, 10 a.m. to 5 p.m.

Phone: (518) 587-1935   **Web:** www.SaratogaAutoMuseum.org

PENNSYLVANIA

AMERICA ON WHEELS
Allentown, PA

To appeal to a general audience, not just automotive enthusiasts, this museum focuses on presenting vehicles in the context of how they were actually used. Because it's based in Allentown, the former long-time headquarters of Mack Trucks, several antique Macks are on display in dioramas showing them in action. The rich automotive history of the local Lehigh River Valley is also highlighted, including the "first horseless carriage" built locally by Hendy Nadig in 1889.

The interactive exhibits highlight the educational component of the museum. Visitors leave knowing more about the science, engineering, and creative thinking that went into developing over-the-road transportation, as well as the effects it had on American culture. The Hubcap Cafe is reminiscent of a '50s ice cream parlor; look up at the ceiling to see how it got its name. NAAM member.

Number of vehicles: 75+ cars, trucks, motorcycles, and bicycles. Some exhibits change every six months.

Highlights: 1940 Mack ED Heavy Hauler; a 1955 Chevy Custom Kopper Kart, based on car customizer George Barris's original design.

Location: 5 N. Front Street, Allentown, PA 18102

Admission: $ **Hours:** Tuesday through Saturday, 10 a.m. to 5p.m.; Sunday, noon to 5 p.m. From January through March the museum closes at 4 p.m.

Phone: (610) 432-4200 **Web:** AmericaOnWheels.org

ANTIQUE AUTOMOBILE CLUB OF AMERICA MUSEUM
Hershey, PA

This museum is affiliated with the Antique Automobile Club of America and is a member of the Smithsonian Institution Affiliations Program. In keeping with its mission of highlighting antique cars, there are several pre-1900 autos on display, including an **1895 Chicago Benton Harbor**.

One of the museum's claims to fame is the Cammack Tucker Gallery. Opened in 2014, it contains **a trio of Tucker automobiles** – the most of any museum in the world – along with Tucker-related paraphernalia including engines, parts, and mechanical drawings. When combined with the two Tuckers on view at the **William E. Swigart Jr. Antique Automobile Museum** (see separate entry) located 105 miles west in Huntingdon, visitors to central Pennsylvania can see five Tuckers in a single day.

One of the highlights of the museum is the "Cruise Through

Time" exhibit, where cars are artfully arranged by decade from the 1890s through the 1980s, in front of giant murals depicting a cross-country road trip from New York City's Battery Park to San Francisco's Golden Gate Bridge. Cars from the '50s are parked facing a drive-in movie screen where an actual movie is playing. In another gallery, visitors can press a button in front of a working machine shop to watch the machinery grind and spin.

One of the coolest cars in the collection is a **1929 Ford Model A Roadster**. What makes it interesting is that it's a one-owner vehicle. Frank Hartmaier, who drove it his entire life, purchased it new when he was 17 years old, and the speedometer stopped working at 400,000 miles.

Celebrity and film cars abound. The museum provided period vehicles for the TV series *Boardwalk Empire,* including a **1924 REO Funeral Hearse**. You'll find that alongside Whitney Houston's **1986 Rolls-Royce Silver Spur**. Don't miss the Alphabet Ford Collection, consisting of every lettered model Ford from A through T.

Miscellaneous sections of the museum include over 300 radiator mascots; a huge, working "O" gauge model train display; and the Floinn Café, a 1940s-era roadside diner that was shipped here from Wichita, Kansas. Every year from May through October there is a special exhibit related to motorcycles.

The Antique Automobile Club of America is also the home of the **Museum of Bus Transportation**. More than a dozen buses show the development of bus transportation in America, including the **1959 GM Coach** that made an appearance in *Forrest Gump;* a **1952 Beaver** that was manufactured in Beaver Falls, Pennsylvania; and a **1951 Checker** made by the company famous for producing Checker cabs. A collection of bus ephemera including vintage schedules, toys, models, and dinnerware shows just how much the service on long-distance bus rides has declined. NAAM member.

Number of vehicles: 150+ (usually 80-100 on display) **Highlights:** Three Tucker 48 cars (models #1001, #1022 and #1026), 1925

Stearns-Knight, Hershey's Kissmobile Cruiser; 1955 Flajole 2DR Sports Coupe (a bizarre-looking custom car that never made it into full production).

Location: 161 Museum Drive, Hershey, PA 17033. Near Route 39 and Hersheypark in central Pennsylvania. If you're in the area, consider visiting the **Rolls-Royce Foundation** (see separate listing), only 30 miles west of here.

Admission: $$

Hours: Daily, 9 a.m. to 5 p.m. (open until 9 p.m. the first Thursday of each month)

Phone: (717) 566-7100   **Web:** www.AACAMuseum.org

Side Trip: Put the Pedal to the Metal

The **Seiverling Car and Pedal Car Museum** in Ephrata, PA offers over 140 pedal cars from around the world; some of them have full suspensions and one even has a transmission. A few have been shown at regional *Concours d'Elegance* events. There are also three full-sized vintage cars: a **1930 Graham Sedan, 1932 Chrysler CP Cabriolet,** and **1967 Ford T5** (the name the Mustang was sold under in Germany). The museum is open by appointment only (evenings and weekends) and select open house Sundays from March through November. To schedule a visit, call them at (717) 431-7257. Ephrata is 45 minutes east of Hershey and the **Antique Automobile Club of America Museum**. More information at www.PedalCarMuseum.com.

Museum of Bus Transportation
Hershey, PA

Remember the days of service like this on a bus? Me neither.

(Housed in the **Antique Automobile Club of America Museum** in Hershey. See the prior listing for more information, or go to www. BusMuseum.org.)

*You can almost hear the Mister Softee jingle
and taste the cherry topping.*

Founded in 1965, this extensive collection includes gasoline-, steam-, and electric-propelled vehicles as well as toy cars, carriages, and sleighs. The main exhibit area occupies the former Boyertown Auto Body Works, where truck bodies were built from 1926 through 1990. A few of these trucks have returned home and are now on display. The focus is on Pennsylvania-built cars, reflecting the Keystone State's importance in the early development of the automobile.

The **1872 Hill** is one of the earliest autos in existence. Teenager James Hill built it in **Fleetwood, Pennsylvania.** (See following sidebar for more information about Fleetwood's influence on the auto world.) Ironically, the first model was too weak to climb hills. The **1913 SGV Touring Car,** built just west of here in Reading, featured a push-button transmission. Six Duryeas built nearby are on display, including a **1917 Duryea GEM Roadster,** a hybrid of a motorcycle and a car.

Note the joysticks for steering on the Duryeas. The stubborn Charles Duryea didn't like steering wheels and was late to the game in using them. The extensive bicycle collection highlights how many car companies grew from bicycle manufacturers; there are two Acme bicycles and an Acme car from the same company.

One of my favorite vehicles is a **1958 Ford Mister Softee Ice Cream Truck** just like the one that blared the ubiquitous theme song around my neighborhood when I was a kid; they were all manufactured in this building. (If you miss that cloying song, you can download it as a ringtone at www.MisterSoftee.com. Be careful though, once you hear it it's difficult to get out of your head.)

The museum also features roadside architecture, with a 1921 Sun Oil cottage-style service station and the 1938 Reading Diner. Another attraction is the restored 1872 Jeremiah Sweinhart Carriage Factory; it was the launch pad for the Boyertown vehicle industry. A must-see event is the annual Duryea Day Antique, Classic Car and Truck Show that takes place Labor Day weekend and attracts over 700 entrants. NAAM member.

Number of vehicles: 50+ (plus another 50 carriages, wagons and bicycles).

Highlights: 1942 International, built at Boyertown Auto Works and used as an ambulance in World War II; 1953 Masano, a one-of-a-kind fiberglass car built in Boyertown features three tail fins.

Location: 85 S. Walnut Street, Boyertown, PA 19512

Admission: $ **Hours:** Tuesday through Sunday, 9:30 a.m. to 4 p.m. The Jeremiah Sweinhart Carriage Factory operates on limited hours, usually every other Saturday, so check ahead if seeing it is in your plans.

Phone: (610) 367-2090

Web: www.BoyertownMuseum.org

Note: The Antique Truck Club of America is also based in Boyertown. More information is at www.AntiqueTruckClubOfAmerica.org.

Side Trip: Fleetwood, PA

The hamlet of Fleetwood is just 15 miles northwest of Boyertown. Fleetwood Metal Auto Body started operations here in 1909. At that time, customers purchased the engine and chassis from a car company, then had the coach custom-built. Fleetwood produced coaches for Packard, Pierce-Arrow, Cadillac, and other high-end brands. Fisher Body Company acquired Fleetwood in 1925, moving operations to Detroit several years later. The Fleetwood name was long associated with Cadillac models, until it was retired in the 1990s. Visiting Fleetwood today, you'll still find manufacturing buildings marked "1909 Fleetwood Auto Bodies" at the corner of Locust and South Franklin Streets as a tribute to that long-ago legacy. To go from Fleetwood to Mack, visit the **Mack Trucks Historical Museum** in nearby Allentown.

EAGLES MERE AUTO MUSEUM
Laporte, PA

The Eagle Mere Auto Museum really ups the "wow" factor.

The first word that comes to mind when entering the **Eagles Mere Auto Museum** is "Wow!" Its collection of more than 75 cars, with a focus on American-made cars and trucks from the 1950s and '60s, is an unexpected find in this remote section of upstate Pennsylvania. Because this era of collecting is a sweet spot for many car buffs, it's a place you can really spend hours ogling the vehicles. As a bonus, it's located adjacent to a vintage aircraft museum. At both museums, the vehicles and airplanes on display are in working order and ready to drive or fly.

Muscle car fans will gravitate to the **"Class of '69"** section, with its collection of ten **Camaros** from that year sporting different styles and engine configurations. The mezzanine overlooking the main floor holds an assortment of six "woody" station wagons.

One of the coolest is a **1947 Ford Sportster Woody Convertible;** it was considered an upscale Jeep for deer hunting, which is a major activity in Pennsylvania. There's also a range of **1955 and '57 Chevy Bel Airs** outfitted for racing.

A reconstruction of local mechanic Lefty's Garage ("We do things right!") includes his shop-worn tools and equipment. The place is also chock-full of vintage neon signs, gas pumps, and automobilia.

Number of vehicles: 75+

Highlights: 1940 Packard Station Wagon; 1966 Shelby GT350; 1987 Buick Grand National; driven only 43 miles, it still has the original plastic covering on the steering wheel.

Location: Merritt Field, PA Route 42, Laporte, PA 17731. About 65 miles west of Scranton, the fictional setting for the television show *The Office.*

Admission: $

Hours: Open Memorial Day Weekend through mid-October: Saturday and Sunday, noon to 4 p.m.

Phone: (570) 220-2429

Web: www.EaglesMereAutoMuseum.com

Note: The owner of the Eagles Mere Auto Museum has over 350 vehicles, so the stock is rotated periodically. An additional 40 cars are on display in the nearby **Turbotville Auto Museum** on Fridays. Saturdays, and Sundays at 4905 State Route 54, Turbotville, Pennsylvania. Call (570-649-6731) for specific opening times.

EASTERN MUSEUM OF MOTOR RACING
York Springs, PA

Dedicated to preserving all forms of motor racing, this museum offers displays devoted to "Big Cars"/Indy 500, midget racers, sprint cars, modified stock cars, drag racing, winged sprint cars, Winston Cup, Formula, motorcycle, airplane, and boat racing – even solar-powered race cars. One of its highlights is the re-creation of the garage of Tommy Hinnershitz, the legendary Pennsylvania racer from the 1930s through 1950s who was inducted into the first class of the **National Sprint Car Hall of Fame** in Knoxville, Iowa. (See separate listing.)

The building overlooks the historic Latimore Valley Fairgrounds and Racetrack where races are still held throughout the year, making this a "living" museum. Aficionados of historical cars will appreciate the motorsports research library that includes the huge archives of legendary automobile journalist, and the "Dean of American Motorsports," Chris Economaki. There's also a collection of 30 engines.

Number of vehicles: 80+

Highlight: ¾-size midget racer in which Pennsylvania native son Mario Andretti started racing.

Location: 100 Baltimore Road, York Springs, PA 17372. About 20 miles northeast of Gettysburg.

Admission: Free, but a small donation is requested

Hours: April through October: Friday, Saturday, Sunday, 10 a.m. to 4 p.m.; November through March: Friday, 10 a.m. to 4 p.m.

Phone: (717) 528-8279   **Web:** www.emmr.org

FRICK CAR AND CARRIAGE MUSEUM
Pittsburgh, PA

The Car and Carriage Museum is part of a much larger complex called the Frick Art & Historical Center, known locally as "the Frick." It reopened in November 2015 after a major renovation of its exhibit of cars and carriages, which highlights themes related to the automotive revolution's effects on society.

Of special interest are two cars owned by Henry Frick and fellow Pittsburgh industrialist Howard Heinz (of ketchup fame): Frick's **1914 Rolls-Royce Silver Ghost** and Heinz's **1898 Panhard**, which may be the first automobile driven around the streets of Pittsburgh. There is always a sleek American Bantam on display; these diminutive cars were produced just north of Pittsburgh. NAAM member.

Number of vehicles: 20+

Highlights: 1909 Stanley Model R Roadster; 1923 Rolls-Royce Silver Ghost Salamanca Town Car; 1940 American Bantam Convertible Coupe.

Location: 7227 Reynolds Street, Pittsburgh, PA 15208

Admission: Free

Hours: Tuesday through Sunday, 10 a.m. to 5 p.m.

Phone: (412) 371-0600

Web: www.TheFrickPittsburgh.org

GRICE CLEARFIELD COMMUNITY MUSEUM
Clearfield, PA

You never know what might pop up in this wild collection.

Its not often you find a museum where there's a wild turkey rambling among the cars, well the turkey in question is a stuffed one that's frozen in time alongside a **1957 Chevrolet Bel Air**, but that's the case at the Grice Clearfield Community Museum in upstate central Pennsylvania. Lynn "Scoot" Grice, an avid hunter, founded the museum where more than 800 stuffed trophy game mounts share space with over 75 automobiles. It's also the type of museum where you'll find a **2007 Ford Mustang Shelby GT500** parked next to a **1913 International Harvester Auto Wagon**. The latter is a remnant of the famous tractor maker's foray into automobile production. Another unexpected find is a snow-white **1936 Cord**.

On the automotive side, one of the highlights of the collection is the display of seven Crosley cars. The Cincinnati-based company was known more for it appliances, and naming rights to the Cincinnati Reds former stadium, than it was for cars. The Crosleys on display include a **1947 Crosley Convertible**, **1949 Crosley Station Wagon** and a **1951 Crosley Panel Delivery Truck.**

A car that's rarely found in museums is a **1932 Rockne.** It was produced for two years by Studebaker as a tribute to the legendary Notre Dame football coach who had died in an airplane crash the year before. Studebaker and Notre Dame are both from South Bend, Indiana.

Number of vehicles: 75+

Highlights: Collection of Crosleys; 1917 Buick D35 Touring Car; 1948 Allard; 1986 Zimmer

Location: 119 N. 4th Street, Clearfield, PA 16830

Admission: $ **Hours:** Memorial Day through September; daily, Monday, 10 a.m. to 4 p.m.; through Saturday, 10 a.m. to 4 p.m.; Sunday, noon to 4 p.m. Early October through Columbus Day; Saturday and Sunday, noon to 4 p.m.

Phone: (814) 768-7332   **Web:** www.GriceMuseum.com

JERRY'S CLASSIC CARS AND COLLECTIBLES MUSEUM
Pottsville, PA

Jerry and Janet Enders converted a circa-1900 building that once housed a Morgan Studebaker dealership into this eye-catching museum. It's a repository of automobile culture of the 1950s and '60s. Murals of mid-century Americana represent the service stations Jerry worked in and the drive-in movie theaters he and Janet attended.

They also form the perfect backdrop for such iconic cars as a **1951 Studebaker Land Cruiser "Bullet Nose."** Jerry's museum also features over 20,000 items from more than 100 years of automobile lore. Other than cars, there's something for everyone including a millinery, library, kitchen, appliance store, vintage jukebox, and a playable 1960s pinball machine.

Number of vehicles: 15

Highlights: 1939 Oldsmobile 60 Series, a locally driven car with just one owner; 1958 DeSoto Firesweep Convertible (1 of 700 built, only 12 survive); 1964 Plymouth Belvedere Coupe with a 426 V8 engine.

Location: 394 S. Centre Street, Pottsville, PA 17901

Admission: $ **Hours:** May through October: Friday, Saturday and Sunday, noon to 5 p.m.

Phone: (888) 802-6605   **Web:** www.JerrysMuseum.com

MACK TRUCKS HISTORICAL MUSEUM
Allentown, PA

This museum is housed in Mack Trucks' former Engineering Design and Test Center. There are 30 vehicles on display, with vintages ranging from 1905 through 1990. Visitors also view a timeline and artifacts relating to the history of the iconic brand. Staff members are experts on Mack Trucks and are available to answer questions or help sift through the extensive archives of build records, photos, and literature.

There's also an exhibit of early chain-driven trucks. Powertrain components on view include cutaways to see what's going on inside.

Kids will like the assortment of Mack Truck toys and replicas. Definitely take one of the tours given by former Mack employees.

Number of vehicles: 30+ (rotated regularly)

Highlights: 1905 Mack Bus (oldest known operational Mack vehicle).

Location: 2402 Lehigh Parkway South, Allentown, PA 18103

Admission: Free

Hours: Monday, Wednesday, Friday, 10 a.m. to 4 p.m. Tours are offered during the day.

Phone: (610) 351-8999

Web: www.MackTrucksHistoricalMuseum.org

ROLLS-ROYCE FOUNDATION AND MUSEUM
Mechanicsburg, PA

Blink and you might miss the **Rolls-Royce Museum.** For such a valuable collection, it's tucked away on a winding, two-lane country road near the state capital of Harrisburg. As the headquarters for the Rolls-Royce Owners Club, the Rolls-Royce Foundation offers an extensive library of materials for anyone interested in these ultra-luxury vehicles. It has gradually expanded into its current role as a museum open to the public.

The main room holds the library and around a dozen Rolls-Royces and Bentleys. Initially Rolls-Royce was known for its high-end engines, not the complete vehicles we see today. When a customer bought a Rolls they were buying only the engine and chassis, which they took to an independent coach builder to customize. A **1934 Rolls-Royce Phantom** shown without a body demonstrates just what the discriminating buyer got for all that money.

A **1929 Rolls-Royce Springfield Phantom I** demonstrates the economic effect of the Roaring Twenties. Unable to meet increased demand at its English factory, Rolls-Royce started producing autos in the industrial town of Springfield, Massachusetts. (See separate listing for the **Wood Museum of Springfield History**.) One thing that set the American version apart was the drum-shaped head lamps. Eventually the Great Depression shuttered the Springfield plant. Rolls-Royce purchased Bentley in 1931, so they're on display here too. NAAM member.

Number of vehicles: 15+

Highlights: 1925 Bentley; 1929 Rolls-Royce Springfield Phantom I; 1961 Rolls-Royce Phantom V. (Careful you don't bump into this leviathan, it's almost 20 feet long!)

Location: 189 Hempt Road, Mechanicsburg, PA 17050. Look for the brick building with the letters "RROC" on the side. If you're in the area you should stop in at the **Antique Automobile Club of America** in Hershey (see separate listing), which is only 30 miles east of here.

Admission: Free

Hours: Monday through Friday, 10 a.m. to 4 p.m.

Phone: (717) 795-9400

Web: www.RollsRoyceFoundation.org

Throughout the year **Carlisle, PA** lives up to the first three letters of its name as multiple vintage car events take place here. Three of the biggest events, drawing tens of thousands of people, are the "Carlisle Nationals" Ford, GM and Chrysler shows that occur on separate weekends during the summer. Each is a combination car show, swap meet, carnival, auction, and celebration of the particular brand. If you need a part to finish your restoration, this is the place to find it. For more information, go to www.CarlisleEvents.com.

SIMEONE FOUNDATION AUTOMOTIVE MUSEUM
Philadelphia, PA

The 1909 American Underslung Traveler
is from arguably America's first pure sports car company.

The Simeone is a hidden gem stashed away in a former engine remanufacturing facility near the Philadelphia airport. Despite its low profile, it won the prestigious "Museum of the Year" award in 2011 at the International Historic Motoring Awards, and in 2014 it was awarded "Car of the Year" for its **1964 Shelby Cobra Daytona Coupe**. The museum owes its existence to the passion of one man, neurosurgeon Fred Simeone. Over the course of a half-century he's collected over 60 of the world's greatest racing cars, all of which still run. Come for the popular twice-monthly "Demonstration Days," when you can see, and hear, some of the cars while they are taken for a spin on the 3-acre back lot.

The oldest vehicle here is a **1909 American Underslung** that raced in long-distance events. Other cars are displayed according to where they raced (Watkins Glen, Bonneville Salt Flats, Brooklands, and more) or by the races they entered. Among them are Le Mans, the Targa Florio in Sicily, and the Mille Miglia. With so many sleek Italian racing cars on display, the museum sometimes looks more like a modern sculpture gallery.

The **1921 Duesenberg French GP Race Car** is a sister car to the one that was driven by Jimmy Murphy in the 1921 Le Mans for the first American victory in an international race. NASCAR is well-represented, with cars including a **2002 NASCAR Dyno Mule**. NAAM member

Number of vehicles: 65+

Highlights: 1964 Shelby Cobra Daytona Coupe; 1938 Alfa Romeo 8C 2900 B MM, which won the 1938 Mille Miglia and is Dr. Simeone's favorite.

Location: 6825 Norwitch Drive, Philadelphia, PA 19153. If you have a long enough layover at Philadelphia International Airport, it's only a five-minute taxi ride to the museum.

Admission: $$

Hours: Tuesday through Friday, 10 a.m. to 6 p.m. (last entry at 4:30 p.m.); Saturday through Sunday, 10 a.m. to 4 p.m. (last entry at 2:30 p.m.).

Phone: (215) 365-7233   **Web:** SimeoneMuseum.org

WILLIAM E. SWIGART JR. AUTOMOBILE MUSEUM
Huntingdon, PA

This gem in the central Pennsylvania countryside highlights the collecting prowess and dedication of the father/son team of W. Emmert Swigart and William E. Swigart Jr. Over the years they purchased around 150 cars, about of which 35 are on display at any one time. The **1903 curved-dash Oldsmobile** was the favorite car of William Swigart.

The museum also has bragging rights for its two Tuckers on display side-by-side, the **1947 Tucker Tin Goose Prototype** (the very first Tucker made) and a **Tucker 48 #1013,** which was seen in the film *Tucker: The Man and His Dream*. The Tucker prototype was the fifth vehicle placed by the Historic Vehicle Association on the National Historic Vehicle Register, an exclusive list of vehicles that boast a significant cultural and historical impact. For more information about the register go to www.HistoricVehicle.org.

Aside from the cars on display, the museum includes a large collection of auto ephemera (license plates, radiator brand emblems, vintage lamps, hood ornaments, and more); bicycles from the late 19th century; and vintage toys. NAAM member.

Number of vehicles: 35 (rotated from a larger collection)

Highlights: 1916 Scripps-Booth; 1936 Duesenberg 12-Cylinder Gentlemen's Speedster (one-of-a-kind prototype); 1947 Tucker Tin Goose Prototype.

Location: 12031 William Penn Highway (Route 22), Huntingdon, PA 16652

Admission: $

Hours: Memorial Day weekend through October 31: daily, 10 a.m. to 5 p.m.; open until 6 p.m. on Friday.

Phone: (814) 643-0885   **Web:** www.SwigartMuseum.com

Note: The Swigart Museum is about a 90-mile drive northwest of Harrisburg. It's easy to combine with a visit to the **Antique Automobile Club of America Museum** in Hershey.

The Pennsylvania Tucker Trail

The release of the 1988 film *Tucker: The Man and His Dream* really pushed the quirky auto into the national zeitgeist, with even non-car buffs learning about its central headlight that swiveled when the car turns. Only 51 of these cars were ever built, with about 47 on display worldwide. The Swigart Museum was once the only museum in the world where you'd see two Tuckers, but as of 2014 there are another three at the **Antique Automobile Club of America** in nearby Hershey. The two museums are only about an hour-and-a-half drive apart, making central Pennsylvania the only place to view five Tuckers in one day. Although you may get "tuckered" out, it's well worth a road trip.

Tucker trivia: The man who directed the Tucker film, Francis Ford Coppola, was given his middle name by his parents in honor of Henry Ford himself. (Coppola was even born in Detroit's Henry Ford Hospital.) His musician father knew the auto titan from his work with the Detroit Symphony Orchestra.

WASHINGTON, D.C.

SMITHSONIAN NATIONAL MUSEUM OF AMERICAN HISTORY
Washington, D.C.

Get your kicks on Route 66 at the Smithsonian.

This museum is massive, and includes such treasured bits of Americana as the flag that inspired Francis Scott Key to write the lyrics to the *The Star Spangled Banner*. There is also a well-curated display, "America on the Move," highlighting the history of Americans in transit via planes, trains, automobiles, and more. The automotive area alone is as large as many individual car museums.

The first-floor gallery starts out from driving's early days as Americans first took to the road. The exhibit devoted to electric vehicles includes a **1904 Columbia Electric Runabout**; a mirror on the floor below the car reveals its innovative power source.

It was a top-selling car in the U.S. around the turn of the 20th century.

A mid-century Portland, Oregon automobile showroom is recreated, complete with a couple purchasing a **1950 Buick Sedan Dynaflow**. The area devoted to the birth of the Interstate Highway System is really cool: the floor is poured in various surfaces, such as concrete and asphalt, that were actually used in road construction in different parts of the country. Riding along those roads in all its glory is a **1967 Pontiac Grand Prix Convertible**. A car not often found in museums, a **1977 Honda Civic**, demonstrates the rise of imports and their impact on the automotive scene.

The Route 66 exhibit includes information about country singer Merle Haggard's family, who trekked from Oklahoma to Bakersfield, California where he was born. Children will enjoy the **1953 "Kidillac" Pedal Car**. Pylons with touchscreens throughout the displays allow visitors to delve deeper into automotive history. There are even episodes of the hit radio show *Car Talk* that explain some technical aspects of cars. The free museum is a must-visit for those touring the nation's capital.

Number of vehicles: 15+   **Highlights:** 1903 Winton Touring Car "Vermont," driven by Horatio Nelson Jackson and Sewall Crocker and accompanied by their dog Bud on the first successful cross-country road trip in 1903 (which took 64 days); 1936 Dodge School Bus; 1950 Studebaker Champion Starlight Coupe.

Location: On the National Mall at 14th Street and Constitution Avenue, NW, Washington, D.C., 20001.

Admission: Free   **Hours:** Open every day except Christmas from 10 a.m. to 5:30 p.m. During the summer they are open until 7:30 p.m.

Phone: (202) 633-1000   **Web:** amhistory.si.edu/OnTheMove

Recommended Viewing

Horatio's Drive, a documentary by noted filmmaker Ken Burns, recounts the tale of the first trans-American road trip, taken in the 1903 Winton displayed at the Smithsonian. It was an incredible accomplishment by two intrepid travelers, Horatio Nelson Jackson and Sewall Crocker, at a time when roads didn't even exist outside towns and cities. Burns retraced the route of their journey for the filming; in many areas, not much has changed. Tom Hanks provides the voice of Jackson.

3

THE SOUTH

It's hard to think of the American South without thinking of NASCAR. Starting from humble roots, it has grown into a uniquely American global phenomenon. NASCAR's early days are on display at the **Occoneechee Speedway** in Hillsborough, North Carolina. Now a hiking trail, it's the last surviving dirt track from NASCAR'S inaugural Strictly Stock season in 1949.

The Charlotte area is home to over a dozen attractions, including racing team headquarters and the **NASCAR Hall of Fame.** The Tar Heel legacies of Richard Petty and Dale Earnhardt, Sr., are visible at the Petty Museum in Level Cross and the **"Dale Trail"** in "The Intimidator's" hometown of Kannapolis.

Muscle cars are well presented at **Rick Treworgy's Muscle Car City** in Punta Gorda, Florida and at **Wheels of Yesteryear** in Myrtle Beach, South Carolina. For those looking for something a bit slower, try the **C. Grier Beam Trucking Museum** in Cherryville, North Carolina.

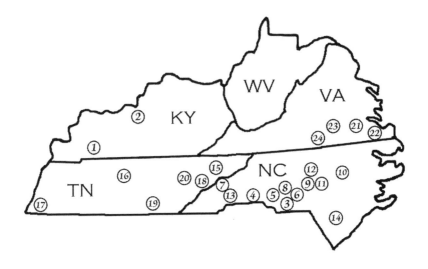

THE SOUTH — MAP ONE

KENTUCKY

    1) Bowling Green Corvette Assembly Plant
       National Corvette Museum

    2) Swope's Cars of Yesteryear Museum

NORTH CAROLINA

    3) Backing Up Classics Museum
       Chip Ganassi Racing
       Hendrick Motorsports Museum
       JR Motorsports
       Kasey Kahne Racing
       Kyle Busch Motorsport

NASCAR Hall of Fame
Roush Fenway Racing
Stewart-Haas Racing
Wood Family Racing

4) Bennett Classics Antique Auto Museum

5) C. Grier Beam Truck Museum

6) Curb Music and Motorsports Museum
Dale Earnhardt Trail

7) Estes-Winn Antique Car Museum

8) Memory Lane Museum
Michael Waltrip Racing
Mooresville, NC-Race City USA
North Carolina Auto Racing Hall of Fame

9) North Carolina Transportation Museum

10) Occoneechee Speedway

11) Petty Museum

12) Richard Childress Racing Museum

13) Wheels Through Time

14) World's largest tire

TENNESSEE

15) City Garage Car Museum

16) Lane Motor Museum
Marathon Village

17) Elvis Presley Automobile Museum at Graceland
Stax Museum (Isaac Hayes' 1972 Cadillac)

18) Floyd Garrett's Muscle Car Museum

19) International Towing & Recovery Museum

20) Women's Basketball Hall of Fame

VIRGINIA

21) Keystone Truck and Tractor Museum

22) United States Army Transportation Museum

23) Virginia Museum of Transportation

24) Wood Brothers Racing Museum

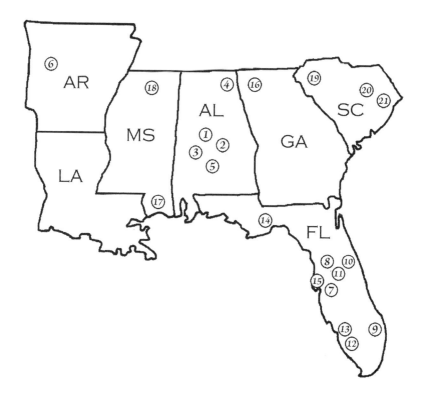

THE SOUTH — MAP TWO

ALABAMA

1) Barber Vintage Motorsports Museum

2) International Motorsports Hall of Fame

3) Mercedes Benz Visitors Center

4) Oldest Army Jeep

5) Wellborn Musclecar Museum

ARKANSAS

6) Museum of Automobiles

FLORIDA

7) Airstream Ranch

8) Don Garlits Museum of Drag Racing

9) Elliott Museum

10) Living Legends of Auto Racing
Racing's North Turn Bar & Grille

11) Mount Dora Museum of Speed

12) Revs Institute for Automotive Research:
Collier Collection

13) Rick Treworgy's Muscle Car City

14) Tallahassee Automobile Museum

15) Tampa Bay Automobile Museum

GEORGIA

16) Old Car City

MISSISSIPPI

17) Busted Wrench Garage & Museum

18) Tupelo Automobile Museum

SOUTH CAROLINA

19) BMW Zentrum

20) Darlington Raceway Stock Car Museum

21) Wheels of Yesteryear

ALABAMA

Barber Vintage Motorsports Museum
Birmingham, AL

Although dairy tycoon George Barber came from a Porsche racing background, he wanted to create a museum that preserved motorcycle heritage. Once he got rolling on motorcycles, he never stopped. There are about 1,400 vintage and modern motorcycles in the collection (according to Guinness World Records, it's the largest in the world), with about half of those on display at any given time. You'll see bikes produced by over 200 manufacturers from 20 countries. There are over 80 Harleys alone. Among the motorcycles are a **1912 Indian Board Track Racer** and a **1913 Flying Merkel** that date from an era when motorcycles looked like glorified bicycles with engines.

Auto racing fans are not left out with, among others, a **1959 Lotus Type 16 Formula Two** and a world champion **1964 Ferrari 158**. Barber boasts the world's largest assemblage of Lotus racecars, with over 50 on hand.

The museum is adjacent to the Barber Motorsports Park, home of the Honda Indy Grand Prix of Alabama and the Triumph Superbike Classic, and the Barber Proving Grounds. In 2015 they started Barber Historics, a vintage racecar event, which is held in the spring along with the cleverly named Barber-Que competition. NAAM member.

Number of vehicles: 700+   Mostly motorcycles, with even more in storage so the collection is rotated regularly.

Highlights: 1951 Vincent Black Shadow (motorcycle that could reach 125 mph); 2008 Ducati Desmosedici; largest collection of Lotus racecars in the world.

Location: 6030 Barber Motorsports Parkway, Birmingham, AL

Admission: $$ **Hours:** April 1 through September 30: Monday through Saturday, 10 a.m. to 6 p.m.; Sunday, noon to 6 p.m. October 1 through March 31: Monday through Saturday, 10 a.m. to 5 p.m.; Sunday, noon to 5 p.m.

Phone: (205) 699-7275 **Web:** www.BarberMuseum.org

INTERNATIONAL MOTORSPORTS HALL OF FAME
Talladega, AL

Located at the legendary Talladega Superspeedway, this is definitely a must-see for NASCAR fans. But the exhibits also turn to other areas of racing, including Indy Car, NHRA, Formula One, modified, motorcycle, and many one-of-a-kind vehicles. Also located on the premises are the Automobile Racing Club of America (ARCA) Hall of Fame, the Quarter Midgets of America Hall of Fame, the Alabama Racing Pioneers Hall of Fame, and the Alabama Sports Writer's Hall of Fame.

A crowd favorite is Richard Petty's **1974 Dodge,** in which he won his fifth NASCAR Winston Cup championship. He liked the car so much he drove it again the next year for, naturally, his sixth NASCAR Winston Cup championship. Also on view is the high-performance **1966 Chevelle** raced by Ray Owen. It won an incredible 676 runs out of 692 starts.

A sobering display shows cars that have been wrecked while racing. It reminds me of those Ohio State Trooper films they showed us in high school driver's education class, with names like *Blood on the Highway* to scare us into driving straight. One of the cars is Michael Waltrip's **1990 Pontiac #30**, which he rammed into a wall at Bristol International Raceway in 1990 for one of the most devastating crashes in auto racing history. Miraculously, Waltrip walked away from the accident.

Number of vehicles: 150

Highlights: Jimmie Johnson's #48 Chevrolet, winner of the 2006 Daytona 500; 1977 Chevrolet Monte Carlo (Darrell Waltrip's "Bertha," in which he won 12 races).

Location: 3366 Speedway Boulevard, Lincoln, AL 35096. Right off I-20, twelve miles north of Talladega.

Admission: $$

Hours: Daily, 9 a.m. to 4 p.m. Extended hours during race weeks.

Phone: (256) 362-5002

Web: www.MotorsportsHallOfFame.com

MERCEDES-BENZ VISITORS CENTER AND PLANT TOURS
Tuscaloosa, AL

When Mercedes-Benz announced they were opening a plant in Alabama in 1993, it was a major coup for the state. It's now a popular car buffs' destination due to its visitor center, which underwent a major revamping in 2015. Expect to see about a dozen of the latest Mercedes-Benz models, antique autos, and even a cracked-up one that demonstrates the safety of this luxury German brand. Plant tours are offered on Tuesday and Thursday at a minimal fee. Advance reservations are required. Call (205-507-2252).

(***Note:*** Children must be at least 12 years old to tour the manufacturing facility.)

The visitor's center and gift shop are free.

Location: 11 Mercedes Drive, Vance, AL 35490. About halfway between Tuscaloosa and Birmingham.

Visitors Center Hours: Monday through Friday, 8:30 a.m. to 4 p.m.

Web: www.mbusi.com/visitorcenter

WELLBORN MUSCLECAR MUSEUM
Alexander City, AL

This monument to muscle cars is housed in a restored vintage 1940s car dealership. At one time, museum founders Tim and Pam Wellborn owned a good chunk of the 1971 Dodge Hemi Chargers produced, but they sold off part of their collection in 2015 with a 22-car Mecum auction. Despite that sale, plenty remains, enough that the museum has to rotate its collection with items in storage. If you're into Dodge, this is the place to go.

Tim's love of all things Mopar started at age 16, when his dad drove home in a 1971 Hemi Charger. Although the collection frequently changes, some mainstays are the **1969 K&K Dodge Daytona Charger #71** that Buddy Baker drove in the NASCAR fastest lap ever (a record that held for 17 years); **1966 Charger "Barn Find," 1971 Hemi GTX, 1971 Shaker Challenger "Barn Find,"** and a **1971 Hemi Charger** in Jamaica Blue.

If you're not a Mopar fan there's also a cool collection of Mercury Cougar Eliminators, Aero Cars designed for NASCAR, Ford Boss Mustangs, Chevrolet Chevelle SS, and many more. The whitewashed brick walls make a great backdrop for the cars, vintage gas pumps, and lighted dealer showroom signs. The museum also hosts popular annual Mopar muscle car events that sometimes end with a ride to Talladega Superspeedway.

Number of vehicles: 40+

Highlights: 1969 K&K Daytona Daytona Charger #71; 1971 Hemi Charger, possibly the last Hemi Dodge Charger ever produced.

Location: 124 Broad Street, Alexander City, AL 35010. Located about 120 miles southwest of Atlanta, GA and 75 miles southeast of Birmingham, AL.

Admission: $$

Hours: Saturday, 10 a.m. to 4 p.m. Open Tuesday through Friday by appointment only.

Phone: (256) 329-8474

Web: www.WellbornMusclecarMuseum.com

Side Trip: The Oldest Army Jeep

In the early days of World War II, before the United States entered the conflict, the Army was seeking an all-purpose vehicle from auto manufacturers. The oldest known survivor of the early prototypes produced by Ford, Willys, and American Bantam is a **1940 Ford Pilot Model GP-No. 1 Pygmy**, which was delivered to the Army for testing in November 1940. The name GP, for General Purpose, was later shortened to Jeep. If it looks a bit familiar, that's because it bears the trademark vertical grill that eventually became an icon for the Jeep brand we know today. It's featured at the **U. S. Veterans Memorial Museum** in Huntsville, Alabama, where over a dozen other military vehicles are also on display, including a Humvee prototype designed by Lamborghini. www.MemorialMuseum.org.

ARKANSAS

MUSEUM OF AUTOMOBILES
Morrilton, AR

Part of the toy collection revving up.

Located on the former estate of Winthrop Rockefeller, this museum is reached via a steep hairpin-turn-studded road in the Arkansas countryside. The autos range from 1904 to 1967, but the real focus is on pre-1950 vehicles.

Some of the more unusual cars include a **1924 Auto Red Bug,** which looks like a child's Flexible Flyer sled on wheels, and the **1923 Climber Touring,** a Little Rock, Arkansas marque and the only survivor of 200 made. Two autos facing each other represent an unsuccessful early attempt to introduce aerodynamic bodies to American car buyers – a **1935 DeSoto Airflow** and a **1937 Chrysler Airflow**. While the cars were ahead of their time, they still look pretty cool today. The **1967 Cadillac Fleetwood 75** was once owned by museum founder and former Arkansas governor Winthrop Rockefeller, and is painted in the Rockefeller family's favorite color, maroon.

The museum is not far from Memphis so naturally there's an Elvis Presley vehicle, the King's **1967 Ford Fairlane 500 Ranchero**. It's on loan, as are about a third of the vehicles, so the collection changes a bit each year. There's also a modest gun collection and a group of antique coin-operated arcade games that still work. Special events throughout the year include "Mustangs on the Mountain" in May, "Car Show & Swap Meet" in June, and the "MidSouth Econoline Meet" in September. NAAM member.

Number of vehicles: 50

Highlights: 1908 Sears Model J Runabout (Yes, the Sears department store made a brief foray into automobile manufacturing, which they tried again in 1952); 1923 Star Station Wagon; 1948 Willys-Overland Jeepster Phaeton; plus 7 motorcycles, including a 1913 Harley-Davidson wood-track racer and a 1969 Rokon.

Location: Petit Jean Mountain, 8 Jones Lane, Morrilton, AR 72110. The museum is about 15 miles southwest of Morrilton. Although I-40 passes near town, plan on driving another 20 miles after exiting the interstate to reach the museum.

Admission: $

Hours: Daily, 10 a.m. to 5 p.m.

Phone: (501) 727-5427

Web: www.MuseumOfAutos.com

FLORIDA

Don Garlits Museum of Drag Racing/Drag Racing Hall of Fame/ Museum of Classic Cars
Ocala, FL

Anyone into drag racing grew up hearing about "Big Daddy" Don Garlits, the legendary "King of the Dragsters." His museum follows the rapid rise of the sport from its birth in the 1940s to the present day. In 1991 he added a Drag Racing Hall of Fame, which selects new inductees every year. There are two buildings, one for drag racers and one for classic cars.

Garlits called his personal racing cars "Swamp Rats." There are over 30 of them here, starting with Don's favorite, **Swamp Rat I,** in which he hit 182 mph at the Bristol Raceway in 1988, up through **Swamp Rat 34,** Garlits' last top-fuel car, in which he sped to 323 mph. There's also a handful of the most famous Slingshot dragsters from the late 1960s.

The Classic Car building includes a rare **1937 Ford Roadster,** a Hemi air-raid siren from the Cold War, and a **1942 Mercury Convertible,** of which less than a dozen survive. It's a rare model year because car factories were shut down and retooled for military production after the Japanese attack on Pearl Harbor. President Eisenhower's **1956 Chrysler Imperial,** which was completely restored by Garlits, rounds out the collection.

Gearheads rejoice! Not only are there way too many cars to list, there's also a large selection of Hemi and flathead engines, rare manifolds, and carburetors that have been restored by Garlits. The walls are festooned with so much automobilia (posters, uniforms, vintage oil cans, old advertising signs, and more) it's hard to tell if there actually are walls behind them.

As the "Big Daddy" himself says, "We show everything, nothing is in storage, and it is 'cluttered' as some tend to think. But my fans love the informal atmosphere!" For an extra fee, Garlits personally leads tours of the garage and takes visitors behind the scenes.

Number of vehicles: Just under 300

Highlights: Swamp Rat IV, the first rear-engine top- fueled dragster in the world.

Location: 13700 SW 16th Avenue, Ocala, FL 34473. About 75 miles northwest of Orlando.

Admission: $$$

Hours: Daily, 9 a.m. to 5 p.m.

Phone: (352) 245-8661

Web: www.Garlits.com

Elliott Museum
Stuart, FL

The "Wheels of Change" car exhibit is part of a comprehensive museum that includes displays on baseball, maritime history, local history, and more. Because museum namesake Sterling Elliott held many early auto-related patents, including the pneumatic tire and a revolutionary steering system, visitors learn how the development of the automobile impacted everyone's lives.

The setting for the cars is a bit unusual. About a dozen are on display on the main floor, which you can walk around. Another 51 autos are held in a three- story parking structure. You select the vehicle you want to see, and after a series of fits and starts it mechanically descends to the main floor, where it is placed on a turntable for viewing. During the wait for the vehicle to arrive the docent shares its history.

The cars in the multi-level garage and on the turntable are behind glass, so you can't walk right up to them. Due to the logistics of this process, you probably won't get to see as many cars as you would in an ordinary auto museum. However, engineering types may like to see the automatic parking structure, which is quite popular in land-constrained places like Tokyo.

For Ford Model A/AA lovers, there are 55 of them in the collection. An extremely rare, locally built car is the sleek **1953 Cunningham C-3 Convertible**. West Palm Beach businessman Briggs Swift Cunningham started his own company to build cars that competed at LeMans; this is one of the legacies of that venture. The bizarre **1976 Citicar Electric Coupe** (it looks like the back half of an AMC Gremlin driving forward) was built in Daytona. NAAM member.

Number of vehicles: 65+ on display, with additional cars in storage that can be seen by appointment.

Highlights: 1903 Stanley Steamer (with original upholstery) owned by museum namesake Sterling Elliott, who was a friend of the Stanley Brothers; 1910 Moline Dreadnought; 1914 Detroit Electric; 1920 Hudson Super Six Limousine once owned by Enrico Caruso.

Location: 825 Northeast Ocean Boulevard, Stuart, FL 34996. On the Atlantic coast, about 100 miles north of Miami.

Admission: $$

Hours: Monday through Sunday, 10 a.m. to 5 p.m. Behind-the-scenes garage tours every Thursday at 11:30 a.m. or by special appointment. Call for details.

Phone: (772) 225-1961   **Web:** www.ElliottMuseumFL.org

LIVING LEGENDS OF AUTO RACING
South Daytona, FL

A very early NASCAR sign is a real survivor.

If you want to meet people who hearken back to the days when drivers actually raced on the beach in Daytona, this small museum tucked into a shopping center is the place for you. The guides are former drivers who regale visitors with fascinating stories from their dirt track racing days. Volunteer and former racer Fred McKaig proudly pointed out the display devoted to his wife, Dot Gladis, who won the 1951 Women's National Stock Car Championship. Dot is also a popular guide at the museum; as Don says, "She could still get out on a racetrack and drive." I noticed a program promoting her appearance at a track in Freeport, New York. It brought back memories for me – that's the same Long Island track where my dad took me to watch races and demolition derbies. The site is now a BJ's Wholesale Club.

The display includes a **1937 Ford** original racecar and replicas of cars raced by Junior Johnson and Bobby Allison. The walls are lined with photos, plaques, trophies, signed helmets, scale cars, uniforms, and other memorabilia from the early days of Daytona racing. A vintage wooden sign was used by NASCAR founder Bill France to promote the Daytona Speedway in the 1950s. A reproduction machine shop similar to one used by legendary mechanic Red Vogt (he came up with the name for NASCAR) shows off several engines, including a 1940 Ford Flathead V8. If you're here for race week in Daytona this is a must visit spot.

Number of vehicles: 5

Highlights: The guides, who represent a living history of racing.

Location: Sunshine Park Mall, 2400 S. Ridgewood Avenue (US 1), South Daytona, FL

Admission: Free

Hours: Tuesday through Saturday, 10 a.m. to 5 p.m. Summer hours are sporadic. Volunteers staff the museum, so it's best to call ahead.

Phone: (386) 763-4483

Web: www.lloar1993.com

Pit Stop: Racing's North Turn Bar & Grille

While you're in Daytona, head out to the beach to see NASCAR's humble roots. The **Racing's North Turn Bar & Grille** sits at the spot where racers churned off the beach and turned onto paved Highway A1A to head back south. In the lobby there's a small museum stuffed with NASCAR and racing memorabilia; there's even a **1934 Ford Sedan** in the foyer. The dining room is also full of NASCAR items and overlooks the beach where the original races took place. The races started in 1936 and continued through the 1950s, except for a break during World War II. Plaques at both the north and south turns commemorate the historic racing landmark.

Racing's North Turn Bar & Grille, 4511 S. Atlantic Avenue, Ponce Inlet, FL 32127. Just over three miles south of the Dunlawton Avenue Bridge. Phone: (386) 322-3258 Web: www.RacingsNorthTurn.com.

A "Kiddie" car parked below the real thing.

It's hard to know where to begin at this museum that bills itself as the "Ultimate Man Cave." Museum founder Kerry Bogard and his supportive wife, Cindy, created an incredible private collection that ambles around their purpose-built Art Deco building. Vintage cars are an important component of displays that include celebrity autographed guitars, jukeboxes, toy planes, militaria, road-trip nostalgia, surfboards, quarter midget race cars, memorabilia from roadside stalwarts Howard Johnson's and Greyhound, and more.

Kerry has always been fascinated with hearses, related funerary paraphernalia (such as a 1940s embalmer's make-up kit) and medical vehicles. There are quite a few on display, including a **1952 Cadillac S&S Florentine Hearse/Flower Car, 1957 Ford**

F-100 Custom "Superior" Ambulance, and a **1948 Barnette Ambulance**, complete with a fake body in the back.

The **1963 Chevrolet Corvette** (with split rear window) holds a special place for Kerry. He sold it in 1980, then just by luck found it for sale years later and couldn't resist buying it back. There are also several kiddie cars, including a **1957 "Kidillac."** Kerry also recreated a vintage Mount Dora gas station, chock-full of petroleum memorabilia, inside the museum. And did I mention all the neon signs on the walls? The Museum of Speed has so much cool stuff on display, you'll want to take a few laps around the building.

To add to the retro vibe, there are old televisions scattered around, playing black-and-white programs from the past. Says Kerry, "Some visitors show up and are so fascinated they just sit there and watch." The Bogards also operate Classic Dream Cars, a vintage dealership, so many of the cars are available for purchase.

Number of vehicles: About a dozen cars from their personal collection, plus another dozen or so for sale.

Highlights: Collection of antique hearses; 1989 Porsche Speedster.

Location: 206 N. Highland Street, Mount Dora, FL 32757. It's 45 miles northwest of Orlando International Airport, but with the town's "old-time Florida" vibe it is worlds away.

Admission: $$ **Hours:** Monday through Friday, 10 a.m. to 5 p.m. Children under 14 not admitted. Call in advance to make sure they will be there. *Note:* Due to damage from prior visitors, no cameras with long lenses are permitted.

Phone: (352) 385-0049

Web: www.ClassicDreamCars.com/and scroll down to the museum.

REVS INSTITUTE FOR AUTOMOTIVE RESEARCH: COLLIER COLLECTION
NAPLES, FL

The founder of the Revs Institute is Miles Collier, whose father and uncle founded the precursor to the Sports Car Club of America. The museum features rare and exclusive automobiles covering a century from 1896 through 1995. Pride of place goes to the **1939 Mercedes W154 Grand Prix (Silver Arrows)**. The V-12 is perhaps the last and greatest pre-war racing car. Its only race was on September 3, 1939, the day Great Britain and France declared war on Germany, suddenly putting a halt to European auto racing.

The oldest vehicle is an **1896 Panhard et Levassor Wagonette**. Along the way there are over 20 Porsches, including Bruce Jennings' **1958 Porsche Carrera GT Speedster**. Many cars are rarely seen in museums, including the **1919 Ballot** and **1952 Cunningham C-4RK** racers. And just to show it's not all high-brow, there are a **1956 Volkswagen Beetle** and an East German **1989 Trabant** of Cold War fame among a host of daily drivers also on display. The cars are all restored and in peak working condition. The renowned research library contains over a million books, magazines, photographs, and ephemera related to automotive history.

Number of vehicles: 100+

Highlights: 1927 Packard Prototype Speedster; 1937 Delahaye 135 MS Special Roadster; 1939 Mercedes W154 Grand Prix (Silver Arrows); 1954 Osca Sports-Racer.

Location: 2500 S. Horseshoe Drive, Naples, FL 34104

Admission: $$ **Hours:** Tuesday, Thursday and Saturday, 10 a.m. to 4 p.m. Must purchase tickets in advance, which are available online or by phone. *Note:* Closed August 1 through September 14.

Phone: (239) 687-7387   **Web:** RevsInstitute.org

RICK TREWORGY'S MUSCLE CAR CITY
Punta Gorda, FL

A 1971 Chevy El Camino boasts a 454 V8.

If seeing almost two acres of General Motors cars packed in under one roof revs your engine, then head to the west coast of Florida. Rick Treworgy has assembled an astonishing collection. He's on site often to answer questions and chat with visitors. The museum tells an almost complete history of GM from the early 1900s to the 1980s, but the focus is on muscle cars. The emphasis is on performance, with **Camaro Z28s, SS Chevelles, SS El Caminos, Big Block Impalas, Pontiac GTOs, Oldsmobile 442s,** and many hot rods and antique Chevys.

There are also one or more **Corvettes** of each model year from 1954 through 1975, as well as a few from each series from 1975 through 2006. Rick's first car was a '55 Chevy he bought used for

$75, so he has a soft spot for them. On display are ten mid-1950s **Chevrolet Bel Airs** of almost every style available. There are no ropes or barriers around the vehicles, so you can really explore them. The hoods of many of the autos are open so you can check out the engines.

Vintage gas pumps are spread throughout the museum. A hot rod and speed shop on the premises provides hard-to-find parts. In case you get hungry after spending hours ogling Detroit metal, there's a '50s-themed diner on site. If you're more into two-wheeling, there's also an assortment of motorcycles and antique bicycles. The gift shop carries many car-related t-shirts that are hard to find elsewhere. NAAM member.

Number of vehicles: 200

Highlights: 1935 Chevrolet Phaeton (one of seven built and the last one known to exist); rows of over 60 Corvettes, including an unrestored 1965 Corvette with 16,000 original miles.

Location: 3811 Tamiami Trail, Punta Gorda, FL 33950. *Note:* At press time they were planning a move nearby to 10175 Tamiami Trail, where fewer cars may be on display. Check the website for the current location.

Admission: $$

Hours: Tuesday through Sunday, 9 a.m. to 5 p.m.

Phone: (941) 575-5959

Web: MuscleCarCity.net

TALLAHASSEE AUTOMOBILE MUSEUM
Tallahassee, FL

The full name of this colossus of collecting, sprawling over 100,000 square feet on two floors, is the **Tallahassee Automobile and Collectibles Museum**. In addition to the extensive car collection, there are pedal cars, spark plugs, Batmobiles, boats, motorcycles, toys, Barbie dolls, cash registers, knives, golf clubs, and more. The founder, successful businessman DeVoe Moore, started collecting things when he was nine and apparently never stopped.

The breadth of cars is awe-inspiring, stretching from an **1893 Duryea** to a **1992 Dodge Viper**. Along the way there are a few detours for a **1931 Duesenberg Model J Dual Cowl Phaeton Convertible**; a **1954 Kaiser Darrin Roadster** (one of my dream cars; check out how the doors slide into the body); and three **Batmobiles** from the *Batman* films. The focus is on American-made vehicles; of the 148 on display, only 7 are foreign. NAAM member.

Number of vehicles: 148

Highlights: 1911 Ford Model T Torpedo Runabout; 1948 Tucker #1005.

Location: 6800 Mahan Drive, Tallahassee, FL 32308

Admission: $$

Hours: Monday through Friday, 8 a.m. to 5 p.m.; Saturday, 10 a.m. to 5 p.m.; Sunday, noon to 5 p.m.

Phone: (850) 942-0137

Web: www.tacm.com

TAMPA BAY AUTOMOBILE MUSEUM
Pinellas Park, FL

This first-rate collection of primarily European cars represents the passion of French-born mechanical engineer Alain Cerf. It includes many obscure brands that introduced leading-edge technology, with a focus on front-wheel-drive vehicles and the engineers who created them.

There are several cars from the Czechoslovakian maker Tatra, including a **1936 Tatra T26-30**, of which only 181 were produced, and a **1938 Tatra T97**. Practically a VW Beetle clone, production of the T97 was stopped by the Germans after they invaded Czechoslovakia; about 500 rolled off the assembly line. French automakers are also well-represented with a **1933 Derby V8** (only 11 produced) and a bizarre cracked-egg-shaped **1946 Mathis VL 333**. Unveiled to the public in 1946, the car is the only survivor of less than a dozen that were built secretly by the French during World War II.

Rare vehicles from this side of the Atlantic include a **1929 Ruxton** prototype. This competitor to the Cord was the first attempt at front-wheel drive in the United States. Its unusual cat's-eye headlights never caught on with the public. Moving up a few decades, there's a **1966 Oldsmobile Toronado,** which was the first American attempt at front-wheel drive since the '37 Cord. A full-time, in-house mechanic ensures that all the vehicles are up and running. NAAM member.

Number of vehicles: 65

Highlights: 1929 Ford Model A with a working Gas-O-Gen system to produce its own hydrogen; 1929 Tracta A race car that won the 1930 LeMans in the 2-liter class; 1965 Ford Mustang with All-Wheel Drive. You read that right; this one-off was sent to the UK to be fitted with AWD and disc brakes.

Location: 3301 Gateway Centre Boulevard, Pinellas Park, FL 33782

Admission: $ **Hours:** Monday, Wednesday through Saturday, 10 a.m. to 4 p.m.; Sunday, noon to 4 p.m. *Note:* Closed Tuesday.

Phone: (727) 579-8226 **Web:** www.tbauto.org

Side Trip: Airstream Ranch

If you're driving between Tampa and Orlando, take a look at **Airstream Ranch,** a series of seven-and-a-half recreational vehicles (to celebrate Airstream's 75th anniversary) angled into the ground. It's similar to the famed **Cadillac Ranch** in Texas. Frank Bates, who had to fight the local authorities for several years to keep it standing, placed it there. To view it, take exit 14 off of I-4 at McIntosh Road; head south, make a right on U.S. 92, and then a right on Castlewood Road.

GEORGIA

Old Car City Usa
White, GA

If you ever wanted to see what 4,000 rusting cars sprawling over 34 acres looks like, then this is the place. It's easy to see why it touts itself as the "world's largest known classic car junkyard." Some of the cars have been here for decades, with so many trees and roots burrowing through them that they look like part of the natural landscape. Owner, and local character, Dean Lewis presides over the place. Old Car City USA is located about 75 miles southeast of Chattanooga's towing museum, which (given the condition of the autos here) seems highly appropriate.

Number of vehicles: 4,000+

Location: 3098 Highway 411 Northeast, White, GA 30184. 50 miles northwest of Atlanta. *Tip:* The cars are deep in the Georgia woods, so bring plenty of bug spray.

Admission: $$$ if you have a camera or are going to have your picture taken, $$ for entry without a camera and without having your picture taken.

Hours: Wednesday through Saturday, 9 a.m. to 4 p.m.

Phone: (770) 382-6141

Web: www.OldCarCityUSA.com

KENTUCKY

NATIONAL CORVETTE MUSEUM
Bowling Green, KY

The phrase "I've got a sinking feeling" could definitely apply to the National Corvette Museum. On February 12, 2014, a rumble was heard around the automotive world when a voracious sinkhole opened up below the floor of the museum, taking eight Corvettes with it. Fortunately, the incident occurred after business hours so no one was injured. The affected cars, including a **1993 40th Anniversary Corvette,** are on display in their as-found condition in a special "Sinkhole Experience" exhibit. Sinkholes aside, this is one of the nation's premier destinations for 'Vette lovers. Visitors can also take tours of the **Bowling Green Corvette Assembly Plant** right across the street. (See the next page for information.)

"Nostalgia Alley" focuses on the 1950s and '60s through TV shows such as *Route 66,* whose stars drove a Corvette (a new one every season) as they traversed the country seeking adventure. Corvette's racing history is shown in the "Performance Area," where visitors can participate in the "Pit Crew Challenge." The "Design and Development" exhibit illustrates how new Corvettes make their way from the drawing board to the streets.

You can also eat breakfast or lunch in the 1950s-themed Corvette Café. Visitors may also sit inside a recent Corvette for a photo op. The exterior design of the museum is unique, just like the automobile it honors. Through a special program, Corvette buyers can take delivery of their vehicle at the museum and get a VIP tour of the assembly plant. NAAM member.

Number of vehicles: 80+

Highlights: Corvettes from 1953 to present day.

Location: 350 Corvette Drive, Bowling Green, KY 42101

Admission: $$

Hours: Daily, 8 a.m. to 5 p.m.

Phone: (800) 538-3883 or (270) 781-7973

Web: www.CorvetteMuseum.org

SWOPE'S CARS OF YESTERYEAR MUSEUM
Elizabethtown, KY

This museum was started by World War II veteran Bill Swope, who went on to much success as the owner of the Swope's Family of Dealerships, where the collection that specializes in Packard, Hupmobile, Pierce-Arrow, and other discontinued marques is located. The display ranges from the 1920s through the 1960s, with some real gems in the hangar-like buildings, including a **1931 LaSalle Convertible Rumble Seat Coupe** that was an early success of legendary General Motors designer Harley Earl.

The swooping black **1935 DeSoto Airflow Sedan** stuck out like a sore thumb when it was introduced, its aerodynamic styling so far ahead of its time that it never quite caught on with the public. The **1970 Cobra Torino SCJ** won the nod as *Motor Trend's* Car of the Year. Each of the autos has a descriptive placard telling its history. Some of the cars are for sale, so you never know what you might drive off the lot. NAAM member.

Number of vehicles: 50+

Highlights: 1910 Brush is on long-term loan; 1925 Pierce-Arrow Model 80; 1955 Dodge Custom Royal Lancer; 1964 Chevrolet Impala 409 SS Convertible.

Location: 1100 N. Dixie Avenue, Elizabethtown, KY 42701. It's only 75 miles northeast of the National Corvette Museum and Corvette Assembly Plant in Bowling Green, KY.

Admission: Free   **Hours:** Summer (April through October): Monday through Saturday, 10 a.m. to 5 p.m. Winter (November through March): Monday through Saturday, 10 a.m. to 4 p.m.

Phone: (270) 765-2181   **Web:** www.SwopeMuseum.com

MISSISSIPPI

BUSTED WRENCH GARAGE & MUSEUM
Gulfport, MS

As the name implies, the Busted Wrench is a working auto garage that happens to have an attached 6,000-square-foot exhibition space stuffed with cars, motorcycles, and boats. Some items are even dangling from the ceiling. Owner and mechanic John Hans is a vintage car fanatic who loves sharing his collection with the public. You can also watch cars being worked on in the garage. The large gift shop is stocked with car nostalgia items, making it a good place to get a set of fuzzy dice to hang from your rear-view mirror.
NAAM member.

Number of vehicles: 25+

Location: 2311 29th Street, Gulfport, MS

Admission: Free   **Hours:** Monday through Friday, 8 a.m. to 5 p.m.; Saturday by chance or appointment.

Phone: (228) 864-9082   **Web:** BustedWrench.com

TUPELO AUTOMOBILE MUSEUM
Tupelo MS

The official car museum of the state of Mississippi opened in 2002. Over 100 vehicles from North America and Europe are on display, starting with a three-wheeled **1886 Benz** and hitting the finish line with a **1994 Dodge Viper** with only 12 miles on the odometer.

A **1948 Tucker #1028** gives visitors the opportunity to ogle this rare make. But why does the open hood reveal a set of vintage leather suitcases? Just like the Volkswagen Beetle, the Tucker was a rear-engine vehicle. A slick **1954 Kaiser Darrin** is unusual because of its pocket doors that slid forward into the body. It was meant to compete with the Corvette, but it never caught on so only 435 were built. A **1982 Barrister Corvette** turns heads. It was built on an '82 Vette by customizer George Barris for Las Vegas entertainer Liberace.

Being located in Tupelo, the birthplace of Elvis Presley, gives the museum an Elvis connection. The "King" famously gave out cars to friends both far and wide. On display is a bright blue **1976 Lincoln Mark IV** he gave to Jerry Kennedy, captain of the Denver Police Vice and Drug Control Bureau for handling Presley's security when he appeared in Denver. NAAM member.

Number of vehicles: 150+

Highlights: 1886 Benz 3-wheeler; 1928 Hispano Suiza; 1948 Tucker; 1983 Camarovette (part Camaro, part Corvette) with 16-port nitrous oxide injection.

Location: 1 Otis Boulevard, Tupelo, MS 38804. Across from BancorpSouth Arena.

Admission: $$ **Hours:** Monday through Saturday, 9 a.m. to 4:30 p.m.; Sunday, noon to 4:30 p.m.

Phone: (662) 842-4242 **Web:** www.TupeloAutoMuseum.com

NORTH CAROLINA

BACKING UP CLASSICS MUSEUM
Concord, NC

Located less than a mile east of the Charlotte Motor Speedway, the **Backing Up Classics Museum** is a real throwback. Visitors meander through a winding hodgepodge of vehicles, vintage auto items, and country music memorabilia, most of which is for sale. Some of the cars have prices on them, while others just state their availability. It's hard to highlight certain vehicles because the collection is always changing, but the focus is on American cars from the 1950s and 1960s and muscle cars. There is a display devoted to *Talladega Nights: The Ballad of Ricky Bobby,* that includes one of the **2004 Chevrolet Monte Carlo** Wonder Bread cars driven by Will Ferrell's character in the movie.

An old camper is set up with all the items an outdoorsman would have needed circa 1940. There are also vintage bicycles, toy scooters, fire engine pedal cars, and license plates. You can purchase track-worn pit crew apparel in the gift shop.

Number of vehicles: 50+

Highlights: Tons of auto memorabilia, focused on American cars from the 1950s and 1960s.

Location: 4545 Highway 29, Concord, NC 28027. Next to Charlotte Motor Speedway.

Admission: $

Hours: Monday, Tuesday, Thursday, Friday, Saturday; 10 a.m. to 4 p.m. Closed Wednesday and Sunday.

Phone: (704) 788-9500   **Web:** www.MorrisonMotorCo.com

BENNETT CLASSICS ANTIQUE AUTO MUSEUM
Forest City, NC

Founded in 2007 by brothers Buddy and Joe Bennett, this attraction has already won a National Antique Automobile Club of America Museum Award. When the Bennetts were boys, their uncle owned a Ford dealership where they picked up their love of cars. Their collection has something for everyone, including automobiles, tractors, and B Series Mack trucks. There's even a **1979 American LaFrance Fire Truck**. The focus is on vehicles in unrestored original condition with low mileage.

TV fans will enjoy the **1963 Ford Mayberry Sheriff's Car** signed by actor Don Knotts, *aka* Deputy Barney Fife. Joe Bennett has owned the **1935 Chevrolet Standard** since he was 14 years old; it's quite a car for a teenager to handle. Those interested in performance will enjoy the **1968 Shelby GT 350**. A unique feature of the museum is the weathered-wood walls, which the Bennett brothers salvaged from an 1890s-era house that was demolished.

Number of vehicles: 70 (some of the cars are for sale, so the collection changes periodically.)

Highlights: 1928 Star Depot Hack; 1931 Ford Model A; 1955 Pontiac Chieftain.

Location: 241 Vance Street, Forest City, NC 28043. About 60 miles west of Charlotte, midway between Charlotte and Asheville.

Admission: $$ **Hours:** Monday through Friday, 10 a.m. to 5 p.m.; Saturday, 10 a.m. to 3 p.m.

Phone: (828) 247-1767   **Web:** www.BennettClassics.com

C. Grier Beam Truck Museum
Cherryville, NC

Keep on trucking!

If you're over a certain age, you remember the ubiquitous Carolina Freight trucks barreling down America's interstates. This is where the long-haul empire began. This ode to trucking is housed next to the original Shell gas station where C. Grier Beam founded Carolina Freight in 1932. If you're wondering why the colors of a North Carolina-based company were red and black and not Carolina blue, Beam graduated from University of North Carolina rival North Carolina State.

Fourteen trucks are on display, along with related Carolina Freight memorabilia. One Fruehauf trailer is rather unusual: It's outfitted with the sleeper located in the nose of the trailer. This type of sleeper became illegal after 1949. A mini-theater located in a **1946 Fruehauf trailer** shows a video highlighting the history of Carolina Freight and its founder. The oldest truck in the collection is a **1927 Chevrolet** with wooden spoke wheels. There are also four stake-bed body trucks that were used in the early days of Carolina Freight's operation. Sadly, the company was bought by ABF in 1995 and the new owners closed the once bustling Cherryville facility.

Extensive information and photos that depict each decade that Carolina operated, beginning with the 1930s and going through the 1980s, is also on view. The gift shop sells Carolina Freight die-cast collectibles along with other items, mostly with the Carolina logo. They also hold an annual car show in the spring. Check the website for details.

Number of vehicles: 14

Highlights: History of the local trucking industry and related memorabilia.

Location: 111 N. Mountain Street, Cherryville, NC 28021. It's 40 miles northwest of Charlotte.

Admission: Free

Hours: Thursday through Saturday, 10 a.m. to 3 p.m.

Phone: (704) 435-3072

Web: www.BeamTruckMuseum.com

CURB MUSIC AND MOTORSPORTS MUSEUM
Kannapolis, NC

Museum founder Mike Curb has had so many successful careers you'd almost think he's more than one person. The son of an FBI agent from Georgia, he's been a musician, record label impresario (Tim McGraw, LeAnn Rimes, and more), Lieutenant Governor and Acting Governor of California, co-chair of Ronald Reagan's presidential election committee, generous philanthropist, and racing team owner. In the latter capacity he raced Richard Petty and a young Dale Earnhardt. In fact, the museum is located in Earnhardt's boyhood town of Kannapolis and is a stop on the **"Dale Trail"** (see following sidebar) of sites related to The Intimidator's life.

Take a look at the unusual photo of Dale Earnhardt posing with the **1980 Chevrolet Monte Carlo** in which he won his first Winston Cup. Curb sponsored the racing legend so early in his career that the car was emblazoned with #2, predating Earnhardt's signature #3. Richard Petty briefly returned to Curb Racing late in his career, and the **1984 Pontiac STP** which he drove to his 199th win is on display. In addition to the stock cars. there's also a row of Indy 500 cars and a few Outlaw Series sprint cars.

A **2004 Ford** is the last car that drove with tobacco advertising before it was banned; in this case it was promoting Red Man snuff. LeAnn Rimes' **1995 Dodge Viper** is also on display. The teen singing star bought the car before she had a driver's license and just drove it around her farm. There's an unusual reason the car has less than 500 miles on it. When Curb found out his protégé was driving this high-powered sports car, he was so concerned for her safety that he swapped the car with Rimes and gave her a full-time driver. While half the museum is devoted to racing, the other half consists of the **North Carolina Music Hall of Fame,** where such local stars as Charlie Daniels, Ben E. King, and Andy Griffith (Sheriff Taylor had a singing career too) are honored.

Number of vehicles: 35

Highlights: 1980 Chevrolet Monte Carlo with distinctive blue and yellow colors, in which Dale Earnhardt Sr. won his first Winston Cup; Richard Petty's 1984 Pontiac, which he drove to his 199th win.

Location: 600 Dale Earnhardt Boulevard, Kannapolis, NC 28081

Admission: Free, donations accepted.

Hours: Monday through Friday, 9 a.m. to 4 p.m.

Phone: (704) 938-6121

Web: http://www.mikecurb.com/motorsports/
museum.cfm?PAGE=097

The Dale Trail:
A Tribute to Hometown Hero Dale Earnhardt

A statue of NASCAR legend Dale Earnhardt, Sr.
is a poignant reminder of a life cut short.

Kannapolis, North Carolina honors "The Intimidator," its most famous native son, with a nine-foot-tall statue at Dale Earnhardt Plaza on the corner of Main Street and West B Street downtown. It's part of "The Dale Trail," a collection of 20 sites related to the life of Dale Earnhardt. Attractions include the appropriately named Car Town section of Kannapolis where Earnhardt grew up and honed his racing skills on his bike (the neighborhood is so named because the streets are named after automotive companies like Ford, Buick, Cadillac, and DeSoto); **Curb Motorsports** (see prior listing), where Earnhardt's 1980 Winston Cup Championship car is on display; "Idiot Circle" downtown, where Earnhardt cruised as a teenager; Punchy's Diner, which serves his favorite tomato sandwich; and more.

Free color maps of the trail are available at the Cabarrus County Visitor Center, 10099 Weddington Road Ext., Concord, NC 28027. For more information, go to www.VisitCabarrus.com/cabarrus-county-dale-trail.

ESTES-WINN ANTIQUE CAR MUSEUM
Asheville, NC

This museum is part of a larger attraction called the Grovewood Gallery that highlights furniture, arts, and crafts. On the grounds you'll find this compact auto collection that features cars from a **1913 Ford Model T Touring** (Tin Lizzie) to a **1956 Cadillac Eldorado**. The sweet spot of the collection is from the 1920s including: a **1922 REO Flying Cloud Touring, 1922 American LaFrance Fire Truck** and a **1927 LaSalle Phaeton**.

Number of vehicles: 20

Highlights: 1922 REO Flying Cloud Touring; 1928 Chandler Sedan; 1950 MG TD Roadster.

Location: 111 Grovewood Road, Asheville, NC 28804

Admission: Free, but donations welcomed.

Hours: Seasonally, April through December: Monday through Saturday, 10 a.m. to 5 p.m.; Sunday, 11 a.m. to 5 p.m. *Note:* Closed January through March.

Phone: (828) 253-7651

Web: www.Grovewood.com/about-us/estes-winn-antique-car-museum/

HENDRICK MOTORSPORTS MUSEUM
Charlotte, NC

Hendrick Motorsports sprawls over a campus with manicured lawns that looks larger than some colleges. They've set aside one building for a substantial museum and gift shop. The museum is packed with at least two dozen racing vehicles, trophies, posters, artwork, and paraphernalia including commemorative checkered flags, racing uniforms, and helmets. Several of the vehicles appeared in the Tom Cruise racing film *Days of Thunder,* for which Rick Hendrick was a technical consultant.

Sitting side by side are the confetti-covered 2014 Daytona 500 winner driven by Dale Earnhardt Jr. and the 2013 Daytona 500 winner driven by Jimmie Johnson. Elsewhere are the cars raced to victory in the same event by Jeff Gordon in 1997 and 1999. He won the latter race by beating Dale Earnhardt Sr. by just 0.128 seconds. Check out the side of the car, where Earnhardt's congratulatory tire rub left its mark on the driver's side.

Visitors can also climb inside a custom carbon-fiber composite seat to get a feel for the cramped quarters in which the drivers operate. The gift shop offers tires from winning races that are marked with the track and date. (Sounds like a good acquisition for the man cave.) Across from the museum are athletic fields where the drivers and pit crews go through their exercise routines, prepping for physically grueling race days. Their schedule is available inside.

Number of vehicles: 25+

Highlights: 1997, 1999, 2013, and 2014 Daytona 500 winners; Jeff Gordon's #4 1989 Sprint Car, which held the Indianapolis Raceway Park (now the Lucas Oil Raceway at Indianapolis) qualifying record for 15 years.

Location: 4400 Papa Joe Hendrick Boulevard, Charlotte, NC 28262. It's located in Concord just north of Charlotte, about a mile north of the Charlotte Motor Speedway – which despite its name is also in Concord.

Admission: Free   **Hours:** Museum and Team Store: Monday through Friday, 10 a.m. to 5 p.m.; Saturday, 10 a.m. to 3 p.m. (Extended hours during race weeks at Charlotte Motor Speedway.) Racing shops: Monday through Friday, 8 a.m. to 4:30 p.m.

Phone: (877) 467-4890   **Web:** www.HendrickMotorsports.com

Memory Lane Museum
Mooresville, NC

This museum is accessed through a door at the back of a bicycle shop, which makes it all the more surprising to pass through and behold a massive collection of over 150 vehicles and related paraphernalia. Owner Alex Beam has been collecting since his youth in the 1960s and it appears that no one ever told him to stop. He must have good taste: Hollywood came calling for vehicles to use in *Days of Thunder, Talladega Nights, Driving Miss Daisy, The Color Purple,* and *Leatherheads,* among others. If you watch *Leatherheads,* you may notice that some of that 1920s-era football movie was filmed in the Mooresville environs.

About half the collection is made up of racing cars, mostly NASCAR, while the rest is vintage and antique autos, including many Model T Fords. There's also a section highlighting Dale Earnhardt, including the **1978 Oldsmobile Cutlass #2** in which he won the 1980 Busch Clash. Some of the more unusual cars are the pocket-sized **1926 Whippet** and a diminutive **1938 Austin Bantam Roadster.** If the latter looks a bit familiar, long-time auto rumor is that Donald Duck's car was based on the Austin Bantam.

Either way, it does look like it could leap out of the pages of a comic book. A **1939 Ford Deluxe** is set up with the obligatory moonshiner's gear in the open trunk.

One corner is dedicated to car crashes and features the veterans of some real fender-benders, including Michael Waltrip's car that he flipped at Daytona in 2000. It was such a total loss that it was compacted. If you want to see what a race car looks like as an engine-sized cube, this is it. (For those paying attention, there are two cars in this book featuring Waltrip's wrecked vehicles. The other is at the **International Motorsports Hall of Fame** in Talladega, Alabama.)

On the offbeat side are Soap Box Derby cars, pedal toy tractors, and what Beam claims is the largest collection of racing go-karts in the world. Darla's Toy Store in the rear contains hundreds, or perhaps thousands, of collectible toy trucks, cars, Western gear, dolls, and doll houses. You should be able to find your favorite toy from your childhood. There's also an incredible collection of plastic model car kits by AMT, Revell, and Monogram in their original boxes. NAAM member.

Number of vehicles: 150+

Highlights: 1912 Republic Truck (one of three remaining); 1930 Ford Model A Coupe Fire Chief Car; Bill Elliot's 1982 Ford Thunderbird.

Location: 769 River Highway (Highway 150), Mooresville, NC 28117. One mile west of I-77, exit 36. 30 miles north of Charlotte.

Admission: $$

Hours: Daily, Monday through Saturday, 10 a.m. to 5:00 p.m.; Charlotte Raceweek, Monday through Sunday, 10 a.m. to 5 p.m. (May & October Races); Winter Hours, mid-November through February, same hours as rest of year but closed Wednesday.

Phone: (704) 662-3673

Web: www.MemoryLaneAutoMuseum.com

Mooresville, North Carolina: Race City USA

You can easily spend a full day in Mooresville. It's home to at least six racing teams, along with the **North Carolina Auto Racing Hall of Fame**, the **Memory Lane Motorsports Museum**, and the **North Carolina Auto Racing Walk of Fame**. The latter is a plaque-filled sidewalk honoring racing's greats, located in front of the Charles Mack Citizen Center downtown. Don't miss the Franklin Automobile Company mural on the side of the Epic Chophouse at 104 South Main Street.

For more information on Mooresville, go to www.RaceCityUSA.org.

NASCAR HALL OF FAME
Charlotte, NC

Racecars lined up on the steep banked track look ready to fly.

Since the **NASCAR Hall of Fame** opened in 2010, it has become a popular and exciting place to spend an afternoon. The thrill level jumps up right away on "Glory Road," a massive banked curve inside the building that supports several legendary racing cars, including a **1952 Hudson Hornet** and a **1966 Ford Galaxie**, known as the "Yellow Banana." The aerodynamically altered car only raced once, but impacted how cars would be inspected and standardized in the future.

Placards highlight the history of famous NASCAR tracks, including some notables from the early days of dirt racing like **Occoneechee Speedway** (see separate entry.) The coolest feature of Glory Road is its two-story banking curve that mimics the slope found on regulation tracks. Near the top, visitors can walk up a

33-degree angled roadway to get a true feel of how sharp that is for drivers. It really is steep!

The "Hall of Fame" is very hands-on, making it a great attraction for children. You can try being a pit-crew member and see how fast you can change the wheels of a car. Elsewhere, tool carts are set up with auto parts that have QR codes affixed to them. Just scan the code, and a description and use of the part pops up on a monitor. For an extra fee, visitors can climb into actual vehicles and compete in a simulated race that is displayed on the dashboard.

Because the Hall of Fame is interactive, it makes sense that the racer's plaques in its "Hall of Honor" are different than at other sports museums. Each one has a monitor that runs highlights of the driver's career. It's much more entertaining than reading a plaque citing career statistics and highlights (although they have that too). The cars of the current year's inductees also are on display in the Hall of Honor.

Upon entry, visitors are given a Hard Card (same size as a credit card) that they insert at various monitors to get even more information or take trivia challenges. This comes in handy at the display of NASCAR's "Greatest Finishes." The **2003 Pontiac Grand Prix,** that was driven by Ricky Craven in the closest win in NASCAR history, is on display. (Two tight finishes in 2016 – at Daytona and Phoenix – came close to breaking that record.) Visitors can swipe their Hard Cards on the adjacent monitor and choose from over 50 exciting race finishes to view. The top floor of the museum is devoted to the history of NASCAR and shows assorted memorabilia, like Dale Earnhardt's racing gloves.

Number of vehicles: 50+

Highlights: 1952 Hudson Hornet driven by Marshall Teague; 1977 Oldsmobile Cutlass that Richard Petty drove to his sixth Daytona 500 win in 1979.

Location: 400 E. Martin Luther King Boulevard, Charlotte, NC 28202

Admission: $$ **Hours:** Daily, 10 a.m. to 6 p.m.

Phone: (704) 654-4400   **Web:** www.NASCARhall.com

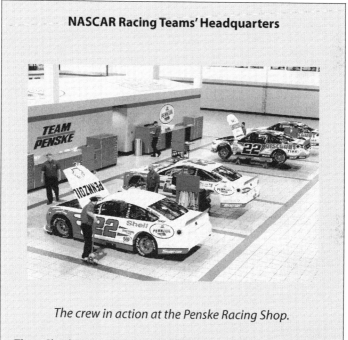

NASCAR Racing Teams' Headquarters

The crew in action at the Penske Racing Shop.

The Charlotte area is jam-packed with racing team headquarters. The ones listed below allow visitors to watch them working on the cars and also sell memorabilia of their most popular drivers. Best of all, most are free attractions. Check their websites for fan days, when drivers are on hand to sign autographs. (See next page for information.)

Chip Ganassi Racing with Frank Sabates (Jamie McMurray, Kyle Larson) 8500 Westmoreland Drive, Concord, NC 28027 www.ChipGanassiRacing.com. (704-662-9642)

Hendrick Motorsports (Jimmie Johnson, Kasey Kahne, Dale Earnhardt Jr.) 4400 Papa Joe Hendrick Boulevard, Charlotte (it's in Concord), NC 28262 www.HendrickMotorsports.com. (877-467-4890) (See separate listing.)

Roush Fenway Racing (Greg Biffle, Bubba Wallace, Trevor Bayne, Ryan Reed) 4600 Roush Place NW, Concord, NC 28027 www.RoushFenway.com (704-420-4350) (See separate listing.)

Stewart-Haas Racing (Tony Stewart, Danica Patrick, Kevin Harvick, Kurt Busch) 6001 Haas Way, Kannapolis, NC 28081 www.StewartHaasRacing.com (704-652-4227)

Penske Racing Shop (Brad Keselowski, Joey Logano, Will Power, Helio Castroneves) 200 Penske Way, Mooresville, NC 28115 www.TeamPenske.com (704-799-7178)

Richard Petty Motorsports (Jeb Burton, Aric Alminola, Brian Scott) 112 Byers Creek Road, Mooresville, NC 28117 www.RichardPettyMotorsports.com

Kyle Busch Motorsports (Kyle Busch, Daniel Suarez, Christopher Bell) 351 Mazeppa Road, Mooresville, NC 28115 www.KyleBuschMotorsports.com

JR Motorsports (Dale Earnhardt Jr, Chase Elliott) 349 Cayuga Drive, Mooresville, NC 28117 www.jrmracing.com

Kasey Kahne Racing 265 Cayuga Dr., Mooresville, NC 28117 www.KaseyKahneRacing.com

Michael Waltrip Racing (Martin Truex Jr., Mark Martin, Clint Bowyer) 20310 Chartwell Center Drive, Cornelius, NC 28031 www.MichaelWaltrip.com *Note:* fee charged.

Wood Family Racing (Ryan Blaney) 7201 Caldwell Road, Harrisburg, NC 28075 www.WoodBrothersRacing.com

North Carolina Auto Racing Hall of Fame
Mooresville, NC

*Local treasures await at the
North Carolina Auto Racing Hall of Fame.*

This museum celebrates the birth of auto racing in North Carolina, which was intertwined with the advent of the moonshiners. The first car on display is a 1940s Ford, with its trunk opened to reveal Mason jars full of "moonshine" (illegally distilled whiskey, a popular local product). The tour guide explains some of the tricks early moonshiners used to camouflage their cars from law enforcement, such as cranking up the shocks so the car wouldn't ride low from the heavy load.

There are also car displays related to NASCAR, drag racing, and the Indy 500. There's even a **1929 Ford Model A** car that set a land speed record for its class in 1992. Mooresville native Don Miller pushed it to 152 mph on the Bonneville Salt Flats, making it the fastest flathead supercharged street roadster in the world. Another unique Ford is a **1997 Ford Lincoln Mark VIII Aero Research Vehicle**. The Thunderbird had been discontinued and because Ford was seeking a NASCAR replacement they used this vehicle for wind tunnel testing. Due to cost issues it was cast aside for the Ford Taurus.

Racing fans will enjoy seeing Rusty Wallace's **1980 Chevrolet Impala,** which he drove in his first NASCAR Winston Cup race and nailing a second-place finish in Atlanta. The **1960 Chrysler 413** dragster, with huge tail fins that make it look like the Batmobile, was driven by NASCAR Hall-of-Famer Rex White when he was the Grand National Champion. Other exhibits include engines, framed driver's racing suits, model cars, and an exhibit devoted to the "First Lady" of racing, Louise Smith, one of stock car racing's pioneer women. The Hall of Fame in the back of the museum displays bronze plaques honoring some of the greats such as Richard Petty, Bill France, and Dale Earnhardt Sr.

Number of vehicles: 40+

Highlights: Four generations of Petty family race cars; 1963 Corvette dragster with only 2,300 miles on the odometer – added one hard-earned quarter-mile at a time.

Location: 119 Knob Hill Road, Mooresville, NC 28117

Admission: $

Hours: Monday through Friday, 10 a.m. to 5 p.m.; Saturday, 10 a.m. to 3 p.m.

Phone: (704) 663-5331

Web: www.ncarhof.com

North Carolina Transportation Museum
Spencer, NC

This 57-acre museum occupies Southern Railroad's largest steam locomotive repair facility on the east coast. While the focus is on trains, there is also a compact and worthwhile auto exhibit spread over several buildings. Most of the cars were bought and driven in North Carolina. A prime example is the **1935 Ford North Carolina Highway Patrol Car**. The 90-horsepower V8 was the car of choice for gangsters, so the highway patrol drove them too. This is the last of the original order of 28 patrol cars. The **1959 DIVCO (Detroit Industry Vehicle Company)** milk truck was driven on a local, you guessed it, milk run. Notice how it used ice as refrigeration.

The **1917 Brockaway Ladder Fire Truck** was operated in Elizabeth City by the first all-volunteer African-American fire department in the state and was in use until the 1950s. There are four other fire trucks in the exhibit. You'll also find automotive memorabilia, highway signage, traffic control equipment, fuel and oil pumps, firefighting equipment, and more.

Number of vehicles: 35   **Highlights:** 1901 Stanhope, a steam auto built by a Cleveland- based sewing machine company; rare 1907 Ford Model R; 1948 Lincoln Continental with a V-12 engine.

Location: 411 S. Salisbury Avenue, Spencer, NC 28159. Five minutes off exit 79 of I-85, 45 miles northeast of Charlotte.

Admission: $ **Hours:** Spring/Summer/Fall (March 1 through October 31): Tuesday through Saturday, 9 a.m. to 5 p.m.; Sunday, 1 p.m. to 5 p.m. Early Winter (November 1 through December 31): Wednesday through Saturday, 9 a.m. to 5 p.m.; Sunday, 1 p.m. to-5 p.m. Winter (January 1 through February 28): Wednesday through Saturday, 9 a.m. to 5 p.m.

Phone: (704) 636-2889   **Web:** www.nctrans.org

Side Trip: Occoneechee Speedway
—NASCAR's Early Dirt Days

Ten miles north of Chapel Hill, North Carolina are the remains of one of NASCAR's earliest tracks, the **Occoneechee Speedway**. It's the last surviving track from NASCAR's inaugural Strictly Stock season in 1949. Races took place on the .9-mile dirt oval until 1968, when the track had to close because local clergymen objected to racing on Sundays.

Richard Petty, who won the last race held here, recalls, "It was a good little track for us. You know, there aren't too many tracks where both my father and I won, but Occoneechee was one of them." After the track closed, the races moved on to bigger venues like the Talladega Superspeedway in Alabama.

Renamed the Orange Speedway, the track languished in obscurity and almost surrendered to the onslaught of the surrounding forest. However, in 1997 it was saved. Its location along the Eno River provided a pastoral setting for nature lovers, so it was converted into a hiking trail.

While not much remains of the original buildings, a group called the Historic Speedway Group has been busy restoring the ticket office and concession stands. Other than the occasional aggressive tree root, the concrete stands have held up pretty well. A stroll across the infield reveals a faded wooden advertising sign touting the "Hillsborough Savings and Loan Association," one of the track's sponsors.

PETTY MUSEUM
Randleman, NC

Richard Petty's iconic #43 Plymouth Superbird.

This shrine for NASCAR fans is dedicated to the racing legacy of the Petty family. It's next to the house where Richard "The King" Petty and his brother (and fellow NASCAR Hall-of-Famer) Maurice, were born. Also on the grounds are buildings for Petty Enterprises, where you can poke your head inside and watch the crew working on vehicles.

A highlight is the **1936 Chevrolet Street Rod** that family patriarch, Lee Petty, drove at Daytona when they still raced on the beach. Maurice later purchased it as his first car. There's also a replica of the **1984 Pontiac Grand National Stock Car** that Richard Petty drove to his 200th win.

The museum houses memorabilia and an incredible number of championship trophies, rings, and belt buckles from the Petty family's illustrious careers, along with pocketknives, guns, and dolls collected by Richard's late wife Lynda. If you're lucky, you might even run into The King himself during your visit.

For children, there's an area to color pictures they can leave for Petty to sign, which the museum will then mail to them. How cool is that? When I was 12 years old, I was thrilled to get a signed photo from Richard Petty with his distinctive loop-filled autograph. On display is the handwriting book he used as a child to practice his signature. Kids will also like the #43 amusement park bumper car painted in Petty's livery.

Number of vehicles: 20+

Highlight: 1992 Pontiac Grand Prix SE #43, in which Petty drove his last lap before his retirement.

Location: 309 Branson Mill Road, Randleman, NC 27317. The mailing address is Randleman, but the museum is located a few miles north in Level Cross, the small hamlet in which Petty was raised; it's about 20 miles south of Greensboro, NC.

Admission: $$ **Hours:** Monday through Saturday, 9 a.m. to 5 p.m.

Phone: (336) 495-1143   **Web:** RPMuseum.com

RCR MUSEUM
Welcome, NC

The museum arm of Richard Childress Racing, it's located on the site of the original #3 Goodwrench team race shop. This attraction especially appeals to fans of racing legend Dale Earnhardt Sr. Childress owns over 40 of the cars that Earnhardt raced and displays over two dozen of them, including the **1998 Chevrolet**

Monte Carlo in which he won the Daytona 500. It still has the lucky penny glued to the dashboard that was given to Earnhardt the day before the race by a child from the Make-A-Wish Foundation.

Cars driven by Ricky Rudd, Kevin Harvick, and Clint Bowyer are featured, along with NASCAR Camping World Truck Series championship Silverados raced by Mike Skinner and Austin Dillon. There's also the Silverado that Dillon drove to victory in the Camping World Truck Series first dirt race at Eldora Speedway in 2013. Kevin Harvick's 2001 Atlanta winner is here, along with his 2007 Daytona 500 car.

The Wall of History near the entrance explains the history of RCR. Visitors can also stroll the Fan Walk overlooking the activities in the race shop. For something different, you can watch No.3 Goodwrench Gas Man Chocolate Myers broadcast SiriusXM's *Tradin' Paint* live from the Richard Childress Racing Museum store, Mondays through Thursdays from 11 a.m. to 3 p.m. Childress is well known for his interest in hunting, so there's also a display devoted to wildlife and outdoor conservation.

Number of vehicles: 50+

Highlights: Over two dozen black #3 cars driven by Dale Earnhardt Sr.

Location: 236 Industrial Drive, Lexington, NC 27295

Admission: $$

Hours: Monday through Friday, 10 a.m. to 4 p.m.; Saturday, 10 a.m. to 2 p.m. (Come during the week to watch the crews working on the cars.)

Phone: (800) 476-3389

Web: www.RCRRacing.com

WHEELS THROUGH TIME
Maggie Valley, NC

This museum, owned by the legendary Dale Walksler, offers a huge collection of rare motorcycles from 1903 through present day, plus one-off cars. It was the setting for the TV show *What's in the Barn* on the Velocity Channel and the newer series *American Restoration* on the History Channel.

The exhibits are incredibly designed and laid out to best feature the motorcycles and cars. One of the popular displays is "Military Might," which features Harley-Davidsons that saw military service. The "Swim Shop" shows a Harley dealer from the late 1940s and early '50s. From an automotive standpoint, one of the highlights is a rare **1915 Locomobile**, made in Bridgeport, Connecticut.

Number of vehicles: 300+   **Highlights:** 1916 Traub, considered the world's rarest motorcycle.

Location: 62 Vintage Lane, Maggie Valley, NC 28751

Admission: $$ **Hours:** Open early April through end of November: Thursday to Monday, 9 a.m. to 5 p.m. Check website for exact dates.

Phone: (828) 926-6266   **Web:** www.WheelsThroughTime.com

Side Trip: The World's Largest Working Tire

On the grounds of **Hester Tire** in North Carolina you can see the world's largest functioning tire. The Michelin 59/80R63 is 14 feet tall, weighs over 10,000 pounds, and fits on a Caterpillar 797B Dump Truck. All that rubber costs over $40,000. At the intersection of Highway 131N and the 211 Bypass in Bladenboro, North Carolina, about 40 miles south of Fayetteville.

SOUTH CAROLINA

BMW Zentrum
Greer, SC

Located next to the BMW manufacturing plant, the **Zentrum** serves as part marketing tool and part museum, highlighting the history of BMW and its racing heritage. Displays cover M-series vehicles, Formula Two racing, and off-road motorcycle rallies. Guided tours of the adjacent plant are also offered. (See information below.) If you can't make the factory tour, a video reveals what you missed.

There's a mix of vintage autos and milestone vehicles, such as the first **BMW Z3** produced there. Current vehicles produced next door are also on display. You'll also see the crash-test **BMW X5,** which has been beaten and battered by Insurance Institute for Highway Safety tests. There are also 15 BMW motorcycles on display. Plenty of BMW paraphernalia are on sale in the gift shop.

Number of vehicles: 17

Highlights: 1930 Dixi (Dixis were the first cars made by BMW); 1995 BMW Z3 (seen in the James Bond film *Goldeneye*).

Location: 1400 Highway 101 South, Greer, SC 29651

Admission: Free   **Hours:** Monday through Friday, 9:30 a.m. to 5:30 p.m.

Phone: (864) 989-5300   **Web:** www.BMWUSFactory.com/zentrum

BMW Factory Tours: Guided tours are available Monday through Friday. You must make an advance reservation by calling (888) 868-7269. For the latest information on touring the BMW plant, go to www.bmwusfactory.com/zentrum/tours/guided-factory-tour.

DARLINGTON RACEWAY STOCK CAR MUSEUM & NATIONAL MOTORSPORTS PRESS ASSOCIATION HALL OF FAME
Darlington, SC

This museum opened in 1965 as a counterpoint to Indy car racing's **Indianapolis Motor Speedway Museum**. The winningest car in the history of stock car racing is on display: the **1956 Ford #26,** driven by Curtis Turner to first place 22 times in a single year in the short-lived Convertible Division. You'll also find the **1985 Ford Thunderbird** Bill Elliott drove to victory in the Southern 500 at Darlington raceway, winning a $1-million bonus. A touching exhibit is devoted to Dale Earnhardt Sr., featuring his handprints in concrete. He won nine times at Darlington. For kids (and adults) who are fans of the movie *Cars,* there is a **1951 Hudson Hornet** driven by Herb Thomas. It was the inspiration for Doc Hudson's car (voiced by Paul Newman) in the film. Thomas won the 1951 Southern 500 at Darlington in this one.

Also stop in at the **National Motorsports Press Association's Hall of Fame** to see memorabilia and interactive exhibits related to over 75 past inductees, including Lee and Richard Petty, Alan Kulwicki, David Pearson, Junior Johnson, and more. In addition to NASCAR races, the track hosts various events throughout the year including classic car shows, barbeque contests, and marathons.

Number of vehicles: 14

Highlights: 1950 Plymouth in which Johnny Mantz won the first Mountain Dew Southern 500; 1991 Chevy Lumina that Darrell Waltrip rolled eight times in the '91 Pepsi 400, but still managed to walk away.

Location: 1301 Harry Byrd Highway, Darlington, SC 29532

Admission: $ **Hours:** Monday through Friday, 10 a.m. to 5 p.m.; Saturday, 10 a.m. to 4 p.m.

Phone: (843) 395-8821   **Web:** www.DarlingtonRaceway.com/About-Us/Museum-Giftshop.aspx

WHEELS OF YESTERYEAR
Myrtle Beach, SC

This collection focuses on American muscle, primarily Chrysler, Dodge, and Plymouth. With more than 100 cars in stock, owners Paul and Carol Cummings rotate the display every winter to give the museum a fresh look for the new year. The Cale Yarborough **1969 Mercury Cyclone,** with its 428-cubic-inch, 360-horsepower CJ V8, gave street drivers a chance to emulate their NASCAR heroes. The cars here are restored, but the Cummings try to keep them as original as possible. The extensive gift shop also offers a wide array of toy muscle cars.

Number of vehicles: 50+

Highlights: 1963 Corvette Split Window Sting Ray Coupe; 1969 Dodge Charger Daytona from the movie *Joe Dirt*; 1971 Plymouth "Hemi" Barracuda convertible.

Location: 413 Hospitality Lane, Myrtle Beach, SC 29579

Admission: $ **Hours:** Daily, 10 a.m. to 6 p.m., extended hours in summer.

Note: The museum is closed around the last two weeks of January, when they rotate the collection.

Phone: (843) 903-4774

Web: www.WheelsOfYesteryearMB.com

TENNESSEE

CITY GARAGE CAR MUSEUM
Greeneville, TN

Museum founder Kurt Bewley descends from a long line of Greeneville automotive history, with a family that's been in the business since 1937. His father, R.R. Bewley, was a Pontiac-Cadillac-Packard dealer and the museum hosts auto memorabilia related to the long-time family business. It's located in a circa-1950 car dealership and is broken down into five sections: 1) An antique 1920s Texaco service station; 2) the historic Bewley Motor Company dealership showroom; 3) the Popcorn Sutton moonshine section, highlighting a **1940 Ford Coupe** moonshiner vehicle; 4) a NASCAR section, including Sterling Martin's **1994 Chevrolet Monte Carlo #4 Kodak,** in which he won the Daytona 500 that year, and a street version of Dale Earnhardt's **1985 Monte Carlo Special Edition #3** stock car, which was sold only at the Dale Earnhardt Chevrolet Dealership in Newton, North Carolina; and 5) the Suzie Q Diner, used for special events.

While this compact collection tends toward Big Three Detroit autos, there are also a few quirky vehicles added to the mix, like a **1933 Hudson Essex Terraplane** and a **1936 Auburn Boattail Speedster.** Gullwing fans can compare a **1981 DeLorean** (only 726 miles) with a **1982 Bricklin.** Truck lovers will enjoy the **1923 Ford Model T Texaco Truck** and **1929 Ford Model A Texaco Truck.** A cross-section of an automobile engine exposes the pistons, crankshaft, valves, and other parts. There's also a selection of antique car tags. NAAM member.

Number of vehicles: 40

Highlights: 1939 Cadillac Sedan, 1970 Subaru 360 Coupe that was the first in America, 1972 DeTomaso Pantera Sports Car with only 4,900 miles.

Location: 210 S. Main Street, Greeneville, TN 37743. About an hour east of Knoxville, TN.

Admission: $ **Hours:** Wed through Sat, 10 a.m. to 4 p.m.

Phone: (423) 638-6971   **Web:** www.CityGarageCarMuseum.com

ELVIS PRESLEY AUTOMOBILE MUSEUM AT GRACELAND
Memphis, TN

A collection of more than a dozen vehicles once owned by Elvis Presley is located across the street from his mansion; admission is included in the ticket price of Graceland tours. Visitors can view a **1956 Cadillac Eldorado Convertible**, a **1975 Dino Ferrari,** and several Harley-Davidson motorcycles. The **1973 Stutz Blackhawk** is the car he rode in through the storied gates of Graceland for the final time on August 16, 1977. Elvis played around like a kid, so there's also his dune buggy, go-kart, motorized three-wheelers, and a snowmobile he had reconfigured to run on lawns. Stop by the adjacent Rockabilly's Burger Shop for Elvis' favorite, a grilled peanut-butter-and-banana sandwich.

Number of vehicles: 18

Highlights: Pink 1955 Cadillac Fleetwood Series 60 that Elvis gave his mother as a gift, even though she couldn't drive; 1966 Rolls-Royce Silver Cloud that was later owned by Michael Landon and Charlie Rich.

Location: 3765 Elvis Presley Boulevard, Memphis, TN 38116

Admission: $$$$ includes admission to Graceland.

Hours: Hours vary slightly throughout the year but are generally Monday through Saturday, 9 a.m. to 5 p.m.; Sunday, 9 a.m. to 4 p.m. Closing times during the week are usually an hour earlier from November through May.

Phone: (800) 238-2000   **Web:** www.Graceland.com

Get the Shaft

To see another car in Memphis with a musical connection, head to the **Stax Museum of American Soul Music.** There you'll find the **1972 Cadillac Eldorado** custom-built for the original "Soul Man," Isaac Hayes. It sits on a rotating turntable to better show off its flashy, 24-carat gold trim; it also came with a refrigerator and TV. Four years later the *Shaft* composer declared bankruptcy, but he no doubt enjoyed a wonderful ride along the way. Stax Museum of American Soul Music, 926 E. McLemore Avenue, Memphis, TN 38106, www.StaxMuseum.com.

FLOYD GARRETT'S MUSCLE CAR MUSEUM
Sevierville, TN

American-made muscle cars from the '50s, '60s, and '70s, especially Chevy products, are the focus here. But there are other makes, too, including Ford Mustangs and Mopar muscle. It's hard to replace that feeling of awe you get seeing all that horsepower lined up in shiny rows.

Note: As this book went to press, Floyd Garrett was trying to sell the museum building and retire. That's been the plan for a few years, so it may not happen anytime soon. He'll keep the museum running while it's on the market, but check their website before visiting to confirm that it is still open. Most of the cars are on loan from collectors, so they are not part of the sale.

Number of vehicles: 90 (cars rotate in and out of the collection, so each visit will be a bit different).

Highlights: 1965 Dodge Coronet with 426-cid Hemi engine; 1969 Chevrolet Camaro; 1971 Plymouth GTX; chatting with Floyd Garrett himself as he shares personal memories about the vehicles.

Location: 320 Winfield Dunn Parkway, Sevierville, TN 37876

Admission: $$ **Hours:** January through March: Daily, 9 a.m. to 5 p.m. April through December: Daily, 9 a.m. to 6 p.m.

Web: www.MuscleCarMuseum.com

International Towing & Recovery Hall of Fame & Museum
Chattanooga, TN

Who didn't want to ride in a tow truck when they were a kid? Only to be smacked with reality when they finally got that chance, which meant their car had broken down yet again by the side of the road. (But enough about my first car.) This museum is dedicated to those who race out into any weather to help us when we're stranded. The Chattanooga location is appropriate; the industry's first wrecker was fabricated nearby at the Ernest Holmes Company. Also on display is the world's largest collection of toy wreckers and gas station memorabilia. The "Wall of the Fallen" outside memorializes tow truck drivers who died helping others.

Number of vehicles: 20

Highlights: A replica of the first wrecker ever built; 1929 Packard with a Manley crane; Locomobile.

Location: 3315 Broad Street, Chattanooga, TN 37408

Admission: $$

Hours: Summer (March 1 through October 31): Monday through Saturday, 9 a.m. to 5 p.m.; Sunday, 11 a.m. to 5 p.m. Winter (November 1 through February 28): Monday through Saturday, 10 a.m. to 4:30 p.m.; Sunday 11 a.m. to 5 p.m.

Phone: (423) 267-3132

Web: www.InternationalTowingMuseum.org

Side Trip: A Stretched-Out Station Wagon

If your Tennessee travels take you through Knoxville, the **Women's Basketball Hall of Fame** features a stretch station wagon that squired the Moore's All-American Red Heads traveling basketball team around the country. The 1966 Pontiac Airporter Limousine is so big it had to be wheeled into the building before all the walls were put up. Women's Basketball Hall of Fame, 700 Hall of Fame Drive, Knoxville, TN 37915 www.WBHOF.com

LANE MOTOR MUSEUM
Nashville, TN

The Lane Motor Museum specializes in non-American cars.

Founded by Jeff Lane in 2002, the **Lane Motor Museum** focuses on cars from Europe, boasting the largest European collection in the United States. That said, they still offer up a few vehicles from the Americas and Asia.

What really sets the museum apart is the amount of quirky, oddball cars that you won't find anywhere else. You want to see a car with a propeller? Check. A car that converts to a bed? Sure. A car that folds up? No problem. It's really wild to walk around and see one crazy vehicle after another. Because many of the cars are rather compact, over 150 are packed into the former Sunbeam Bakery space.

The bulbous, Czech-built **1964 Tatra T-603 MKII Saloon** was only available to high-level Communist Party officials. Because the front bench seat also folds down into a bed, one wonders if there was a connection somehow. A **1954 Simca Weekend Prototype** is a one-off that was given to French bombshell Brigitte Bardot for her promotional appearances on behalf of the automaker. What may be the oddest car in the collection (and that's really saying something) is a wood-bodied **1932 Helicron**. This French-made vehicle with a giant wooden propeller attached to the front looks like some fantasy car from a Dr. Seuss story. Believe it or not, it still drives.

What's cool about most of the cars is that although they're rare, they are not shiny baubles that sold for six figures, but autos that regular people drove. So you might find a **1967 Saab 95 Station Wagon** parked next to a shiny red **1957 Messerschmitt KR200** three-wheeled microcar with handlebar steering. Hey, did you expect a full steering wheel for half the price of a Volkswagen? There's also a formation of unusual military vehicles in the parking garage, and around 30 motorcycles. A play area keeps the kids entertained – which is a good thing because you can easily spend several hours at the Lane. NAAM member.

Number of vehicles: 150+ on display (total collection is over 400)

Highlights: 1935 Adler Trumpf Junior; 1959 Weidner Condor; 1955 MG that Jeff Lane restored when he was a teenager.

Location: 702 Murfreesboro Pike (Route 70), Nashville, TN 37210. Three miles southeast of downtown Nashville.

Admission: $$ **Hours:** Monday, Thursday, Friday, Saturday, Sunday: 10 a.m. to 5 p.m.; Closed, Tuesday and Wednesday. *Note:* If you visit on a weekend, ask if they are offering tours of the basement, where many more cars are stored – or check the website for special events.

Phone: (615) 742-7445 **Web:** www.LaneMuseum.org

Side Trip: The Marathon Man

The former Marathon factory is still in use today.

Marathon Village is a cluster of brick factories where Nashville's automotive industry was launched in the early 20th century. Here Marathon cars were produced from 1910 through 1914. Today it is a mixed-use complex, with an eclectic array of tenants that includes the automotive-themed Garage Coffee Company, along with Antique Archaeology (owned by Mike Wolfe of *American Pickers* fame). Best of all for car buffs, developer Barry Walker has been collecting the few remaining Marathon cars known to exist. So far he has acquired a half-dozen, which now sit proudly in the original Marathon showroom. Once Marathon closed its doors no more cars were manufactured in Tennessee until the 1980s with the advent of Saturn, now also departed. Marathon Village is located at 1200 Clinton Street, Nashville, TN 37203. www.MarathonVillage.com.

Nissan Plant Tour

Twenty miles southeast of the **Lane Motor Museum** in Nashville, the **Nissan plant** in Smyrna offers free tours on Tuesdays and Thursdays. Visitors are driven through the factory on a tram for a close-up view of production. To reserve a spot, e-mail them at: nissansmyrnapublictours@nissan-usa.com. They book up early, so contact them several weeks in advance – or even sooner during the summer.

Side Trip: Dodge City

For an almost-vanished piece of automotive archaeology, head to the corner of Broadway and 16th Avenue South in downtown Nashville to see the Beaman GMC/Buick dealership. Although the building is modern, along the Broadway façade you'll see memories of a lost era: two century-old columns that were salvaged from an old Dodge Brothers dealership that stood on this site and survived until the 1960s. Notice the spoked wheel, car parts, and tools etched into the columns along with the "DB" logo. 1531 Broadway, Nashville, TN.

VIRGINIA

Keystone Truck and Tractor Museum
Colonial Heights, VA

A 1938 version of farming in style.

Here you'll find more than 70,000 square feet of gleaming tractors, autos, and trucks. As the name implies, the focus is on tractors but there are enough other vehicles to keep everyone happy. Museum founder Keith Jones bought his first tractor – a **1950 John Deere M** – in 1997 from his late uncle's estate. That's when he "got the collecting fever"; which hasn't broken.

The coolest tractor in the museum is a **1938 Minneapolis-Moline UDLX**. It boasts a car-like appearance, with an enclosed cab and amenities including a radio, heater, and clock. The slogan was "farm during the day, drive to town at night." Hard to believe with all that bling it wasn't a sales success. But according to the museum guide, "it was too expensive, and farmers thought you were a wuss if you had a cab on your tractor." A **1917 International Harvester Titan** was left in its original beat-up condition to show what amazing workhorses these were.

Despite the focus on tractors, cars are also well represented. Highlights include a trio of **1955/'56/'57 Ford Thunderbirds;** a **1967 Chevrolet Chevelle Custom** hot rod; and a **1992 Shelby Cobra** with a $500,000 MSRP. Owner Keith Jones is the CEO of trucking firm Abilene Motor Express so trucks are also on display. The **1957 Diamond T "Pig Nose Truck,"** so named because the owner wanted more power and added an extra engine to the front, is an odd one. A dozen fire trucks and a vintage fire chief's car tempt even the most stoic visitor to make siren noises.

Kids can sit on a **1959 John Deere 430 Wide** for a photo op. The walls are lined with a collection of over 1,800 model trucks. Old-time gas pumps, a moonshining display, and tobacco-farming memorabilia round out the collection.

Number of vehicles: 200+ (170 tractors, 20+ cars, 25+ trucks)

Highlights: 1917 International Titan 90; 1923 Ford Model T American LaFrance Fire Engine; 1932 Massey Harris GP Tractor, the first with four-wheel drive.

Location: 880 W. Roslyn Road, Colonial Heights, VA 23834. It's 20 miles south of Richmond and right off I-95 exit 53, just north of Petersburg.

Admission: $

Hours: Monday through Saturday, 10 a.m. to 6 p.m.; Sunday, 11 a.m. to 5 p.m.

Phone: (804) 524-0020   **Web:** www.KeystoneTractorWorks.com

UNITED STATES ARMY TRANSPORTATION MUSEUM
Fort Eustis, VA

*A 1941 Plymouth Deluxe Sedan, identical to this one,
served in the Pacific in World War II.*

Fort Eustis was the long-time headquarters of the United States Army Transportation Corps. It's now Joint Base Langley-Eustis – and home to a museum that highlights the history of repositioning troops and war materiel from the American Revolution through the present day. The display devoted to motorized transport begins in the early 20th century with one of America's most influential road trips, the Army truck train that drove from Washington, D.C. to San Francisco in 1919 to inspect America's roads. (They were found to be either non-existent or sorely lacking.) Lieutenant Colonel Dwight D. Eisenhower was on this journey, which influenced him as President decades later, when he signed the act creating the Interstate Highway System.

Many exhibits are devoted to transportation in World War II, including the famed Red Ball Express, which hauled fuel to Allied tanks after the Normandy invasion. A **1943 GMC 2-½ Ton Truck,** which GIs called a "Deuce and a Half," highlights that mission. A Jeep that was converted to drive on rail tracks in the Pacific Theater is an outstanding example of American ingenuity. From a later era, the jet-black "Eve of Destruction" gun truck looks like something from a *Mad Max* movie and is the only one to return from Vietnam. The **M-Gator Utility Vehicle** is a conversion of a John Deere ATV used in desert terrain. There are separate outdoor pavilions for trucks, Jeeps, aviation, rail, and marine vehicles.

Number of vehicles: 30+ (not including boats, trains, and aircraft).

Highlights: World War II-era vehicles including a Dodge WC-52 Weapons Carrier, Willys-Overland Jeep, and M29 Weasel Cargo Carrier snow vehicle; modern transports include an M998 Troop Cargo Carrier Humvee.

Location: 300 Washington Boulevard, Fort Eustis, VA 23604. On Joint Base Langley-Eustis, about 15 miles southeast of Williamsburg. *Note:* The museum is on an active military installation, so you and your vehicle must pass a thorough inspection at the gate. Bring a government-issued photo ID.

Admission: Free

Hours: Tuesday through Sunday, 9 a.m. to 4:30 p.m. Closed on Federal holidays.

Phone: (757) 878-1115

Web: www.transportation.army.mil/museum/transportation%20 museum/museum.htm

Virginia Museum of Transportation
Roanoke, VA

If you liked the movie *Planes, Trains and Automobiles,* you'll love the **Virginia Museum of Transportation,** because they've got them all here. Start out with the **1923 Piedmont Touring Car Model 4-30.** One of only three known to exist, it was built by the only auto company ever chartered in Virginia. A **1918 Kline Kar** (yes that's the correct "cute" spelling) was also made in Virginia. There's even an electric charger in front of the museum, in case you drove up in a Chevy Volt. I wonder if it works on the **1913 Detroit Electric** car inside; talk about a car ahead of its time!

An unusual, and rather morbid, vehicle is a **1936 Siebert Ford Combination Ambulance/ Hearse.** Can you imagine getting into an accident and seeing a hearse roll up to take you away? That's how it was done back then, with the car and driver serving double duty. Moving forward a few decades, glide over to the **1957 Desoto Fireflite Sportsman** to get your tail-fin fix.

On the railroad side of the museum there are more than 50 exhibits, the stars of which are two historic steam engines. The "Wings Over Virginia Aviation Gallery" is dedicated to the history of flight in Virginia. NAAM member.

Number of vehicles: 25   **Highlights:** Federal Aviation Administration Tucker Sno-Cat (technically not a car, this snowmobile on steroids is fun to gaze at, and probably even more fun to take out on the snow); Jeep-Oren-Industrial Fire Truck; 1955 Studebaker President Speedster.

Location: 303 Norfolk Avenue SW, Roanoke, VA 24016

Admission: $ **Hours:** Monday through Saturday, 10 a.m. to 5 p.m.; Sunday, 1 p.m. to 5 p.m.

Phone: (540) 342-5670   **Web:** vmt.org

WOOD BROTHERS RACING MUSEUM
Stuart, VA

Founders of the longest active running NASCAR team, the Wood family boasts one of the finest pedigrees in the racing world. It all started in 1950 with brothers Glen and Leonard Wood. Glen went on to be selected as one of NASCAR's "50 Greatest Drivers," and both brothers are enshrined in the NASCAR Hall of Fame. The family business now includes the third generation of Woods, who are running the #21 Sprint Cup Ford team.

From the back-and-white checkered flag floor of the museum, to the garage out back, you know you're in a special place for NASCAR history buffs. There's a **1963 Ford Galaxie** tribute car built by Leonard Wood. He built the original car that won the Daytona 500 in 1963, with Tiny Lund behind the wheel. The walls are lined with racing memorabilia attesting to the family's long racing history. (Their racing operations can be visited in Harrisburg, North Carolina.)

Number of vehicles: 15+

Highlights: 1937 Ford Coach tribute car, one of Glen Wood's most famous cars; 1971 Mercury driven by David Pearson.

Location: 21 Performance Drive, Stuart, VA 24171

Admission: Free

Hours: Monday through Friday, 8:30 a.m. to noon and 1 p.m. to 5 p.m.

Web: www.WoodBrothersRacing.com

4

MIDWEST

Michigan is the heart of American auto manufacturing, and it shines with more than two-dozen car museums and attractions. The biggest of them all is the **Gilmore Car Museum** in Hickory Corners. This colossus of car collecting contains over 10 museums within its 90-acre campus. Another major player is the **Henry Ford Museum,** which offers highlights of American history along with its well-regarded automobile collection. Ohio and Indiana produced their share of cars too, which is reflected in the automotive heritage sights in those states. The town of Auburn, Indiana boasts several car attractions, a highlight being the **Auburn Cord Duesenberg Automobile Museum.**

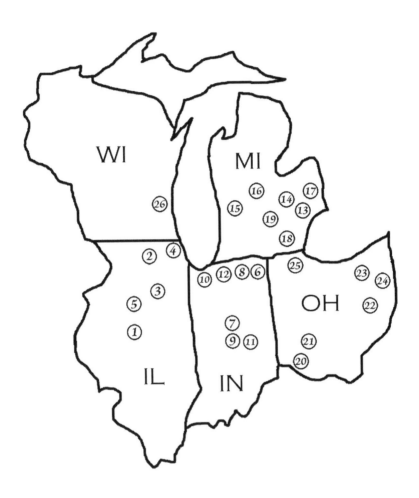

MIDWEST

ILLINOIS

    1) Caterpillar Visitors Center
       Peoria Riverfront Museum

    2) Historic Auto Attractions

    3) Pontiac-Oakland Museum & Resource Center

    4) Volo Auto Museum

    5) Wheels O'Time Museum

INDIANA

    6) Auburn Cord Duesenberg Automobile Museum
       Early Ford V8 Foundation and Museum
       International Monster Truck Museum
       Kruse Automotive Museum
       National Automotive & Truck Museum
       National Military History Center

    7) Elwood Haynes Museum
       Kokomo Automotive Museum
       Ray's Drive-In

    8) Hostetler's Hudson Auto Museum

    9) Indianapolis Motor Speedway Hall of Fame Museum

10) Kesling Auto Collection

11) Model T Museum

12) Recreational Vehicle and Manufactured Home
    Hall of Fame
    Studebaker National Museum

MICHIGAN

13) Automotive Hall of Fame
    Detroit Historical Museum
    Edsel and Eleanor Ford House
    Ford Rouge factory tour
    GM Heritage Center
    Henry Ford Museum
    Model T Automotive Heritage Complex
    Packard Motor Car factory
    Packard Proving Grounds Historic Site
    Stahls Automotive Foundation
    Walter P. Chrysler Museum

14) Buick Gallery at the Sloan Museum

15) Gilmore Car Museum
        Cadillac LaSalle Club Museum
        Campania Barn
        Classic Car Club of America Museum
        George & Sally's Blue Moon Diner
        H. H. Franklin Collection
        Lincoln Motor Car Heritage Museum
        Model A Ford Museum
        Pedal Car Collection
        Pierce-Arrow Museum
        Shell Station

16) R. E. Olds Transportation Museum

17) Wills Saint Claire Auto Museum

18) Uniroyal Tire Ferris Wheel

19) Ypsilanti Automotive Heritage Museum

OHIO

20) American Sign Museum
Crosley Building

21) British Transportation Museum
Citizens Motor Car Company/
America's Packard Museum

22) Canton Classic Car Museum

23) Crawford Auto Aviation Collection

24) National Packard Museum

25) Snook's Dream Cars

WISCONSIN

26) Wisconsin Automotive Museum

ILLINOIS

Historic Auto Attractions
Roscoe, IL

Cars and a somewhat eclectic collection of Americana fill this
rambling museum, which includes wax figures of American
presidents and other presidential memorabilia. A display devoted
to John F. Kennedy includes the **1956 Cadillac Limousine** that
was trailing behind him that fateful day in Dallas. The collection
of Presidential limousines includes cars that have squired the likes
of Dwight Eisenhower, Lyndon Johnson, and Ronald Reagan.
Transportation for overseas leaders includes Benito Mussolini's
1939 Lancia Astura Parade Car. Historic-themed cars include
vehicles owned or driven by Elvis Presley, John Dillinger, and other
notables.

The "World of Speed" exhibit includes five-time NHRA Top
Fuel champion Joe Amato's **1998 Hemi-Powered Top Fuel
Dragster** and a Richard Petty **1960 Plymouth Stock Car,** along
with helmets and racing suits worn by both Dale Earnhardt Sr. and
Jr. Conway Twitty's all-original **1957 Lincoln Continental Mark
II** highlights an exhibit devoted to country music memorabilia.

One somewhat auto-related item is a tire from the Space
Shuttle. There are too many artifacts from the automobile world
and American history to list. It's fair to say there are many things
here you definitely won't see anywhere else.

Number of vehicles: 75

Highlights: 1928 Delage Limousine that belonged to the King of
Siam; NHRA exhibit.

Location: 13825 Metric Road, Roscoe, IL 61073. About 75 miles
northwest of Chicago, near the Illinois/Wisconsin state line.

Admission: $$

Hours: Memorial Day weekend through Labor Day weekend: Tuesday through Saturday, 10 a.m. to 5 p.m.; Sunday, 11 a.m. to 5 p.m. September through November: Saturday, 10 a.m. to 5 p.m.; Sunday, 11 a.m. to 5 p.m. Closed December through just before Memorial Day.

Phone: (815) 389-7917

Web: www.HistoricAutoAttractions.com

PONTIAC-OAKLAND MUSEUM & RESOURCE CENTER
Pontiac, IL

Acres of chrome in a 1959 Bonneville.

This incredible display illustrates how one man's obsession can become a museum. Tim Dye has been collecting all things Pontiac since his teen years, and is supported in his quest by his patient wife, Penny. The museum is immaculately curated and provides a thrill to any auto aficionado cruising nearby Route 66. The Pontiac location leads many visitors to assume the car was made here, but they were not. The Dyes started their collection in Oklahoma and were seeking to expand. When the mayor of Pontiac learned of their plans, he attracted them here with an offer of space in the charming downtown to house the museum.

The Oakland Motor Car Company started out in 1907 in Pontiac, Michigan and was a subsidiary of the Pontiac Buggy Company. After being gobbled up by General Motors, Oakland started producing Pontiac automobiles, a respected name that lived on until its sad demise in 2010. The brand that arguably launched the muscle car era with the 1964 GTO was no more, making it even more important to preserve the Pontiac legacy. A **1965 GTO** in the museum recalls those heady days.

A **1964 Pontiac Parisienne Safari Station Wagon** is set up in such a lifelike camping tableau with one of those ubiquitous Scotch coolers, Coleman stove and faux fire, that you can almost smell the wieners roasting. The wagon was built in Canada so it features a Chevrolet drive train and chassis.

Any type of Pontiac memorabilia you can think of is on display, including uniforms from Pontiac-sponsored sports teams, vintage advertising, dinnerware, Indian headdresses used for marketing, model cars by year, and much more. The largest Pontiac-Oakland reference library in the world contains thousands of related documents, such as owner's manuals, marketing materials, service manuals, books, and magazines. It was fun to explore the library and find the original owner's manual and sales brochure for my first car. Tim spread his collecting net so wide, he even owns heaps of material related to the Native American Chief Pontiac. NAAM member.

Number of vehicles: 17 (cars are rotated frequently)

Highlights: 1890s Pontiac Buggy (only two exist); 1931 Oakland Sport Coupe (last model year for Oakland); 1965 GTO Convertible.

Location: 205 N. Mill Street, Pontiac, IL 61764. Pontiac is 100 miles southwest of Chicago along historic Route 66.

Admission: Free, but donations accepted.

Hours: Daily: April 1 through October 31, 9 a.m. to 5 p.m.; November 1 through March 31, 10 a.m. to 4 p.m.

Phone: (815) 842-2345

Web: www.PontiacOaklandMuseum.org

Volo Auto Museum
Volo, IL

The tagline for this museum is "Automobile & Military Experience." It rambles over five buildings, including a car dealership where you can buy many of the vintage cars on display. A virtual automotive film festival of movie cars includes a **1975 Ford Falcon Interceptor XB** from *Mad Max*; the **1975 Dodge Monaco Bluesmobile** from *The Blues Brothers*; and the **1976 GMC Mystery Machine Scooby Doo Van.** A **1974 Cadillac DeVille Station Wagon,** custom-made to take Elvis Presley to the airport, rounds out the celebrity vehicles.

The "Bizarre Collection" lives up to its name, featuring such oddities as a replica of James Dean's **1955 Porsche 550 Spyder** with a giant bust of Dean as its hood ornament. The collection of militaria starts with a **World War II Jeep**, detours into Cold War-era armored personnel carriers, and ends at relics from Saddam Hussein's palace.

Note: Because this is also a seller of vintage and historic autos, you never know what you'll find at the Volo Auto Museum. It also means that some of the items noted here might not be there when you visit; call ahead if there is something special you want to see. NAAM member.

Number of vehicles: 200+

Location: 27582 Volo Village Road, Volo, IL 60073. About 50 miles north of Chicago.

Admission: $$ **Hours:** Daily, 10 a.m. to 5 p.m.

Phone: (815) 385-3644   **Web:** www.VoloCars.com

WHEELS O'TIME MUSEUM
Dunlap, IL

A search by two men seeking storage space for their Packards eventually morphed into four buildings devoted to automobiles, fire trucks, farm equipment, an antique locomotive, clocks, and more. There are plenty of mechanical toys and things that make noise, most of the "Please Touch" variety, to keep the kids occupied.

Tons of cars, including a rare **1917 Gem**, are crammed into the building, where a World War I German tri-plane is suspended from the ceiling. A gem of a different kind is a **1931 Peoria Ahrens-Fox Fire Pumper** restored by volunteers. Ford lovers will enjoy the vintage Ford dealership, complete with memorabilia and autos. The Peoria Early Ford V8 Club and several other Ford Clubs update the Ford display monthly. NAAM member.

Number of vehicles: 50+ cars, fire trucks, and tractors.

Highlights: 1916 Glide, made in Peoria Heights; 1933 Packard 12-Cylinder; 1937 Cord.

Location: 1710 W. Woodside Drive, Dunlap, IL 61525. Just outside Peoria, 150 miles southwest of Chicago.

Admission: $

Hours: Seasonally May 1 through October 31: Wednesday through Sunday, noon to 5 p.m.

Phone: (309) 243-9020   **Web:** www.WheelsOTime.org

Side Trip: Will It Play in Peoria?

Peoria boasts a little-known role in early automotive history. Charles Edgar Duryea, one of the Duryea brothers who developed the first commercially successful automobile in Springfield, Massachusetts, lived for a time in Peoria. (He and his brother Frank were born in Illinois.) In 1898, he built a three-wheeled auto dubbed the Duryea Motor Trap in the barn behind his house. (Probably not the best name for marketing – but to be fair, at the time a trap referred to a horse-drawn carriage.) The car is on display in all its quirky glory at the **Peoria Riverfront Museum**, where it is the centerpiece of an exhibit about the Duryea brothers. 222 SW Washington Street, Peoria, IL 61602. www. PeoriaRiverfrontMuseum.org.

Note: While you're in Peoria, take a side-trip to the **Caterpillar Visitors Center**. http://www.caterpillar.com/ en/company/visitors-center.html

---

INDIANA

Auburn's Auto Heritage

Auburn, Indiana is a real magnet for automotive fans. It's home to several car-related museums (**Auburn Cord Duesenberg Museum, National Automotive and Truck Museum, Early Ford V8 Foundation, Kruse Automotive Museum, Northeastern Indiana Racing Museum** and the **International Monster Truck Hall of Fame**) plus the **National Military History Center**.

Here's a taste of what awaits you in Auburn:

NATIONAL AUTOMOTIVE & TRUCK MUSEUM   This museum is in a circa-1920s factory building of the Auburn Automobile Company. It's adjacent to the Auburn Cord Duesenberg Museum, which occupies the former Auburn showroom. Also included is the National Automotive & Truck Model & Toy Museum, which highlights toy and model cars and trucks from 1894 to the present. If you once played with it as a child, it's probably here. NAAM member. 1000 Gordon M. Buehrig Place, Auburn, IN; Admission: $ Hours: March through November – Daily, 9 a.m. to 5 p.m.; December, January, February – Thursday, Friday: 11 a.m. to 5 p.m.; Saturday, Sunday: 9 a.m. to 5 p.m.; (260-925-9100) www.natmus.org.

AUBURN CORD DUESENBERG AUTOMOBILE MUSEUM   (See separate listing)

EARLY FORD V8 FOUNDATION AND MUSEUM (see separate listing)

The museums listed below are in the **American Heritage Village**, 5634 CR 11A, Auburn, IN 46706

KRUSE AUTOMOTIVE MUSEUM Features a unique collection of cars and trucks, like the Batmobile, that have appeared in movies and television shows, plus custom hot rods built by Carl Casper. It's also the home of the **International Monster Truck Museum & Hall of Fame** (see below) and the **Northeastern Indiana Racing Museum**. Paid admission to the Kruse Museum also covers the **National Military History Center**. Admission: $$ (260-927-9144) www.dekalbcvb.org

INTERNATIONAL MONSTER TRUCK MUSEUM Four monster trucks are on display along with related memorabilia. The mission of the museum is "collecting and archiving the history of the monster truck sport and related aspects of the high-performance aftermarket, focusing upon capturing history from the surviving pioneers and legends." There is an annual induction ceremony to add significant people in the history of monster trucks into its Hall of Fame. www. MonsterMuseum.org.

NATIONAL MILITARY HISTORY CENTER Devoted to the history of the Armed Forces of the United States and those who served their country. www.NationalMilitaryHistoryCenter. org

Auburn Cord Duesenberg Automobile Museum
Auburn, IN

*The Cord is one of the most distinctive
American automobiles ever built.*

Without a doubt, Cords are some of the coolest classic cars out there. To find them in one place alongside Auburns and Duesenbergs is a car lover's nirvana. This building's history is distinctive. From 1930 through 1936 the landmark Art Deco structure was the headquarters of the Auburn Automobile Company, making it the only museum in this book that's housed in the original headquarters of the cars it features.

Rare Auburn artifacts include tools, trimming brushes, and quilts created from upholstery scraps. A display of racing helmets ranges from the early days of speed to the modern era. For gearheads, the "Hall of Technology" highlights engines and carburetors so you can see what's purring (or roaring) under the hood. Other brands on display include Packard, Pierce-Arrow, Cadillac, and Stearns-Knight, with a range of cars from the 1890s to present day. NAAM member.

Number of vehicles: 120

Highlights: 1927 Duesenberg Model X Boattail Speedster – only a few were manufactured and this one's a beauty; the row of 12-cylinder Classic Era vehicles.

Location: 1600 S. Wayne Street, Auburn, IN 46706

Admission: $$ **Hours:** Monday through Friday, 10 a.m. to 7 p.m.; Saturday and Sunday, 10 a.m. to 5 p.m.

Phone: (260) 925-1444 **Web:** www.AutomobileMuseum.org

EARLY FORD V8 FOUNDATION AND MUSEUM
Auburn, IN

Specializing in the Ford Motor Company from 1932 through 1953, this museum showcases the era of the flathead V8 engine. You'll find related items produced during this period including cars, trucks, industrial engines, literature, and more. One exhibit, a 1932 chassis without a body, reveals the entire drivetrain. The engine collection includes a wide range of cutaways, along with restored and original engines. There are also displays showing the evolution of dashboards and clocks.

Assorted ephemera includes period advertising and promotional material covering Ford industrial engines, tractors, and other ways that FoMoCo used the flathead V8 engine. The extensive collection includes original dealership banners, vintage neon signs, gas pumps, KR Wilson tools, a FoMoCo parts department, artwork, and a research library.

Number of vehicles: 13

Highlights: 1933 Model 40 4-cylinder Tudor sedan, one of only 2,996 produced; 1941 V8 9-seater School Bus from Washington.

Location: 5634 County Road (CR) 11A, Auburn, IN 46706. Find it in the **American Heritage Village.**

Admission: $ **Hours:** Monday, 9 a.m. to 3 p.m.; Tuesday through Saturday, 9 a.m. to 5 p.m. Hours vary so call before coming, particularly in the winter.

Phone: (260) 927-8022   **Web:** www.FordV8Foundation.org

Hostetler's Hudson Auto Museum
Shipshewana, IN

As a 14-year-old back in 1936, Indiana farm boy Eldon Hostetler was fascinated with his neighbor's 1936 Hudson Terraplane. He was bitten by the "car bug"; thus began a lifetime of collecting all things Hudson. Eventually he and his wife, Esta, donated their automobile collection to Shipshewana Township for a museum.

The result is the world's largest collection of Hudson automobiles and products, along with related brands including Essex, Terraplane, and Dover. All the cars are in primo, shiny condition. The bright-yellow **1936 Hudson Series 65 Convertible Coupe,** complete with rumble seat, would stand out in any collection of fine autos. Mr. Hostetler passed away in January 2016, but his legacy lives on in this museum.

Number of vehicles: 50

Highlights: 1911 Hudson 33 Speedster; an extremely rare 1942 Hudson Series 21 Wood-Bodied Station Wagon; 1951 Hudson Brougham Convertible Parade Car.

Location: 760 S. Van Buren Street, Shipshewana, IN 46565. In the **Shipshewana Event Center,** about 100 miles east of Chicago.

Admission: $

Hours: April 1 through December 31: Tuesday through Saturday, 10 a.m. to 4:30 p.m.

Phone: (260) 768-3021

Web: www.HostetlersHudsons.com

Vintage Memories

You know you're of "a certain age" if you remember driving cars with any of the following features:

- Headlight dimmer switch on the floor

- No seatbelts

- Real chrome front grille

- Non-powered steering

- Gearshift on the steering wheel column ("three on the tree")

- Push-button station changers on your AM radio

- A full-sized spare tire

- Leaded gas

- Roll-down windows

- Front window vents

- You needed two keys for your car: one to unlock the door and one to start it

- Flipping your license plate down to pump gas

- Whip radio antenna

- Car advertisements that included "Body by Fisher"

- Whitewall tires

- Being upset when gasoline cracked 30 cents a gallon

INDIANAPOLIS MOTOR SPEEDWAY HALL OF FAME MUSEUM
Indianapolis, IN

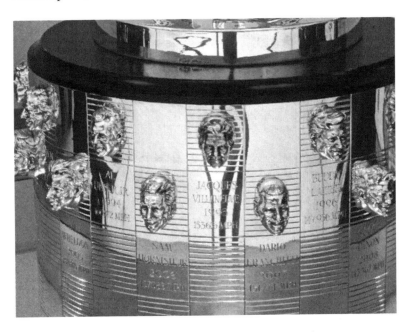

The somewhat quirky Borg-Warner trophy.

Although this is the heart of "Indy Land," the museum's collection includes vehicles from many racing series, including IndyCar, NASCAR, Formula One, Sprint, Midget, motorcycle races, and drag racing. There are also vehicles that have set world land speed records, including Craig Breedlove's **Spirit of America Sonic I**. A variety of passenger automobiles, some of them manufactured in Indiana, are also featured.

Also here are cars that won more than 30 Indianapolis 500 races. The **Marmon "Wasp"** won the inaugural Indianapolis 500 in 1911 with Ray Harroun at the wheel, and was featured on a postage stamp in the U.S. Postal Service's Transportation Series. In the 1920s, the **Duesenberg #12** was the only car ever to win both the Indianapolis 500 and the French Grand Prix at Le Mans.

Also on display is the coveted Borg-Warner trophy, with its iconic bas-relief sculpture of the head of every winning driver of the Indy 500. The original trophy stays here, while the champion driver receives a replica. NAAM member.

Number of vehicles: 75

Highlights: Four cars driven to the checkered flag by A.J. Foyt, Jr., including the 1977 racecar in which he won his record-setting fourth Indy 500 win; Indiana-built cars, including a 1920 Stutz H "Bulldog" Touring car manufactured by Stutz Motor Car Co. in Indianapolis and a 1926 Apperson Jackrabbit Speedster built in Kokomo.

Location: 4790 W. 16th Street, Speedway IN, 46224.

Admission: $$ For an added fee there are grounds tours, as well as track tours, which include a ride around the track.

Hours: March through October: daily, 9 a.m. to 5 p.m.; November through February: 10 a.m. to 4 p.m.

Phone: (317) 492-6784

Web: www.IndianapolisMotorSpeedway.com/at-the-track/museum

Kesling Auto Collection at the La Porte County Historical Society Museum
La Porte, IN

This may seem like an unlikely place to find a **1948 Tucker,** but there's one in this local county history museum. The auto collection is here thanks to the generosity of Peter C. Kesling and his wife, Charlene, who had eclectic tastes. Besides the aforementioned Tucker, you'll see a **1982 DeLorean,** plus Hoosier-built autos including a **1929 Auburn Cabin Speedster** and a **1937 Cord 812 "coffin-nose,"** among others.

The county museum also encompasses an impressive armaments collection, the W. A Jones Collection of Ancient Weapons, which includes over 800 items from around the world. There are also displays of a 1920s kitchen, a Victorian parlor, and a pioneer log cabin.

Number of vehicles: 40

Highlights: Indiana-built 1929 Duesenberg Model J; 1935 Auburn Boattail Speedster; 1948 Tucker.

Location: 2405 Indiana Avenue, Suite 1, La Porte, IN 46350. (About 30 miles west of South Bend, Indiana, home of the **Studebaker National Museum.**)

Admission: $

Hours: Tuesday through Saturday, 10 a.m. to 4:30 p.m.

Phone: (219) 324-6767

Web: www.LaporteCountyHistory.org/museum-exhibits/kesling-auto-collection

Kokomo Automotive Museum
Kokomo, IN

The 1959 Cadillac represented the height of the tail fin era.

This central Indiana museum is a real hidden treasure. It focuses on autos from 1900 through the 1940s, while also reaching back in automotive history to local inventor Elwood Haynes' 1890s vehicles. Cars are laid out by decade, so the visitor travels through time as they stroll through the museum. Paintings on the floor resembling Interstate signs point out the decade, while placards highlight the popular culture of each era.

A replica of an **1894 Haynes Pioneer** is on display. A **1918 Maxwell** chassis is shown without a body, so visitors can see the labeled engine and learn about the inner workings of a car. A **1948 Lincoln Continental Coupe** was donated to the museum by its original owners, Bill and Sue Hough, who drove it on their honeymoon. The **1959 Cadillac Fleetwood** represented the height of the "tail fin" era for cars. If you're not careful, you might poke your eye on one of these chrome-tipped wedges. (*Note:* The tail fin on the cover of this book is from a 1959 Cadillac.)

Visitors can sit in a **1914 Ford Model T "Tin Lizzy"** for a photo op. Exhibits include period clothing, antique license plates, military uniforms, hundreds of colorful motor oil cans with intriguing graphics, food and toys of each era, and a selection of vintage auto radios with the radical push-button technology invented in Kokomo. NAAM member.

Number of vehicles: 100+

Highlights: 1915 Ahrens-Fox fire engine; 1997 General Motors EV-1 Electric vehicle (the battery was developed by Delco Electronics in Kokomo).

Location: 1500 N. Reed Road, Kokomo, IN 46901. In the Ivy Tech Community College Kokomo Event & Conference Center.

Admission: $ **Hours:** Tuesday through Sunday, 10 a.m. to 4 p.m.

Phone: (765) 454-9999

Web: www.KokomoAutomotiveMuseum.org

Pit Stop

If you're in the area you must try the local delicacy, a pork tenderloin sandwich. Head over to **Ray's Drive-In** for a King Tenderloin sandwich. Roughly the size of a '57 Chevy steering wheel, one can feed at least 3 people. The vintage diner is located at 1900 North Courtland Avenue in Kokomo, about two miles west of the museum.

MODEL T MUSEUM
Richmond, IN

This museum is run by the Model T Ford Club of America, which bills itself as the world's largest Model T club. One of the highlights is a **1906 Ford Model N**, a rare entry-level pre-cursor to the Model T. A **1914 Model T Touring** was one of the first built on the assembly line. There's also a diverse collection of rare Model T-era tools and objects, including an original set of magnetos, coil testers, artwork, oil cans, early porcelain license plates, and more. The library contains many rare Model T-related books.

Number of vehicles: 15, with an additional 10 rotated in periodically.

Highlights: 1909 Ford Model T Touring; 1918 Fordson tractor; 1922 Snowmobile mail truck that saw service in Minnesota.

Location: 309 N. 8th Street, Richmond, IN 47374. In the Historic Depot District. Richmond is 75 miles due east of Indianapolis via I-70.

Admission: $

Hours: Tuesday through Sunday, 10 a.m. to 5 p.m.

Phone: (765) 488-0026

Web: www.MTFCA.com

THE RECREATIONAL VEHICLE AND MANUFACTURED HOME HALL OF FAME
Elkhart, IN

You don't have to be into RVs to enjoy this museum, as it presents the long history of Americans taking to the road with examples of mobile living from before World War I through today.

Visitors stroll through the museum along a meandering replica highway, which makes the vehicles look like they just pulled over for the night. The oldest display is a **1913 Earl Trailer** attached to a **Ford Model T.** There's a **1931 Chevrolet Housecar** built for saucy actress Mae West; it wasn't meant for camping, but instead was a mobile lounge for Miss West when she was making movies. For a walk on the wild side, check out the super-custom **1976 Cadillac Eldorado Motorhome.** You can step inside many of the units to view the vintage accessories.

The 300+ member Hall of Fame recognizes those who have made significant contributions to the recreational vehicle and manufactured home industry. There's also an extensive research library and RV-related memorabilia.

Number of vehicles: 50

Highlights: 1931 Tennessee Traveler Housecar, built on a Ford Model AA chassis; 1935 Bowlus Road Chief Trailer, the precursor to the iconic Airstream Clipper; 1964 Coachmen Cadet 15-footer, Coachmen's first production unit.

Location: 21565 Executive Parkway, Elkhart IN 46514. About a two-hour drive east of Chicago, near South Bend, IN.

Admission: $$

Hours: Monday through Saturday, 9 a.m. to 5 p.m.; Sunday, 10 a.m. to 3 p.m. *Note:* There is overnight RV parking for museum visitors, but no water, sewer, or electric hook-ups are available.

Phone: (574) 293-2344

Web: www.RVMHHallOfFame.org

*The head-turning Studebaker "bullet nose"
was a star in The Muppet Movie.*

Studebaker originated as a wagon maker in the 1850s, but embraced the new-fangled automobile in 1902. The super-elegant **1932 President St. Regis Brougham** is one of only five of its kind in existence. The **1934 Bendix SWC** is even scarcer; it's a one-off vehicle that was used by the Bendix Corporation to highlight its automotive components. A **1963 Studebaker Avanti,** with its space-age styling, was one of the last gasps of the car company to stay afloat. But alas, the South Bend factory closed in December of that year.

The "Presidential Carriage" collection includes carriages used by Presidents Lincoln (it's the one he rode in on his final ride to Ford's Theatre), Harrison, McKinley, and Grant. The "Studebaker Super

Service Center" is a great spot for kids to work on scale-model cars, doing everything from checking under the hood to changing the tires. The car is on a mini-lift, so they can even slide under it. For researchers, the archives collection contains the surviving documents (engineering drawings, promotional films, and photos) of the Studebaker Corporation and the Packard Motor Car Company. I'd say that's a ton of paper, but it's actually 70 tons. NAAM member.

Number of vehicles: 120 – about 70 are on display upstairs, with the reminder, including military vehicles, in the "visible storage" area on the lower level.

Highlights: 1950 Studebaker Champion (first of the bullet noses); 1956 Packard Predictor (concept car).

Location: 201 S. Chapin Street, South Bend, IN 46601

Admission: $

Hours: Monday through Saturday, 10 a.m. to 5 p.m.; Sunday 12 to 5 p.m.

Phone: (888) 391-5600

Web: www.StudebakerMuseum.org

MICHIGAN

Buick Gallery at the Sloan Museum
Flint, MI

The **Sloan Museum's Buick Automotive Gallery and Research Center** features 20 classic and concept Buicks, Chevrolets, and other locally built automobiles. It also hosts the Perry Archives chronicling the history of Flint. For car buffs, these archives are a trove of information about autos built in the Flint region, including Buick, Chevrolet, GMC, and Durant.

The collection rotates frequently, but visitors will typically see cars like a **1913 Chevrolet Classic Six,** the oldest running Chevrolet in the U.S.; a "Polo White" **1953 Chevrolet Corvette,** one of 300 built on a temporary production line in Flint to meet unexpected demand for the new vehicle; and a prototype **1954**

Buick Wildcat II two-seat roadster, which with its fiberglass body and style looks rather like a Corvette. Check the website to see what's in their current display before your visit. You'll also found out about any special temporary exhibits.

Number of vehicles: 20

Highlights: 1944 Buick M-18 Hellcat Tank Destroyer; 1958 Buick Roadmaster (with its colossal size, it looks like it could go up against the tank destroyer).

Location: 303 Walnut Street, Flint, Michigan 48503. One block east of the Sloan Museum on the Flint Cultural Center campus.

Admission: $ Includes admission to the Sloan Museum.

Hours: Closed Monday through Thursday, but open by appointment with 24-hour notice; Friday, 10 a.m. to 5 p.m.; Saturday and Sunday, noon to 5 p.m.

Phone: (810) 237-3440

Web: www.SloanMuseum.org/Buick-Gallery

DETROIT HISTORICAL MUSEUM
Dearborn, MI

This free museum offers so much more than cars, but it's difficult to convey the history of the Motor City without including an automotive display. It tells the story of how Detroit built cars and how cars shaped the city in turn. Visitors learn that early on, several cities could have eventually become the Motor City, but Detroit boasted the right combination of visionaries and technology to come out on top.

Car manufacturing is highlighted, from the early days of horseless carriages to the popular Cadillac two-story "body drop" which once operated in the Clark Street assembly plant until it closed in 1987. A Cadillac body is lowered on its frame every twelve minutes. The Automotive Showplace in the lobby houses a rare car, such as a **1935 Stout Scarab** (ironically that's another name for Beetle), that is changed out about twice a year. Permanent exhibits include the World War II-related "Detroit: The Arsenal of Democracy" and the Glancy Trains Collection.

Number of vehicles: 5+

Highlights: Replica of the 1896 Charles Brady King car, the first horseless carriage driven on the streets of Detroit, preceding Henry Ford's Quadricycle by a few weeks; 1901 "Curved Dash" Oldsmobile, one of the first mass-produced, hand-built automobiles; 1911 Ford Model T, with a mural backdrop that visitors can use for "selfies."

Location: 5401 Woodward Avenue, Detroit, MI 48202

Admission: Free   **Hours:** Tuesday through Friday, 9:30 a.m. to 4 p.m.; Saturday and Sunday, 10 a.m. to 5 p.m.

Phone: (313) 833-1805   **Web:** www.DetroitHistorical.org

> The **Motor Cities National Heritage Area** is an affiliate of the National Park Service. Its mission is to preserve and promote the extensive automotive and labor heritage of Michigan. The 10,000-square-mile area contains the largest concentration of auto-related sites in the world, which is certainly befitting of the area surrounding the Motor City. For more information, go to www.MotorCities.org.

GILMORE CAR MUSEUM
Hickory Corners, MI

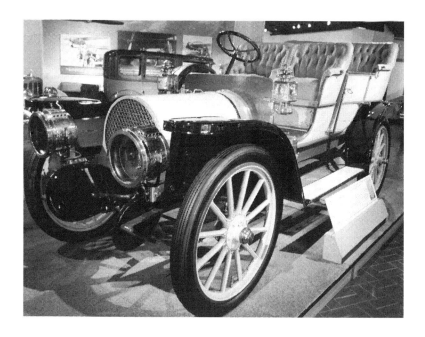

With almost 400 cars, if you want to see it, it's at the Gilmore.

Donald Gilmore's passion for car collecting started in 1963, when he retired as chairman of pharmaceutical giant Upjohn and needed something to keep himself busy. His wife, Genevieve, gave him a 1920 Pierce-Arrow in need of major restoration and his collection grew from there. Today, the 90-acre campus offers over 400 autos in seven independent museums, plus an assortment of attractions that can easily fill a solid day. You know a museum is extensive when the **1948 Tucker** is easy to overlook. The main building includes the Gilmore Heritage Collection, Steam Barn, Lincoln Museum, and Franklin Collection. It's open year-round, while the rest of the campus and other museums and collections are open from April 1 through November 30.

Here's a summary of the attractions that are open year-round and are connected physically to the main building:

Gilmore Heritage Center – Enter the main building to view temporary exhibits, library, gift shop, café, and theater. As a taste of historic things to come, just inside the entrance you'll see an **1886 Benz Motorwagen**. Beyond that, past special exhibits have included museum-owned cars and loaners for themed shows, from hot rods to Packards.

Steam Barn – About 30 cars are lined up in a wooden barn behind the main building. This collection covers the early years of automotive history from horseless carriage days through 1917, when cars were powered by gasoline, steam, or electricity. One leading-edge vehicle is a **1904 Autocar Runabout**. Built in the Philadelphia suburb of Ardmore, it's considered to be America's first car with more than one cylinder that used a drive shaft.

A **1903 Columbia Electric Runabout** is the same model in which Teddy Roosevelt became the first president to ride in an automobile. A **1912 Cadillac Model 30 Touring Car** was revolutionary because it was the first car with an electric starter; no more hand-cranking to get your motor running. A **1911 Stanley Steamer Touring Car** is tilted up to show how power is generated underneath. Vintage license plates line the walls, along with cases stocked with Brass Era headlamps.

H. H. Franklin Collection – 16 Franklin autos and related paraphernalia are on display in a re-creation of Ralph Hamlin's circa-1918 auto dealership in Los Angeles. The Syracuse, New York built air-cooled Franklins were known as good climbers in their day, including the **1909 Franklin Model D Touring**. A rare **1932 Franklin Supercharged Series 17 Sedan** is one of fewer than 200 that were built.

The Continental was the dream car of its era.

Lincoln Motor Car Heritage Museum – Created by the Lincoln Motor Car Foundation, this museum opened in 2014 and is based on an historic Lincoln dealership. Winding among the 25 vehicles are placards relaying the history of Ford's luxury line. Lincoln started out building motors during World War I, but eventually ran into financial difficulties and was taken over by Ford in 1922. Among the highlights are a **1955 Continental Mark II Sport Coupe Prototype**, one of only three built, it was destined for the crusher before it was rescued, and a **1979 Lincoln Continental Town Car**, one of the last pre-gas crisis land yachts. The streamlined **1937 Lincoln-Zephyr Coupe** makes anyone yearn for that name to be brought back. Don't miss the "Lincoln Stones," large engraved limestone panels that were salvaged from the main entrance of the Lincoln Administration building in Detroit. Remember to step outside the back door and pose with a bronze version of Abraham Lincoln happily sunning on a park bench. For more information, go to www.LincolnCarMuseum.org.

Elsewhere on the grounds are the museums and collections that are only open from April 1 through November 30:

Cadillac LaSalle Club Museum and Research Center – This re-creation of a 1948 Cadillac dealership, with 20 cars on display, starts out with an entertaining video about the history of Cadillac. You'll learn that it was originally called the Henry Ford Company, before Ford went off on his own. The **1903 Cadillac Runabout** is a remnant of Ford's early influence on the brand. The **1948 Cadillac Sixty Special** was the first Caddy with tail fins, which set off a tail fin "arms race" that peaked in 1959. Dan Aykroyd drove the **1957 Cadillac Eldorado Brougham** in the film *Driving Miss Daisy*. The walls are lined with vintage advertising and Cadillac plant photos. LaSalle, an early pre-World War II brand of Cadillac, is represented here by a **1937 LaSalle Convertible Sedan**.

Model A Ford Museum – This is the permanent collection of the Model A Ford Foundation Inc. (MAFFI). Its 30+ vehicles highlight the breadth of the Ford Model A in this recreated 1928 Ford dealership. Although the Model A was only produced from 1928 through 1931, it had a massive effect on the automotive scene. In a technological contrast, iPads mounted on stands next to the vehicles provide more information about each one. Here you'll see the versatility of the car in it many incarnations, including a **1928 Ford Model A Tudor Sedan** in its original colors of green, gray, and black; a **1929 Ford Model A Taxi** (only 264 were produced); a **1931 Ford Model A Deluxe Phaeton**, one of the most sought after today; a **1931 Ford Model A U.S. Post Office Truck;** and a **1929 Ford Model A Sears Thrifty Tractor Kit**. A **1929 Ford Model AA Half-Ton Platform Truck** was used in the construction of Hoover Dam.

Gearheads will enjoy the extensive collection of 1920s and 1930s Model A carburetors. For non-car buffs, there are displays of period vintage clothing to match the vehicles. For more information about the Ford Model A Museum, go to www.MAFFI.org.

Pierce-Arrow Museum – An early presidential vehicle, the Pierce-Arrow Motor Car Company existed for only 38 years in Buffalo, New York, but its reputation lives on as one of the premier automobiles ever made. The **1903 Pierce Stanhope** was a best-seller in its day, with a whopping 149 units sold. A **1931 Pierce-Arrow Series 41** enclosed-drive limousine was produced the same year the company hired Margaret Bourke-White to photograph that year's model – the first time a prominent photographer was hired by a car company to shoot their advertising. The museum is decorated with Pierce-Arrow artifacts and memorabilia, including bricks from the original factory floor in Buffalo. For more information about the collection and the Pierce-Arrow Society, go to www.Pierce-ArrowMuseum.org.

Classic Car Club of America Museum – 30 cars from the 1920s, '30s, and '40s are displayed along with over 1,000 automotive mascot figurines. The building is a wooden barn from the 1890s that was disassembled and moved to this spot to house the collection of the Classic Car Club of America. Some of the cars are on loan, so they rotate in and out of the museum. Video monitors relay the history of the cars.

Highlights include a **1928 Stutz Chantilly Sedan** with safety wire in the glass; a **1937 Cord 812 Beverly Sedan**; a **1938 Packard 12 Victoria Convertible**; and a **1939 Delahaye 135M Convertible Coupe**. There's also an unrestored **1926 Marmon 5-Passenger Sedan,** to give you an idea of what many of these shining specimens looked like when they were originally found languishing in a garage or barn. Visit on the first Sunday in June for the annual judged *Concours* event, the Grand Experience. For more information, go to www.CCCAMuseum.org.

Campania Barn – With so many treasures at the Gilmore, it's easy to overlook this collection housed in another 1890s barn that was disassembled and moved here. The bi-level structure houses cars from the 1930s on the upper level and the 1940s on the ground floor. You'll find a **1948 Tucker** that is well, tucked into a corner. It has less than 50 miles on the odometer. Near the Tucker is an interesting juxtaposition: a **1940 American Bantam**, the diminutive-car looking like something out of a miniature circus next to its burly neighbor. You can see how Bantam created the design of the early Jeeps.

Upping the nostalgia quotient, a **1947 DeSoto 9-Passenger Sedan** is the same make the Cunningham family drove on the TV show *Happy Days*. (Theirs was a 1948 model, which you can see at the **LeMay Family Collection** in Tacoma, Washington.) Here it's hauling a **1947 Dufrene Camping Trailer**. There are some wooden tires that museum founder Donald Gilmore developed in reaction to wartime rubber shortages. It turns out they had lousy traction, so the project was abandoned. A **1923 Checker H-2 Taxicab** was one of the first of the legendary Checkers produced in nearby Kalamazoo, Michigan. Period music plays over the loudspeakers to enhance the 1930s and '40s ambience.

Depot – This replica of a train depot houses a massive collection of automotive mascots and hood ornaments that was featured on *Antiques Roadshow*. Initially hood ornaments were just radiator caps that let the driver know the water level in the radiator, but they quickly became decorative status symbols. There seems to have been an ornament for every motif you can think of, including animals, cupids, spaceships, airplanes, ships, and even Egyptian Sphinxes.

Pedal Car Collection - Kids are not left out at the Gilmore, with this assortment of toy pedal cars that were part of the collection of John L. Stegeman. They can even hop into an Assistant Fire Chief's car for a photo-op. In the rear of the building is a larger-than-life recreation of a 1930 Rolls-Royce, used as a set for the 1967 Disney film *The Gnome-Mobile*.

Motorcycle Collection – Vintage motorcycles on display from the 1890s right up through 2006 include a rare **1898 Leon-Bollee**.

The re-created 1930s Shell station even has working restrooms.

Shell Station – This is a re-creation of a 1930s service station complete with original pumps, a work bay, and automobilia inside. Be sure to try the interactive display of car horns from 1899 through 1956; the latter is so loud it may knock you out of your socks. This replica of a service station is so real it actually has working restrooms. (Except you don't have to ask for a key.)

George & Sally's Blue Moon Diner – Since you'll need at least a day to take in all the attractions at the Gilmore Car Museum, it's good to know you'll be well-fed. Stop in at the traditional 1941 Silk City Diner that was moved here from Meriden, Connecticut. The wait staff is dressed in vintage garb and are so friendly you'd swear you stepped into a time warp. I recommend the locally made old-fashioned fruit pies.

As you can see, the Gilmore Car Museum is a one-of-a-kind experience. Allow plenty of time for your visit. During the summer, there are at least a dozen car shows and related activities. NAAM member.

Gilmore Car Museum

Number of vehicles: Almost 400

Highlights: 1929 Duesenberg J-111 Dual-Cowl Phaeton ($20,000 in 1929!); 1948 Tucker; 1963 Chrysler Turbine Concept Car, which ran on rocket fuel – but the project was soon jettisoned.

Location: 6865 W. Hickory Road, Hickory Corners, MI 49060

Admission: $$

Hours: Monday through Friday, 9 a.m. to 5 p.m.; Saturday and Sunday, 9 a.m. to 6 p.m. *Note:* The Main Building, Steam Barn, Franklin Collection, and Lincoln Motor Car Heritage Museum are open year-round. The remaining museums and attractions are open from April 1 through November 30.

Phone: (269) 671-5089

Web: www.GilmoreCarMuseum.org

Side Trip: Kalamazoo Valley Automobile Heritage Tour

As is typical of many Michigan towns, Kalamazoo played a prominent role in the early automobile industry. Its biggest manufacturer was **Checker Cab,** who built taxis here from 1923 through 1982. Another builder in the 1920s was luxury marque **Handley-Knight**. A driving tour around the Kalamazoo Valley highlights some of these automotive sights. More information and a brochure are available online, at www.DiscoverKalamazoo.com/tours-147.

Side Trip: GM—Mark of Excellence

While this book focuses on museums that are open to the general public, the **GM Heritage Center** is so big it's worth knowing about if you have the opportunity to see it. More than 600 cars from a century-plus of General Motors history are on display. Many are chosen because of a unique feature. For example, the **1912 Cadillac** was the first to offer an electric starter. (One is also on display at the **Gilmore Museum** in Hickory Corner, Michigan.) The **1953 Firebird I** was the first gas-turbine auto built and tested in the U.S. Cars are continually added to the growing collection. The museum is open to groups of 30 or more by appointment, but also hosts receptions for various organizations. If you can get on the invitation list for one of these, you'll gain access to this rare collection. GM Heritage Center, 6400 Center Drive, Sterling Heights, Michigan. www.GMHeritageCenter.com. You can also download nifty wallpaper of the cars for your computer.

Henry Ford Museum
Dearborn, MI

Honk if you remember when burgers were 15 cents.

Known locally as "The Henry Ford," this museum is a large complex of which the car collection is just one component. There are also areas devoted to aviation, locomotives, American history, early American antique furniture, clocks, silver, pewter, and jewelry. But you're here for the cars, so let's start there.

The heart of the collection is the "Driving America" exhibit. There are so many "firsts" here that I'll highlight just a few: a **1865 Roper Steam Carriage,** perhaps the first personal, self-propelled carriage built in America and the oldest surviving American automobile; an **1896 Duryea Runabout,** the first production car in America and the only one left from a limited production run of 13; the **1903 Ford Model A Runabout** that was Ford Motor

Company's first car; a **1903 Packard Model F Runabout,** only the second car to cross the United States (it took 61 days); and a **1951 Crosley Hot Shot Roadster**, the first post-World War II American sports car. There's also a **1948 Tucker #1016** and a much more mundane **1984 Plymouth Voyager Minivan** – the vehicle that totally changed the concept of what American families drove, to many a suburban fathers' chagrin.

A neat feature is the sign next to each vehicle that states the original purchase price of the car and how long someone making an average annual salary back then had to work to pay for it. A **1981 Ford Escort** would take five months to purchase, while you would have had to work *ten years* to buy your dream **1931 Duesenberg Model J**. If that seems like a long time, consider the **1931 Bugatti Royale Type 41 Convertible**. You'd have to toil for 31 years to park that baby in your garage. Although realistically, your chauffeur would have done that for you.

Celebrity vehicles include journalist Charles Kuralt's **1975 FMC Motorhome,** in which he drove around America for his "On the Road" segments on CBS Television. Other Americana includes intact neon signs advertising roadside staples such as McDonald's and Holiday Inn. A rebuilt motel room brings back memories of childhood vacations, right down to the Holiday Inn logo towels. The "Presidential Vehicle" collection includes the limousine John F. Kennedy was riding in when he was assassinated in Dallas. Surprisingly, it was put back into service and used for several years before being retired.

The ticket price includes admission to the whole building, so you may as well wander around and view some of the other attractions. Featured artifacts include a copy of Thomas Paine's 1776 pamphlet *Common Sense*; George Washington's campaign chest and bed; the chair Abraham Lincoln was sitting in when he was assassinated; and the bus Rosa Parks was riding when she was arrested for refusing to give up her seat. NAAM member.

Number of vehicles: 150+

Highlights: Presidential vehicles collection; 1902 Ford "999" Race Car; 1931 Bugatti Royale (third of only six built); 1939 Dodge Airflow Texaco Tanker Truck; 1952 Oscar Meyer Wienermobile.

Location: 20900 Oakwood Boulevard, Dearborn, MI 48124. At the corner of Village Road and Oakwood Boulevard, just west of the Southfield Freeway (M-39) and south of Michigan Avenue (US-12). Look for the entrance in the replica of Philadelphia's Independence Hall.

Admission: $$ Ticket packages are available that include the **Ford Rouge Factory Tour** and **Greenfield Village**.

Hours: Daily, 9:30 a.m. to 5 p.m.

Phone: (800) 835-5237

Web: www.TheHenryFord.org/museum

Side Trip: Automotive Hall of Fame

Located next to the **Henry Ford Museum**, the **Automotive Hall of Fame** honors the men and women who developed and revolutionized the automotive industry. Exhibits and galleries highlight the history of automotive design and technology and those who made it possible. The list of almost 300 inductees ranges from Mario Andretti to Ferdinand von Zeppelin, inventor of the eponymous airship that helped pave the way for advanced automobile technology. 21400 Oakwood Boulevard, Dearborn, MI 48124. www.AutomotiveHallOfFame.org.

Ford Rouge Factory Tour

At the **Henry Ford Museum**, you can purchase tickets to watch the F-150 pickup truck being assembled at the **Ford Rouge Factory** in Dearborn, which at one time employed over 100,000 workers. (Today they number about 6,000.) There are five segments to the self-guided tour: Legacy Theater, Manufacturing Innovation Theater, Observation Deck, Assembly Plant Walking Tour (the fun part), and the Legacy Gallery. In the assembly plant you'll stroll a catwalk above the production line. Make sure to check the website for times when the assembly line is down. Tours still go on, but you'll miss the actual vehicle assembly process.

Location: The Henry Ford, 20900 Oakwood Boulevard, Dearborn, MI 48124. You'll board a bus to get to the factory.

Admission: $$ **Hours:** Monday through Saturday, 9:30 a.m. to 5 p.m. Last tour leaves at 3 p.m.

Phone: (800) 835-5237   **Web:** https://www.thehenryford.org/rouge/thetour.aspx

Side Trip: Edsel & Eleanor Ford House

Henry Ford's son, Edsel, became president of Ford Motor Company in 1919 when he was only 25 years old. His home, designed by noted architect Albert Kahn to resemble a Cotswold village, features artwork and gardens that are a popular attraction in southeast Michigan. Unlike his function-over-form father, Edsel was more into style. The garage at his estate contains rotating exhibits that focus on automotive design over the years. There are a handful of autos on display that reflect the theme of the current exhibit. Located at 1100 Lake Shore Road, Grosse Pointe Shores, MI 48236. www.FordHouse.org.

Model T Automotive Heritage Complex
Detroit, MI

Also known as the **Ford Piquette Avenue Plant**, this 1904 building takes you back in time to the early days of Ford. A short film about the early days of Ford sets the stage for visiting the factory floor.

Henry Ford's second-floor office, complete with his messy desk, is set up as it was in 1908. The other executive offices were on the first floor, but the hands-on Ford wanted to be near the second-floor shop where the cars were actually produced. Over 12,000 Model T cars were produced on the age-worn wooden floors. Within a few years the plant was too small for Ford's manufacturing volume, so it was sold to Studebaker.

Check the schedule for daily tours led by knowledgeable docents. The gift shop is notable because almost all the products are proudly "Made in the USA," including winged-logo Ford shirts. NAAM member.

Number of vehicles: 20+

Highlights: 1909 Model T in red (they were available in that color until 1914); a 1923 Ford Model TT Stake Truck.

Location: 461 Piquette Street, Detroit, MI 48202

Admission: $$ On Model T Tuesdays, for an additional fee there is a guided tour, movie, and box lunch. Reservations are required.

Hours: April through October: Wednesday through Sunday; 10 a.m. to 4 p.m. From November through March, tours are available by appointment between 10 a.m. to 4 p.m.

Phone: (313) 872-8759

Web: www.FordPiquetteAvenuePlant.org

Have You Grilled on a Ford Lately?

Early cars were built with wooden frames. Count on Henry Ford to figure out what to do with all those scrap pieces of wood left over from building Model Ts. His company developed a method of creating charcoal briquettes out of them, then built a charcoal factory for that purpose. Originally called Ford Charcoal, the name was later changed to Kingsford, after a Ford relative who found the site for the plant. The rest is barbecue history.

PACKARD PROVING GROUNDS HISTORIC SITE
Shelby Township, MI

This 22-acre site with buildings – once again designed by Albert Kahn – is where Packard started testing their cars in 1927, a vast improvement over putting them through their paces on the streets of Detroit. Considering all the development around it, it's incredible that the grounds, 2.5-mile oval track, and buildings are still intact. The site passed through several hands over the years (including Ford's) and survived a potential date with the wrecking ball. A not-for-profit organization is raising funds to build a museum on the site. For now, visitors can arrange a free tour given by volunteer Packard fans. The track's straightaway has been used as the staging point for vintage road car rallies, which is quite a sight. There are also a few Packards on display, including a **1954 Packard Pacific** and a **1954 Packard Caribbean Convertible**. 49965 Van Dyke Ave., Shelby Township, MI 48317 Between 22 Mile and 23 Mile Road (586) 739-4800 www.PackardMotorFdn.org.

Packard Factory Ruins

Built in 1903 and also designed by Albert Kahn, the 40-acre **Packard factory** was an industrial workhouse and the first factory in Detroit constructed out of reinforced concrete. The buildings now lay in ruins, the largest abandoned factory in America and a silent testimony to the rise and fall of Detroit's automotive legacy. A sign on the property refers to a developer's plans to revitalize it at some point. Located in Detroit at East Grand Boulevard and Concord Avenue, just off I-94. Note the mid-century Packard Motel across the street.

R.E. Olds Transportation Museum
Lansing, MI

The world of Oldsmobiles on display.

The R.E. Olds Transportation Museum boasts a great car museum smell: the musty aroma of oil and lubricants fills the air. The restored circa 1966 stained-glass "rocket wall," which once adorned the Oldsmobile administration building in Lansing, gives the building a retro vibe.

There are several early vehicles here, including an **1897 Olds** – the only surviving example of four that were built. On loan from the Smithsonian, the oldest of Olds resides in a climate-controlled glass case. The **1901 Oldsmobile Curved Dash Runabout** is considered the first high-production auto, while the **1905 Oldsmobile Touring Runabout** was the first vehicle where Olds replaced the steering tiller with a wheel.

Ransom Olds left his namesake company in 1904 to found the REO Motor Company. From that era, a quarter-scale **1905 "Baby" REO** used for marketing purposes sits next to its "Mama," a full-sized **1905 REO**. A **1923 REO Speedwagon** nearby gave its name to a pretty successful rock band. For those who like unrestored cars, the **1927 REO Wolverine** "barn find" has been kept as-is.

Despite all the antique hardware, more modern versions of the marque are not left out. Some of these are cars not typically found in museums, like the gold-colored **1966 Oldsmobile Toronado,** *Motor Trend*'s Car of the Year and America's first front-wheel-drive car in decades; a **1950 Oldsmobile 88 Holiday Coupe,** which was a successful NASCAR racer; and a **1981 Oldsmobile Toronado XSC Diesel V8** with a factory-installed CB radio, reflecting a popular hobby of the day.

R.E. Olds started out as an engine builder, but his company branched out into related fields, so several REO lawn mowers and even a refrigerator are shown. A few engines are suspended from girders, including the last 3800 V6 built in Lansing that was signed by all the factory workers. There are also Olds family items on display, including the original fireplace from their mansion that was torn down (ironically to make way for a freeway). Real Olds diehards can buy a bumper sticker in the gift shop that says, "I don't care what GM says – Oldsmobile will never die." NAAM member.

Number of vehicles: 50+

Highlights: 1909 REO Touring Car Model D; 1930 Viking, Oldsmobile's upscale line which lasted only a year; 1962 Oldsmobile F-85 coupe.

Location: 240 Museum Drive, Lansing, MI 48933

Admission: $

Hours: Tuesday through Saturday, 10 a.m. to 5 p.m.; Sunday, noon to 5 p.m. (Closed Sundays, November through March.)

Phone: (517) 372-0529   **Web:** REOldsMuseum.org

STAHLS AUTOMOTIVE FOUNDATION
Chesterfield, MI

Plan ahead if you want to see the private collection at Stahls. It's only open to the general public on the first Saturday of the month and on Tuesdays. Because many of the cars are one-of-a-kind, it's certainly worth the effort. The display ranges from the late 19th century to 1960s muscle cars. The focus is on the 1930s and 1940s, however, including a **1948 Tucker #1015** touted as "the best on the planet."

Custom car builder "Von Dutch" built a **1904 Winton** replica for the movie *The Reivers* starring Steve McQueen. McQueen ended up owning it after filming was completed. Other automobilia on display includes vintage road signs, gas pumps, oil cans, and pre-World War II items. Some of the cars, including the **1964 Leslie Special** and **1964 Hannibal 8** that appeared in the Jack Lemmon/Tony Curtis movie *The Great Race*, are periodically taken out for cross-country races. NAAM member.

Number of vehicles: 80+

Highlights: 1904 Oldsmobile Model 6C Curved Dash Runabout; 1947 Packard Custom Clipper Club Sedan; 1948 Tucker (#15 produced, it also appeared in the movie *Tucker.*)

Location: 56516 N. Bay Drive, Chesterfield, MI 48051

Admission: Free, but donations accepted.

Hours: Tuesday, 1 p.m. to 4 p.m.; first Saturday of the month, 11 a.m. to 4 p.m.

Phone: (586) 749-1078   **Web:** StahlsAuto.com

WALTER P. CHRYSLER MUSEUM
Auburn Hills, MI

This museum closed in 2012 due to funding issues. But, staffed by volunteers, it reopened with limited hours in 2016. It celebrates the automotive heritage of Walter P. Chrysler, who rose from being a locomotive mechanic to the top of the car industry. For Mopar fans it's a must-see. The displays amble over two floors and a basement, presenting the history of Chrysler vehicles including orphan brands Hudson, Nash, DeSoto, Willys-Overland, Plymouth, and Rambler. One cool feature is the rotating tower that displays Chrysler concept cars. Muscle car fans should head to "Boss Chrysler's Garage" in the basement where vehicles from the 1960s and '70s are featured. This is a rare collection that hasn't been available to view lately, so it's worth heading over during its limited reopening.

Number of vehicles: 65+

Highlights: 1924 Chrysler Model 70 Prototype, one of four prototypes produced; 1963 Chrysler Turbine Car, one of nine left in the world and one of a handful that still run; a rare surviving World War II Multibank tank engine; it employed five Chrysler six cylinder engines and put out almost 700 horsepower.

Location: One Chrysler Drive, Auburn Hills, MI 48326

Admission: $$

Hours: Since its reopening in 2016, it is open on selected weekends; 10 a.m. to 4 p.m. Check the website for the latest details.

Phone: (248) 944-0439

Web: http://www.ChryslerBoyhoodHome.com/

WILLS SAINTE CLAIRE AUTO MUSEUM
Marysville, MI

Because this specialty museum is open only one day a month, you'll have to time your visit carefully. What you'll see in return for your effort is the largest collection of Wills Sainte Claire automobiles in the world. There are ten here, ranging from a **1922 Wills Coupe** to a **1926 Wills 7-Passenger Sedan**.

Wills Sainte Claire cars were produced by C.H. Wills and Company from 1921 through 1925 here in Marysville. C.H. Wills was Henry Ford's chief engineer and invented Vanadium steel, used so successfully in the Model T. He may be even more famous for designing the script Ford logo that's still used today. He left Ford in 1919 (with over $1 million) to start his own line of cars.

The problem with his cars is that while they were advanced technologically – electric fuel pump, hydraulic brakes, overhead cam engine, and more – they were fairly stodgy looking. Pretty much what you'd expect from a car designed by a perfectionist engineer who was more interested in function over form. But the cars were technological marvels that are worth seeking out for gearheads.

The building is pretty cool. A Dow Chemical munitions plant during World War II, it was designed so that only the roof would blow off in the event of an explosion. The white brick walls are covered with vintage Wills Sainte Claire advertising posters and engineering blueprints. Car museums like this that are devoted to one marque are fascinating and offer the opportunity to really learn about more obscure brands in automotive history. NAAM member.

Number of vehicles: 10

Highlight: 1922 Wills Coupe; 1926 Wills Roadster.

Location: 2408 Wills Street, Marysville, MI 48040

Admission: $

Hours: Second Sunday of the month from 1 p.m. to 5 p.m. Group tours possible outside these hours.

Phone: (810) 987-2854

Web: www.WillsAutoMuseum.org

Side Trip: World's Largest "Tire"

This giant structure looks like a tire, but was actually a Uniroyal-sponsored Ferris wheel at the 1964-65 World's Fair in New York City, where over 2 million riders took a spin in it. Weighing 12 tons, it stands 80 feet tall and sits on the eastern side of I-94 in Allen Park, Michigan, about 15 miles southwest of downtown Detroit.

YPSILANTI AUTOMOTIVE HERITAGE MUSEUM
Ypsilanti, MI

Despite a name that's difficult to pronounce, Ypsilanti (Ip-si-lanti) boasts a strong automotive legacy. Car companies with connections to the Ypsilanti region include Apex Motors, Kaiser-Frazer, and Hudson. The museum, partially housed in an old car dealership, also devotes a fair amount of space to the **Chevrolet Corvair,** the car that received unwanted attention in Ralph Nader's book, *Unsafe at Any Speed.* In the museum there's a Tucker on display but it's a fiberglass prop that was used in the film *Tucker: The Man and His Dream.* Preston Tucker himself lived just a few blocks away. (See following sidebar.)

In 2014, the museum also became the home of the **National Hudson Motor Car Company Museum.** It includes a **1957 Hudson Hornet Hollywood** in all its three-tone, red-black-and-white glory – the last car produced by the automaker. The setting is appropriate, because the museum is housed in the last Hudson dealership in the country, which closed in 1958. A **1953 Hudson Hornet** is seen in an episode of *Antiques Roadshow*, which filmed a segment about model cars at the museum.

Each year the museum features a Hudson from a different decade, with a display reflecting that time period. One of the highlights is a **1933 Hudson Terraplane K Series Coach.** To emphasize their speed, aviator Amelia Earhart was hired to promote them. Fans of the animated film *Cars* will appreciate the **1952 Hudson Hornet** driven by Herb Thomas to a NASCAR championship. Don't miss the quarter-scale Hudsons that were used in research and development.

Miller Motors, a fully preserved pre-war automobile dealership, is also part of the museum. It includes a vast collection of advertising, repair, and promotional items that were used at car dealers from the 1920s through the 1950s. There are even greasy mechanic's overalls from the former Hudson dealership hanging on the wall. You really feel like you have stepped back in time and are about to buy a new car. If you visit in the fall, you'll see one of the largest orphan (discontinued brands) car shows in the country. NAAM member.

Number of vehicles: 30+

Highlights: 1933 Hudson Terraplane K Series Coach; 1952 Hudson Hornet; 1960 Chevrolet Corvair (first model year).

Location: 100 E. Cross Street, Ypsilanti, MI 48198. In the historic district known as Depot Town, 35 miles west of Detroit.

Admission: $

Hours: Tuesday through Sunday, 1 p.m. to 4 p.m.

Phone: (734) 482-5200

Web: www.YpsiAutoHeritage.org

Side Trip: Preston Tucker's House

If you're looking for more automotive history in Ypsilanti, the former home of automotive renegade inventor Preston Tucker is only four blocks away from the **Ypsilanti Auto Heritage Museum**. Located at 110 Park Street, it's not open to the public, but still worth a photo op.

OHIO

Canton Classic Car Museum
Canton, OH

*A Chevy Camaro parked next to a BMW Isetta
shows the wide range of cars here.*

Located just a few blocks south of the famous Lincoln Highway, this sprawling museum is a feast for the eyes, with much more than just autos on display. It also includes a well-curated assemblage of collectibles and ephemera from the past century, including petroliana, vintage toys, clothing, movie posters, historic photography, and much more, making it a great attraction for nostalgia seekers. Placards provide detailed background on the cars, placing them in historical context for their era.

The rare **1922 Holmes** was built in Canton; note the ungainly headlamps that look like lug nuts. The 13-horsepower **1957 BMW**

Isetta is one of the smallest cars you'll find in a museum. It's a one-door, two-passenger coupe (and designed for very small passengers at that). For contrast, it sits next to a **1967 Chevrolet Camaro SS Pace Car**. Polar explorer Admiral Byrd owned the **1932 Lincoln KB V-12**. Edsel Ford financed many of his adventures. A **1931 Marmon** sports a V-16 engine. Marmons came with a certificate guaranteeing they had been test-run at the Indianapolis Motor Speedway. The front of the museum was a car dealership and still displays the original tile floor. NAAM member.

Number of vehicles: 40+   **Highlights:** 1937 Ahrens-Fox Quad Fire Engine; 1937 Cord Model 812; 1970 Plymouth Road Runner Superbird.

Location: 123 6th Street SW, Canton, OH 44702

Admission: $ **Hours:** Daily, 10 a.m. to 5 p.m.

Phone: (330) 455-3603   **Web:** www.CantonClassicCar.org

The British Are Coming! The British Are Coming!

The **British Transportation Museum** is dedicated to preserving the U.K.'s transportation history. Currently their collection of 34 cars is located in two warehouses, about 40 miles apart in Dayton and Wilmington, Ohio. Along with the more well-known Minis and Jaguars, some of the unusual marques on display include a **1938 Vauxhall DX 14/6,** a **1960 Peerless GT,** and a **1961 Humber Super Snipe.** They also show vintage bicycles, model cars, engines, and a library. They are raising funds for a permanent museum. Until then, they are open either by appointment or during an Open House. For further information, visit them online at www.BritishTransportationMuseum.org

The Citizens Motor Car Company/America's Packard Museum
Dayton, OH

The cars are displayed in a restored 1917 Packard dealership in Dayton's Motor Car Company Historic District. A rarity is the jet-black **1928 Jesse Vincent Speedster Model 626**, which reached 129 mph at the Packard Proving Grounds in Detroit. It's named after designer Jesse Vincent, who also developed the Liberty aircraft engine that was instrumental in fighting World War I. He was ahead of his time with aerodynamics, insisting that the speed machine have no headlights, fenders, or windshield. The passenger seat, slightly offset behind the driver, was designed for a time when a mechanic came along for the ride to handle the expected breakdowns. NAAM member.

Number of vehicles: 15

Highlights: 1914 Packard with chaperone seat in the rear; 1919 Packard Model E Five Ton Truck.

Location: 420 S. Ludlow Street, Dayton, Ohio 45402

Admission: $

Hours: Monday through Friday, noon to 5 p.m.; Saturday and Sunday, 1 p.m. to 5 p.m.

Phone: (937) 226-1710

Web: www.AmericasPackardMuseum.org

Side Trip: All Signs Point to Cincinnati

A feature of classic American road trips is the vast array of vintage neon signs that still advertise motels and roadside diners. Many of those signs are disappearing, victims of age, weather, and neglect. However, many are being restored at the **American Sign Museum**, located in the Camp Washington section of Cincinnati under the tutelage of Tod Swormstedt.

The French-created technology to produce neon signs owes its American existence to the auto industry, when a Los Angeles car dealer bought two signs from French inventor Georges Claude to advertise his Packard dealership. Since then, America has never looked the same.

Neon signage hit its stride in postwar America. On display are several examples, including a 1950s Howard Johnson's sign from Utica, New York and a 1963 McDonalds Golden Arch (when burgers were only 15 cents!) from Huntsville, Alabama. There are also neon signs advertising service stations and long-gone American car companies.

Not all signage is two-dimensional. This is best displayed by a rotating Earl Scheib sign (remember the "I'll paint any car for $99.95" ads?), which consists of the neon outlines of cars spinning around a rotating globe. It was recovered from a building in Los Angeles.

At 1329 Arlington Street, just around the block from the American Sign Museum, you'll find the abandoned Art Deco former factory and headquarters of the **Crosley Radio Corporation**: note the "C" logo in a crest over the doorways. The radio and appliance maker made a brief foray into automobiles, which were designed in this building. While some very early production took place here, most of the manufacturing occurred in Indiana. The American Sign Museum is located at 1330 Monmouth Street, Cincinnati, OH 45225. www.americansignmuseum.org

CRAWFORD AUTO AVIATION COLLECTION OF THE WESTERN RESERVE
HISTORICAL SOCIETY
Cleveland, OH

This museum is tucked into a large two-story corner of the **Western Reserve Historical Society**. The upper level is devoted to Ohio car manufacturers, while the lower level runs the gamut of automotive history. The museum's namesake, Frederic Crawford, was the president of auto and aircraft engine manufacturer Thompson Products, which through a series of mergers eventually became the "T" in industrial giant TRW.

The "Setting the World in Motion" exhibit on the upper level (which is the street level) highlights Northeast Ohio's prominent early role in the auto industry. Back then there were about 115 manufacturers with names like Packard, Winton, Peerless, Stearns, White, and Baker Electric, making it the automotive center of America. The region was only surpassed by Detroit in 1908, when Ford began cranking out the Model T. View rare Ohio cars like the **1902 American Gas** and the **1916 Owen Magnetic**. The latter was known as the "Car of a Thousand Speeds," because there were no gears to shift. The **1920 Cleveland Roadster,** with its six-cylinder engine, was the last of several cars that earned the "Cleveland" moniker. An aluminum **1932 Peerless**, which weighed only 4,000 pounds, was the last car produced in Cleveland. A neat after-market accessory is the 1906 brass Gabriel 10-note horn. It comes with its own keyboard for the driver to play a tune and was available for luxury autos.

The lower level contains "REVolution – The Automobile in America," an exhibit of 50+ cars highlighting American automotive technology and design from the 1890s through the 21st century. It is divided into seven themes: Invention & Design, Tire Tech, Alternative Fuels, Need for Speed, Road Trip, Accessory Corner, and Stainless Steel. For the latter, a stainless-steel **1981 DeLorean DMC-12** is parked next to three autos that are also rendered in the shiny metal: a **1936 Ford 68 Deluxe**; a **1960 Ford Thunderbird** (one of two produced, with the other at the **AACA Museum** in Hershey, PA); and a **1966 Lincoln Continental Convertible**.

The much-maligned **1964 Chevrolet Corvair** rests comfortably next to an endless loop of a General Motors video promoting the 95-horsepower car. For a bit more pep, the **1972 Dodge Colt**, powered by aviation fuel, cranks out 1,200 horses. Among the rarities are the infamous **1997 General Motors EV1 Electric Car**, this one lucky enough to avoid the crusher, and a **1956 Mercedes Benz 300 SL Gullwing Coupe**. NAAM member.

Number of vehicles: 140+

Highlights: 1897 Panhard Levassor, an unrestored vehicle that may be the oldest enclosed car in the world; 1901 Packard; 1909 Hupmobile, one of the first cars museum founder Crawford collected; 1920 Jordan Playboy, which revolutionized automobile advertising, taking it away from technical specifications and invoking the romance of driving. Vehicles are preserved, not restored, so they are more in their original "as found" condition.

Location: 10825 East Boulevard, Cleveland, OH 44106

Admission: $$ This includes admission to the art and military collections, too.

Hours: Tuesday through Saturday, 10 a.m. to 5 p.m.; Sunday, noon to 5 p.m.

Phone: (216) 721-5722

Web: www.wrhs.org/research/crawford/autos

NATIONAL PACKARD MUSEUM
Warren, OH

The Packard brothers started out in Warren in 1899. Within a decade the company, known for its high-quality cars, was based in Detroit and neither Packard sibling was associated with it. But their legacy lives on in their hometown in northeast Ohio. The museum hosts Packards built from 1900 to 1956, ranging from a **1900 Packard Model B** (the second-oldest surviving Packard) through a rare assemblage of three **1956 Packard Caribbeans**. A sentimental favorite is the **1941 Packard LeBaron** chauffeur-driven limousine that was owned by Mrs. James Ward Packard.

There's an extensive collection of archives from the Packard family and the Packard Electric Company (which still exists as part of Delphi Automotive), memorabilia, and a handful of Packard marine engines. Check their schedule for annual events that include a Packard legacy weekend (devoted to the car whose motto was "Ask the man who owns one") and a motorcycle show. NAAM member.

Number of vehicles: 30, plus special exhibits throughout the year.

Highlights: 1900 Packard Model B (the second-oldest surviving Packard); 1911 Model 30 Detroit Fire Department Squad Car; 1927 Sterling Knight (the last car made in Warren, by a short-lived venture); 1956 Packard Caribbean Push-Button Automatic Convertible.

Location: 1899 Mahoning Avenue N.W., Warren, OH 44483. About 60 miles southeast of Cleveland.

Admission: $ **Hours:** Tuesday through Saturday, noon to 5 p.m.; Sunday, 1 to 5 p.m.

Phone: (330) 394-1899   **Web:** www.PackardMuseum.org

Part of the Texaco collection of petroliana.

Bill Snook bought his first car, a Model A Ford, in 1939 and spent a lifetime collecting autos and related paraphernalia. His son, Jeff, has kept the tradition alive at **Snook's Dream Cars**. While Bill was more interested in classic cars, Jeff is into racing, so the collection reflects both of their interests. All the cars are road-ready; as the affable Jeff says, "I like driving old cars around."

Jeff races cars on weekends and proudly shows off some of the cars he runs, including a **1956 Lotus Eleven** and a **1961 Triumph TR3A**. His father found the surf-green **1957 Chevrolet Bel Air** in a barn and it was the elder Snook's last restoration. Check out the **1959 Ford Galaxie Skyliner**; it takes 19 servomotors to crank open the retractable hardtop.

The front of the warehouse structure housing the museum has been transformed into a 1940s Texaco station. Design students from nearby Bowling Green State University artfully created the interior to look like a 1930s general store, Bowling Green's Main Street in the 1940s, a 1950s diner, and a 1960s Sebring Raceway pit lane.

Beyond pristine autos, the museum also houses pedal cars, vintage bicycles, coin-operated arcade games, auto nostalgia items, and a large variety of Texaco collectibles. There are always a few vintage cars being worked on in the adjacent garage, which visitors can peek at. NAAM member.

Number of vehicles: 30

Highlights: 1936 Auburn; 1954 Kaiser Darren 161 Roadster; 1966 Austin-Healey 100-4/BN1.

Location: 13920 County Home Road, Bowling Green, OH 43402

Admission: $

Hours: Monday through Friday, 9 a.m. to 5 p.m.; Saturday and Sunday by chance or appointment.

Phone: (419) 353-8338

Web: www.SnooksDreamCars.com

WISCONSIN

Wisconsin Automotive Museum
Hartford, WI

Hartford was the home of the Kissel Motor Car Company, which produced the toy-sounding Kissel Kar from 1906 to 1931. (Although the "Kar" moniker was dropped from the logo medallion in 1918, due to anti-German sentiment during World War I.) Kissels were popular with Hollywood stars and even aviator Amelia Earhart. The museum has 25 Kissels on display, including a primo **1921 Kissel Speedster Gold Bug**. Considering there are fewer than 200 surviving Kissels, this place boasts quite the lion's share of this brand. Nash, another Wisconsin auto builder, is also featured with a dozen vehicles, including a bulbous **1950 Nash Statesman Airflyte** and a slick **1953 Nash Healey LeMans Coupe**.

The museum spreads over 75,000 square feet on two floors. The other cars include REOs, Pierce-Arrows, Pontiacs, Studebakers, Chevrolets, Fords and more. You'll also find a large collection of model cars, a multimedia display maintained by the Southeastern Wisconsin Short Track Hall of Fame, and a 1,000,000-mile **1989 Saab 900 SPG.** The Nash Car Club of America has dedicated space in the museum for exhibits. In addition to the cars, there is a collection of automotive memorabilia including license plates, sparkplugs, and oil cans plus industrial engines and outboards built in Wisconsin. There's also a sprawling Lionel Train diorama, and even a Volkswagen-powered airplane overhead. Check their schedule for well-attended car shows throughout the year. NAAM member.

Number of vehicles: 100+ (About half the cars on display are on loan, so the collection changes periodically.)

Highlights: 1902 Rambler Runabout; 1957 Continental Mark II (at $10,000, it rivaled a Rolls-Royce in pricing); 1961 Rambler Convertible featured in the TV show *3rd Rock from the Sun*.

Location: 147 N. Rural Street, Hartford WI   53027. About 40 miles northwest of Milwaukee.

Admission: $$

Hours: May 1 through September 30: Monday through Saturday, 10 a.m. to 5 p.m.; Sunday, noon to 5 p.m. *Note:* From October 1 through April 30, hours are the same as above, except they're closed Monday and Tuesday.

Phone: (262) 673-7999

Web: www.WisconsinAutoMuseum.com

5

HEARTLAND

Bridging the country, the Heartland provides a wide range of automotive sights. The **National Sprint Car Hall of Fame and Museum** in Knoxville, Iowa overlooks a race track where these exciting races take place. If you're driving the Interstate across the country you'll see plenty of trucks. The **Iowa 80 Trucking Museum** provides a salute to the American trucking industry. One of the quirkiest sights in this book is located in Nebraska. There you'll find **Carhenge,** a re-creation of Stonehenge built with vintage American sedans. It's definitely worth a side trip.

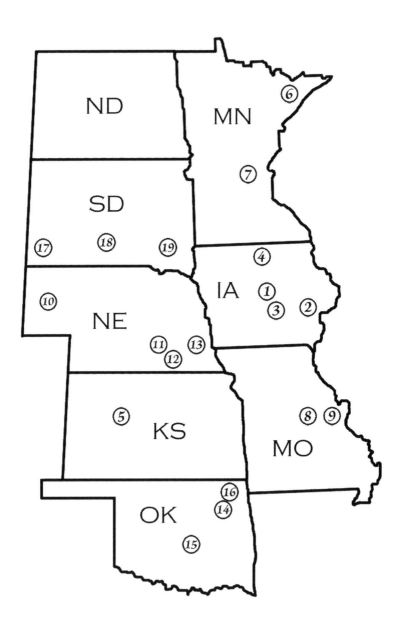

Heartland

IOWA

1) Hemken Collection

2) Iowa 80 Trucking Museum

3) National Sprint Car Hall of Fame

4) Surf Ballroom

KANSAS

5) Walter P. Chrysler boyhood home

MINNESOTA

6) Frank Lloyd Wright service station

7) Veit Automotive Foundation Museum

MISSOURI

8) Auto World Museum

9) Museum of Transportation

NEBRASKA

10) Carhenge

11) Classic Car Collection

12) Harold Warp Pioneer Village

13) Smith Collection Museum of American Speed

OKLAHOMA

14) Afton Station Route 66 Museum
Darryl Starbird's National Rod & Custom Car
Hall of Fame

15) Muscle Car Ranch

16) One lane Route 66

SOUTH DAKOTA

17) Motion Unlimited Museum

18) Pioneer Auto Show

19) Telstar Mustang-Shelby-Cobra Museum

IOWA

HEMKEN COLLECTION
Williams, IA

Daryl Hemken loved cars, particularly convertibles from 1947 and 1948, which make up the cream of the collection. There are also lesser-seen marques (Packard, Studebaker, Stutz, Nash, Hudson, International), plus the usual GM and Ford cars, mostly in unrestored condition. The collection includes a **1947 Oldsmobile Series 66 Convertible**, whose engine shared some mechanical features with World War II tanks; a **1947 Hudson Commodore Brougham Convertible** with only 33,000 original miles; and a **1948 Nash Custom Convertible**, with a foot-mounted button for changing the radio station. One of the rarest cars here is a completely original **1948 Playboy Convertible** with a retractable hardtop, built in Buffalo, New York. Only 97 were built and this is #79. To see another one of these, visit the **Buffalo Transportation Pierce-Arrow Museum** in Buffalo. (See separate listing.)

On a side note, I always appreciate collections that show cars not typically found in museums. One such example here is a **1978 AMC Matador** with the special "Barcelona" package. The remainder of the museum includes picnic coolers, petroleum collectibles, car parts, bicycles, a 1940s kitchen, and a collection of John Deere pedal tractors. NAAM member.

Number of vehicles: 65+ (more off-site, so the selection rotates)

Highlights: 1919 Stutz Phaeton; 1937 Mercedes-Benz 170-V Special Roadster (only a few survive); 1955 Packard Caribbean Convertible (500 produced); 1958 Packard Hawk (these were somewhat derided in their day, because the front grille resembled a set of fish lips.)

Location: 202 Main Street, Williams, IA. Only 65 miles north of the state capital of Des Moines.

Admission: $

Hours: May through October: Wednesday and Friday, 1 p.m. to 5 p.m. or by appointment.

Phone: (515) 689-1047

Web: www.the-hemken-collection.org

Side Trip: The Day the Music Died —Buddy Holly's Last Show

The Hemken Collection is only 50 miles south of a sight that's well worth a road trip detour. Early rock-and-roller **Buddy Holly** played his last concert at the **Surf Ballroom** in Clear Lake, Iowa on February 2, 1959. After midnight the plane in which he was riding crashed, carrying him, Ritchie Valens, J.P. "The Big Bopper" Richardson, and pilot Roger Peterson to an early grave. This event was immortalized in Don McLean's song *American Pie*. The retro, tropical-themed Surf Ballroom still hosts concerts – and a museum dedicated to the performers who played their final shows that fateful night. About six miles north of the ballroom there's a memorial where the plane crashed in the middle of an Iowa cornfield. Although the sight is not car-related, attendance at any "Cruise-In Night" car show reveals that fans of vintage cars are often fans of early rock-and-roll too. Surf Ballroom, 460 North Shore Drive, Clear Lake, Iowa. www.SurfBallroom.com.

IOWA 80 TRUCKING MUSEUM
Walcott, IA

The Iowa 80 Truck Stop bills itself as the "largest truck stop in the world." Its founder, Bill Moon, opened the adjacent museum to share his truck collection with the public. Exhibits range in age from a **1910 Avery** tractor farm wagon (one of only six in existence) through a restored **1983 Ford 9000** cab-over tractor. Known as "Ole Number One," it was the first Con-Way Freight tractor to hit the roads.

A **1911 Walker Electric Truck** shows that the concept of electrically powered vehicles has been around almost since there were vehicles to operate. Used as a delivery van in Chicago, it boasted a range of 50 miles on a single charge. It's always fun to come across vintage tow trucks, and the **1924 White Wrecker Model 40** (seen in the film *Fried Green Tomatoes*) doesn't disappoint. The engine block on another wrecker, a **1941 Freightliner**, shows a casting date of Dec. 8th, 1941, the day after the attack on Pearl Harbor.

One black cab, looking vaguely like Darth Vader, formerly carried a 25-foot-long, 8-ton trailer behind it. It belongs to a **1978 Kenworth Bandag Bandit,** which Martin Carver drove over 150.9 miles per hour at the Bonneville Salt Flats in 1978 to set a new land speed record for its class. To make the feat even more remarkable, it was achieved on a set of retread tires built by the Bandag Company.

Also on display is a collection of antique toy trucks (back when they were made out of metal, not plastic) and assorted petroliana, including vintage gas pumps and signs. Afterwards, stop in the REO Theatre to see films about the American trucking industry.

Number of vehicles: 65+

Highlights: 1912 Mack Jr. (one of three in existence); 1925 Douglas with well-drilling rig.

Location: I-80 exit 284 at the **Iowa 80 Truck Stop**, Walcott, IA

Admission: Free **Hours:** Summer: Memorial Day through Labor Day: Monday to Saturday, 9 a.m. to 5 p.m.; Sunday, noon to 5 p.m. Rest of the year: Wednesday to Saturday, 9 a.m. to 5 p.m.

Phone: (563) 468-5500

Web: www.Iowa80TruckingMuseum.com

NATIONAL SPRINT CAR HALL OF FAME
Knoxville, IA

Normally these sprint cars are covered with dirt and mud.

This is one of the few museums that sells earplugs in its gift shop. That's because it overlooks the second turn of the legendary **Knoxville Raceway**, in the heart of the "Sprint Racing Capital of the World." If you're a sprint car fan, or just want to learn more about this unique sport, you have to visit. The colorful collection of vehicles includes 22 sprint cars plus midget cars, championship cars, super-modifieds, and modifieds.

With their metallic bat wings soaring overhead, sprint cars are bizarre-looking vehicles that look like they're ready to go airborne. The wings create downdraft to keep the cars on track. Watching them in action sliding around a dirt track is one of the most exciting thrills for racing fans.

In addition to the cars on display there's the actual Hall of Fame. One of the inductees is Andy Granatelli; fans of 1970s racing will remember his television ads for STP that introduced the word "viscosity" into the mainstream vernacular.

Auto trivia question: What does STP stand for? See answer below.

A white **1923 Frontenac Racer #7** reveals the dangers of racing in an age before roll bars, windshields, and seat belts. A salute to 12-time Knoxville Nationals and 20-time World of Outlaws (WoO) champion Steve Kinser includes six sprint cars driven by him during his career, including one from each decade (1970's to present). Replica garages of legends John Gerber and Bob Trostle include their racers.

The Hall of Fame is on the second floor, with framed photos representing every member. You also get a bird's-eye view of the racetrack. A movie theater runs continuous loops of sprint car races. The gift shop boasts a huge assortment of sprint car merchandise and is also open online. NAAM member.

Trivia answer: STP is Scientifically Treated Petroleum.

Number of vehicles: 30

Highlights: 1923 Frontenac Racer #7; Steve Kinser cars.

Location: One Sprint Capital Place, Knoxville, IA 50138. (On North Lincoln Street/Route 14) Knoxville is just off Route 5, 30 miles southeast of Des Moines.

Admission: $

Hours: April through September: Monday through Friday, 10 a.m. to 6 p.m.; Saturday, 10 a.m. to 5 p.m.; Sunday, noon to 5 p.m. October through March: Same hours, except it doesn't open until noon on Saturday.

Phone: (641) 842-6176

Web: www.SprintCarHOF.com

KANSAS

Side Trip: Walter P. Chrysler Boyhood Home & Museum

The Chrysler Building in New York is a famous city landmark. Here's another Chrysler building to visit – the childhood home of Walter P. Chrysler in Ellis, Kansas contains many artifacts from his life. The 1924 Chrysler on display was owned by his great-grandson. www.ChryslerBoyhoodHome.com

---

MINNESOTA

VEIT AUTOMOTIVE FOUNDATION MUSEUM
Buffalo, MN

The Veit's mission is to preserve autos and auto memorabilia for future generations and to promote the sport of hot rodding. The hours are extremely limited at this collection in a rural barn setting, but it's worth timing your visit so they are open. The collection focuses on Chevy, Ford (heavy on tricked-out 1933 models), and specialty cars from the 1950s and 60s.

Chevys include a flame-tipped **1950 Chevrolet Bel Air Deluxe** 2-door hardtop that was museum founder Vaughn Veit's first car. He lost track of it over the years before rediscovering it on its way to the junkyard. The current restoration is top-of-the-line. Ford lovers will enjoy over a dozen deuce coupes from the 1920s and '30s. An electric-yellow **1933 Ford Cabriolet Deluxe** sports a '95 Corvette engine. Among the specialty cars is a diminutive **1959 Nash Metropolitan**, so tiny that you had to be shorter than 5' 6" to fit comfortably behind the wheel. There are also three rooms stuffed with 150 antique gas pumps. NAAM member.

Number of vehicles: 30

Highlights: 1931 Duesenberg; 1933 Ford Fordor Model 40 Deluxe; 1957 Chevrolet Nomad wagon.

Location: 914 80th Street NW, Buffalo, MN 55313

Admission: Free, but donations accepted.

Hours: Tuesday and Thursday only, 9 a.m. to 3 p.m.; weather permitting in winter.

Phone: (612) 805-4780   **Web:** www.VeitAuto.com

MISSOURI

AUTO WORLD MUSEUM
Fulton, MO

Local car collector, World War II veteran, and potato-chip king William Backer founded this museum. (Note for history buffs: Fulton, Missouri is where Winston Churchill made his famous "Iron Curtain" speech in 1946.) The cars are displayed with old photos and memorabilia that take you on a nostalgic journey. The building may be a little musty and dusty, but there are some hidden gems here as well. Think of it as an automotive scavenger hunt.

At the Auto World Museum, you'll see almost a century's worth of vehicles from the 1890s through 1986. There are several rarities you won't find at many auto museums, including a three-wheeled **1910 Kelsey Motorette**; **1922 Wills Sainte Claire**, a marque produced by Childe Wills, a refugee from the Ford Motor Company (see separate listing for the **Wills Sainte Claire Auto Museum** in Marysville, MI); and a **1931 Marmon Series 16 Limo** with a V16 (!) engine, which retailed for $5,000 – quite a sum during the Great Depression. Mr. Backer had two favorite cars, the **1913 Ford Model T** and the **1926 Pierce-Arrow Touring** which he liked for its sturdy, solid feel. The collection is larger than the museum space, so call ahead to make sure a specific vehicle is on display.

Number of vehicles: 80

Highlights: 1909 Lambert Model A1; 1917 Scripps Booth Roadster with unique staggered seats; 1929 Cord Cabriolet; 1932 Franklin; 1970 AMC Javelin SST Fastback Coupe.

Location: 200 Peacock Drive, Fulton, MO 65251. Right on Route 54, about 100 miles west of St. Louis. Look for the precariously perched pink Volkswagen.

Admission: $

Hours: Daily, 9 a.m. to 5 p.m.

Phone: (573) 642-2080

Web: www.AutoWorldMuseum.com

MUSEUM OF TRANSPORTATION (Earl C. Lindberg Automotive Center) St. Louis, MO

Part of a much larger museum that includes over 70 locomotives, there are some unique vehicles here. One of most bizarre is a **1963 Chrysler Turbine** car, which could run on any flammable liquid. Only 55 were built, most were scrapped, and this is the only one on public display that is operational. The odd-looking **Bobby Darin Dream Car,** completed in 1960 by Detroit clothing designer Andy Di Dia, featured the first-ever rear-seat radio speakers and hidden windshield wipers. The *Mack the Knife* singer used to own it. Given the museum's location, they are particularly proud of the **1901 St. Louis**, built by the eponymous St. Louis Motor Carriage Company. Check the website for a full schedule of car shows from April through September.

Number of vehicles: 16

Highlights: 1919 Dorris Panel Truck built in St. Louis; 1959 Ford Gas Turbine Truck Tractor.

Location: 3015 Barrett Station Road, St. Louis, MO 63122

Admission: $

Hours: Hours vary by season, so check the website for details. In summer peak season (Memorial Day through Labor Day): Monday through Saturday, 9 a.m. to 4 p.m.; Sunday, 11 a.m. to 4 p.m. During the winter it's usually open Thursday through Sunday.

Phone: (314) 965-6212

Web: TransportMuseumAssociation.org

NEBRASKA

Side Trip: Carhenge

The only things missing are the Druids.

In the town of Alliance, Nebraska you can view one of the most unusual "car-iosities" anywhere in America, a re-creation of Stonehenge made entirely of 39 cars. Some are stuck in the ground, while others are balanced on top of them. They're all painted gray, to resemble the original standing stones at the ancient site in England. Jim Reinders built Carhenge in 1987 as a memorial to his father. At first the town didn't know what to make of the piece, even though it drew people from all over the world. They now embrace it as a visitor attraction. It's definitely worth a side trip. Considering the remote location, I was surprised that there was a steady flow of people coming to see it on a blustery weekday in October. Right next to it is a "Car Art Reserve" with newer sculptures made out of cars and car parts. Admission is free. For updated information, go to www.Carhenge.com.

CLASSIC CAR COLLECTION
KEARNEY, NE

The **Classic Car Collection** is a relative newcomer to the auto museum scene. Opened in 2011, it was developed around the donated 131-car collection of Bernie and Janice Taulborg. They mostly collected cars of the spoke wheel and touring era. The museum fills in other niches, such as muscle cars, with donated and loaned vehicles.

The collection is broken out thematically: The Drive-In, with nine cars parked in rows facing a screen showing highlights from old films; Chrysler Legacy; Cadillac Corral; and the Grand Concourse. There is also an International Corner, but it's not a display of foreign autos. Because this is Nebraska farm country, there is a slew of International Harvester trucks and buggies instead, ranging from a **1907 International Auto Buggy** to a **1969 International Truck.** The **1909 Metz Roadster** was a kit car that was bought in 14 installments. To ensure final payment, the steering wheel was the last part delivered. (Although you'd think someone who had just built a car could figure out a way to get around that.)

Daredevil fans will enjoy Evel Knievel's rare **1974 Cadillac Pickup Truck.** It still has the tie-downs in the cargo area that held his motorcycles. Local color is added with the original starting "Christmas Tree" from the Kearney Dragway.

The guide hands visitors an iPad to take around the collection; after you tap the number corresponding to each vehicle, more information and photos appear on the screen. Depending on how much detail you crave, this is a fantastic tool that could add a few hours to your visit. The placard for each car displays its appraised value, which is always handy for those putting together their wish lists. The slick, metallic burgundy **1968 Chevelle Malibu Convertible** would be mine. The museum is worth a nostalgic road trip, especially since it's located on the Lincoln Highway, America's first transcontinental roadway. NAAM member.

Number of vehicles: 200

Highlights: 1930 Lincoln Phaeton Convertible; 1965 Morgan Convertible (one of just 440 produced); 1938 Rolls-Royce 7-Passenger Limo, the only one made and billed as the "million-dollar car."

Location: 3600 E. Highway 30 (Lincoln Highway), Kearney, NE 68847. (In back of Cabela's.)
Local trivia: Kearney is the midpoint of the historic Lincoln Highway that runs between New York and San Francisco.

Admission: $ **Hours:** Monday through Saturday, 9 a.m. to 5 p.m.; Sunday, noon to 5 p.m.

Phone: (308) 234-1964   **Web:** www.CCCKearney.com

HAROLD WARP PIONEER VILLAGE
Minden, NE

Feeling like a time capsule from yesteryear, the **Harold Warp Pioneer Village** is a sprawling assemblage of antique Americana that just happens to include 350 automobiles. Their "modest" goal is to present artifacts from every field of human endeavor from 1830 to the present day. In addition to the cars there are 100 tractors; 20 aircraft; kitchens, living rooms, and bedrooms representing seven generations; a gun collection; artwork; historic buildings; and more. The **1906 Ford Model K Roadster** was an unusual luxury vehicle for Ford in its pre-Model T days, while a **1937 Cord 812** is distinctive for its "coffin" nose. It was among the first generation of production automobiles with headlights that folded into the fenders. For gearheads there's an **1876 Otto**, an early internal-combustion engine.

Number of vehicles: 350

Highlights: Turn-of-the-century Milwaukee steam-powered car; 1905 Buick, reputedly the world's oldest Buick (it has the earliest flywheel number); 1962 Amphicar (four cylinders and two propellers).

Location: 138 E. U.S. Highway 6, Minden, NE 68959. It's an easy half-hour drive south of Kearney, NE, where the **Classic Car Collection** is located.

Admission: $$

Hours: Winter: daily; 9 a.m. to 4:30 p.m. Summer (Memorial Day weekend through Labor Day weekend): 9 a.m. to 6 p.m. Call for spring and fall hours.

Phone: (308) 832-1181

Web: www.PioneerVillage.org

SMITH COLLECTION MUSEUM OF AMERICAN SPEED
Lincoln, NE

*You'll need to slow down to take in the entire
Museum of American Speed.*

Billed as the "World's Largest Collection of Exotic Racing Engines & Vintage Speed Equipment," the **Museum of American Speed** is a tribute to the obsession of racer Bill Smith. In 1952 he founded Speedway Motors, a leading supplier of after-market street rod and racing parts. He and his wife, Joyce, started the museum in 1992 to house his growing collection. It sprawls over 165,000 square feet of exhibit space on three floors, adjacent to Speedway Motors' distribution facility.

True to Smith's reputation as a gearhead, he started out as an engine collector. The museum is one of the few that focuses on engines as much as cars. An example is the Harry Miller engine gallery, which showcases equipment like the Miller "91" 8-cylinder engine that is the legacy of the automotive pioneer.

Separate displays highlight unique segments of racing, including the Indy 500 pit, sprint cars, NASCAR, midget racing, soap box derbies, and land speed records. Don't miss the stairway leading to the second floor; the walls are blanketed with hundreds of record album covers and movie posters with auto racing themes. The Ford gallery showcases Model Ts and As, along with aftermarket parts for them. Check out the Model T #5,000,000, along with a massive collection of Ford flathead V8 engines. They glisten so much it's hard to believe they were ever used.

A surprise is the world's largest collection of pedal cars, including the oldest in existence from the 1890s. One of them, a **1924 Alamite Paige Roadster,** cost as much as a new Ford at the time. (But to be fair, it did come with a grease gun and tool kit.) If that's not enough, there are also auto racing-themed vintage toys, board games, and pinball machines. NAAM member.

Number of vehicles: 100, plus several hundred engines.

Highlights: Red Baron show car; 1948 Tucker; Tom Cruise's racing car from *Days of Thunder.*

Location: 599 Oak Creek Drive, Lincoln, NE

Admission: $$

Hours: May through September: daily, Monday through Friday, noon to 4:30 p.m. October through April: Friday, noon to 4:30 p.m. Guided tours available at 1 p.m.

Phone: (402) 323-3166

Web: www.MuseumOfAmericanSpeed.com

OKLAHOMA

DARRYL STARBIRD'S NATIONAL ROD & CUSTOM CAR HALL OF FAME
Afton, OK

Darryl Starbird is a legend in the hot rod and custom car field, even earning himself an insider's reference in the nostalgic film *American Graffiti*. Since these cars are all one-of-a-kind and custom-built, you'll see vehicles, some quite bizarre, that you won't find anywhere else. Anyone who was into Monogram plastic car models when they were a kid probably built one based on a Starbird design. You really have to see these cars in person to believe they are even possible.

There are also photos and memorabilia related to well-known custom-built vehicles including street rods, nostalgic cars, vans, sports cars, and futuristic-looking, bubble-topped concept cars right out of *The Jetsons*. NAAM member.

Number of vehicles: 50, about half of which were created by Starbird.

Highlights: Moonbird bubble car (picture a cross between a '59 Cadillac and the Batmobile); Cristina Mark IX, based on a 1941 Lincoln Continental.

Location: 55251 E. Highway 85A, Afton, OK 74331. About 80 miles northeast of Tulsa on old Route 66.

Admission: $$

Hours: March through October: Wednesday through Monday, 10 a.m. to 5 p.m. Closed Tuesday.

Phone: (918) 257-4234

Web: www.DarrylStarbird.com

MUSCLE CAR RANCH
Chickasha, OK

Their tagline is "Like no other place on Earth," an apt description of a place that's hard to describe. Picture a destination for car junkies that also happens to offer three stocked fishing ponds, an RV park, and more, and you just may have the ultimate road-trip destination. Looking like *American Pickers* on steroids, there are hundreds of thousands of artifacts here including vintage signs, car parts and accessories, antique trucks, buses, and motorcycles spread out over 62 acres and several barns. For road-trippers, all this fun is only 45 miles southwest of Oklahoma City, which you'll be driving through if you're taking a Route 66 tour.

Location: 3609 S. 16th Street, Chickasha, OK 73018

Phone: (405) 224-4910

Web: www.MuscleCarRanch.com

Tip: While you're in Chickasha, check out the 1949 **Chief Drive-In Theater** to complete your auto experience. It's only two 2 miles from Muscle Car Ranch on Highway 81, just south of Chickasha. Go to www.ChiefDriveInTheatre.com for show times.

Side Trip: Sleep in a Ford factory

Opened in 2016, the 21c Museum Hotel is located in the renovated Oklahoma City Ford Motor Company Assembly Plant that was designed by the ever-present Albert Kahn. The 1916 building retains much of its original industrial features, providing a unique stay for car buffs. 21c Museum Hotel, 900 W. Main Street, Oklahoma City, OK 73106 www.21cMuseumHotels.com/OklahomaCity

---

Side Trip: Afton Station

This car collection and Route 66 vintage memorabilia museum is housed in a 1930s D-X gas station that the owners, David and Laurel Kane, lovingly restored. **Afton Station** is so authentic that it received a "2009 Route 66 Business of the Year" award at the national Route 66 Festival in Flagstaff, Arizona. There are 17 vintage cars, with the focus on Packards from the 1920s through the 1950s. Among the highlights are a **1917 Packard Motorhome** and a rare **1958 Packard** built in the Studebaker factory after the two companies merged. Afton Station also functions as a rest stop with restrooms, visitor information, and maps. Opening hours from around March through November are 9:30 a.m. to 3 p.m., seven days a week. But it's always best to call ahead to see if they'll be there. (918-257-4044) www.PostcardsFromTheRoad.net.

Side Trip: One-Lane Route 66

*Route 66 looks unchanged since
Bonnie and Clyde drove this road. (See next page.)*

There is no better classic American road trip than a drive on Route 66 from Chicago to Santa Monica, California. Although much of the road has been replaced by modern interstates, there are still plenty of spots where you can drive on the old rutted concrete surface and seek out the tasty and the offbeat. One of my favorites is a run-down section in northeast Oklahoma where Route 66 is a one-lane, nine-foot-wide highway. Now, that's not a single lane in each direction, but a single lane in **total**! When cars arrive from opposite directions they have to pull over onto the shoulder to let the other pass by.

For a three-mile stretch just south of Miami, Oklahoma Route 66 turns into a "ribbon road," at 9 feet wide it's more like a large sidewalk. Back in the 1920s, the state of Oklahoma was trying to save money building Route 66 and this was the result. Motoring along the pitted road and kicking up dust from the orange clay, I felt like I was back in the 1920s. In fact, outlaws like Bonnie and Clyde often drove along Route 66 as they roamed the area. In the last months of their lives, they kidnapped the police chief in the nearby town of Commerce. (There you can also see the boyhood home of Mickey Mantle.)

Pit Stop: Even decades after officially passing out of existence, Route 66 still reveals new surprises to the curious road-tripper. And if you're hungry – and who isn't after all that driving – head back to Miami and stop in at one of the great old-time burger joints: Waylan's Ku Ku Burger. This joint's been flipping patties since the 1960s.

SOUTH DAKOTA

Motion Unlimited Museum and Antique Car Lot
Rapid City, SD

At this part-car museum, part-car dealer, you can look at a vintage auto and maybe even drive it away. Owned by Bill and Peggy Napoli, this hybrid attraction is a pretty cool place to visit. The 13,000-square-foot facility is full of vintage autos, motorcycles, bicycles, pedal cars, gas pumps, toys, oil cans, vintage clothing, and various automobilia.

Some of the classics on display include the unfortunately named **1934 Studebaker Dictator**. For obvious reasons, Studebaker changed the name of this model to Commander in 1937. The Napolis like Chevys, so you'll see them from 1955 through 1960, including El Caminos, Hardtops, and a completely restored, bright-red **1960 Impala Convertible**. Because the Napolis restore their vehicles themselves, they are usually working on a handful at any time.

Their motorcycle collection focuses on Japanese bikes from the 1960s including Honda, Yamaha, and Suzuki. There are also dozens of vintage pedal cars and over 2,000 toy cars including Hot Wheels, Tonka (remember when they were made out of metal?), Japanese tin, Marx tin, Hubley, and many more.

Number of vehicles: 40+

Highlights: 1938 Lincoln Zephyr V-12; World War II Airplane Car; model kit cars, many still in their original boxes.

Location: 6180 S. Highway 79, Rapid City, SD 57702. Rapid City is known as the "City of Presidents" due to its proximity to Mount Rushmore. Just 2-½ hours south of here is a car attraction you don't want to miss, **Carhenge**. (See separate listing.)

Admission: $

Hours: May through October: Monday through Friday, 9 a.m. to 6 p.m.; Saturday, 9 a.m. to 4 p.m.; Sunday by appointment. Antique Car Lot is open year-round.

Phone: (605) 348-7373

Web: www.MotionUnlimitedMuseum.com

PIONEER AUTO SHOW
Murdo, SD

This mega-display of autos is probably as close as most people will come to a barn find. There are so many vehicles here in several buildings that it's hard to know where to begin. Some of the cars are stored inside the main structure, while others look like they were driven into one of the outbuildings years ago and left untouched; with a set-up that is somewhat random.

There are not one, but two **1937 Cords** with their distinctive noses. Muscle cars are represented by a **1968 Shelby Mustang Fastback** and a rare **1970 Pontiac GTO Judge Convertible**, one of only 168 built. Walking among the buildings is like being on an endless scavenger hunt. In one of the barns I finally found a Lamborghini I can afford: a **Lamborghini C603 Tractor**. The noted Italian sports car company started out making farm equipment.

Motorcycles range from a 1914 Indian through a 1976 Harley-Davidson that belonged to Elvis Presley. For those in your group who need to find something else to do while you meander through the buildings, there is the Zeitner Rock, Gem, and Fossil collection, along with hundreds of vintage toys and music boxes. A 1950s diner is also on site.

Number of vehicles: 275 cars, 60 motorcycles, and 60 tractors.

Highlights: 1907 Middleby, perhaps the last survivor of this Reading, PA-based manufacturer; 1914 Beardsley Electric, a rare Los Angeles-built car; a 1954 Kaiser Darrin, the only car with sliding pocket doors; a 1981 Trabant, the infamous East German car that made a Volkswagen Beetle feel like a luxury mobile.

Location: 503 5th Street, Murdo, SD 57559. About halfway across South Dakota, just north of exit 192 on I-90.

Admission: $$ **Hours:** Summer hours (generally May through September 15): Daily, 8 a.m. to 9 p.m. Winter hours: Monday through Saturday, 9 a.m. to 6 p.m.; Sunday, 10 a.m. to 6 p.m.

Phone: (605) 669-2691   **Web:** www.PioneerAutoShow.com

Telstar Mustang-Shelby-Cobra Museum
Mitchell, SD

Jerry and Mavis Regynski own Telstar Motors in Mitchell, South Dakota, where they restore Shelbys and Mustangs. But just restoring the famous muscle cars wasn't enough for them. In their spare time they created the first Shelby and Mustang museum, containing at least one Shelby from every year and model of production.

Naturally, the first year of Mustang production is represented, with a **1964-½** Ford Mustang Convertible. If you rented a car from Hertz in the mid-1960s, you might have gotten lucky and been handed the keys to a limited-edition **1966 Shelby GT 350** in black-and-gold livery. The Rent-A-Racers, as they were known, were very popular with a certain segment of the population.

Just a taste of the remainder of the collection includes a **1965 Shelby GT 350, 1968 Shelby GT 500 convertible, 1969 Shelby GT 350 fastback,** and a **1970 Boss 302.** If you happen to own one of these bad boys or another Shelby or Mustang, Telestar does restorations for customers from around the world. They also offer completely restored cars for sale.

Number of vehicles: 40

Highlights: If you're into Mustangs and Shelbys, everything.

Location: 1300 - 1400 S. Kimball Street, Mitchell, SD 57301. Hometown of the famous Corn Palace.

Admission: Varies by size of group. Since this is a working shop, one of the owners has to carve out time for a tour.

Hours: Guided tours by appointment.

Phone: (605) 996-6550

Web: www.TelstarMotors.com

6

Mountain States

The Mountain States aren't as populated with auto sights as the rest of the country, but they make up for that with quality. You'll find not one, but two, museums related to automotive visionary Carroll Shelby: the **Shelby American Collection** in Colorado and the **Shelby Museum** in Las Vegas. Fans of thriller writer Clive Cussler will be pleased to visit the **Cussler Museum** in Colorado, where several of the cars made cameo appearances in his books. Farther afield, the **Montana Auto Museum** is a unique attraction; it's located in a former prison.

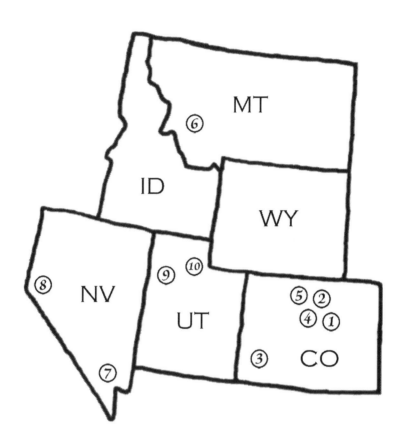

Mountain States

COLORADO

1) Cussler Museum
   Forney Museum of Transportation

2) Dougherty Museum

3) Gateway Canyons Auto Museum

4) Shelby American Collection

5) Stanley Hotel

MONTANA

6) Montana Auto Museum

NEVADA

7) Auto Collection at the LINQ
   Shelby Museum

8) National Automobile Museum: The Harrah Collection

UTAH

9) Bonneville Salt Flats

10) Browning-Kimball Classic Car Museum

COLORADO

CUSSLER MUSEUM
Arvada, CO

This museum arose from best-selling novelist Clive Cussler's long-time love affair with cars. He grew up in Southern California, hot-rodding a 1936 Ford. His hobby totals over 100 vehicles, split between classic cars and 1950s convertibles. Many of the cars were featured in Cussler's "Dirk Pitt" thrillers. A copy of the book each was featured in is placed next to the car, such as the Pepto-Bismol-colored Voisin depicted in *Sahara*.

Some of the classics include a **1921 Rolls-Royce Silver Ghost**; **1937 Cord**; and a **1926 Hispano-Suiza**. The "1950s" room is loaded with convertibles that look ready to hit the road on the first sunny day. Other top cars are a fire engine-red **1957 Chrysler Imperial** and a **1955 Packard Caribbean**, one of only 500 sold. Since the collection is larger than the museum, the displays change periodically. NAAM member.

Number of vehicles: 50+

Highlights: 1911 Locomobile M48 Seven-Passenger Touring; 1913 Marmon; 1932 Auburn Boattail Speedster; 1963 Studebaker Avanti.

Location: 14959 W. 69th Avenue, Arvada, CO 80007. (*Note:* The museum is located only 14 miles west of the **Forney Museum of Transportation.** See separate listing.)

Admission: $ **Hours:** Open seasonally from May through September: Monday and Tuesday only, 10 a.m. to 7 p.m.

Phone: (303) 420-2795   **Web:** www.CusslerMuseum.com

DOUGHERTY MUSEUM
Longmont, CO

In addition to raising turkeys, local farmer Ray G. Dougherty grew this collection of autos that is still run by his family. While there is a strong emphasis on antique farm equipment and musical instruments, there's plenty to keep a car buff happy, too. There are autos going back more than a century, with almost all of them in working order.

The cars are mostly divided between Brass Era (1905 to World War I) and Vintage (around 1919 to 1930) vehicles. There are a few outliers on both ends of this spectrum, including a **1902 Stevens-Duryea** and a **1937 Lincoln Zephyr**. Some little-known makes are also represented here, including a **1909 Fuller**; a **1910 Lozier**; a **1908 Silent Waverley**, so named because it was battery-powered and lacked the loud, clanging engine of early cars; and a **1916 Franklin Series 8**. The **1909 International Auto-Wagon** sprouted from a brief foray into passenger automobiles by farming equipment maker International Harvester.

The Roaring Twenties kicks in with a **1920 Pierce-Arrow Model 48** and a **1924 Rolls-Royce Silver Ghost**, among others. Firefighting buffs will enjoy the **1928 American LaFrance Pumper**. There are also over 50 pieces of farming equipment, ranging from a **1911 John Deere Model "A" Manure Spreader** to balers and corn shellers.

Number of vehicles: 40+

Highlights: 1902 Mobile Steamer, perhaps the first car in Boulder County; 1914 Metz; 1915 Stanley Steamer 12-Passenger Mountain Wagon. The latter was used to ferry guests to the historic Stanley Hotel (developed by F.O. Stanley, one of the twins of Stanley Steamer fame). The hotel is still open and is located 35 miles northwest in Estes Park, the gateway to Rocky Mountain National Park.

Location: 8306 N. 107th Street, Longmont, CO 80504. It's 35 miles north of downtown Denver. You can also pass through Boulder and take in the **Shelby American Museum** on the way up. (See separate listing.)

Admission: $ **Hours:** June through August: Friday, Saturday and Sunday, 11 a.m. to 5 p.m. It's best to call ahead for specific open days.

Phone: (303) 776-2520   **Web:** www.BoulderCounty.org/os/ culture/pages/DoughertyMuseum.aspx

FORNEY MUSEUM OF TRANSPORTATION
Denver, CO

Woodie wagons are always popular cars.
Photo credit: Forney Museum of Transportation

This collection offers something for everyone who is into vintage autos, motorcycles, trains, tractors, and – since this is the Mile High City – the occasional snowmobile.

Aviation enthusiasts shouldn't miss the bright yellow **1923 Kissel Speedster Gold Bug** that Amelia Earhart drove cross-country from Los Angeles to Boston in 1924. One of the most spectacularly bizarre cars you'll see anywhere is a Spanish **1923 Hispano-Suiza Victoria Town Car**. It's also bright yellow, but that's not what is so different about it. The body is so long it requires two sets of wheels in the rear. Posing by some of the cars are mannequins dressed in clothing of the era.

Number of vehicles: 16

Location: 4303 Brighton Boulevard, Denver, CO 80216. (**Note:** The museum is only 14 miles east of the **Cussler Museum.** See separate listing.)

Admission: $$ **Hours:** Monday through Saturday, 10 a.m. to 4 p.m.; Sunday, noon to 4 p.m.

Phone: (303) 297-1113   **Web:** www.ForneyMuseum.org

GATEWAY CANYONS AUTO MUSEUM
Gateway, CO

John S. Hendricks, who also started the Discovery Channel, among many other achievements, founded this adobe-looking museum in western Colorado. At Gateway Canyons, automobiles are treated as performance art. They are presented as if they're occupying a high-end art museum, with detailed descriptions and plenty of room to roam around each vehicle.

There are several galleries to tour. The "Hollywood High Style" gallery includes a **1930 Duesenberg Model J Transformable Cabriolet** and a **1932 Auburn 8-100A Boattail Speedster Convertible**. If muscle is more your speed, head to the "American Muscle Gallery" and drool over a **1970 Plymouth Barracuda Coupe "Hemi Cuda"** or a **1971 Pontiac GTO Judge**. Regular daily drivers are covered in the "Mass Mobility" gallery, with machines like a **1914 Ford Model T Runabout**.

A car you won't find anywhere else is a one-off **1954 Oldsmobile F-88** dream car, designed by Harley Earl for a General Motors "Motorama" show. In 2007, the museum purchased this unique auto at Barrett-Jackson Auctions in Scottsdale for an eye-catching $3,240,000. At that price, its metallic gold patina is highly appropriate.

Number of vehicles: 50+

Highlights: 1913 Pierce-Arrow; 1936 Supercharged Auburn, 1936 Cord Phaeton; 1937 Hudson Terraplane Convertible Coupe; 1953 Cunningham C3 Continental Coupe; 1954 Oldsmobile F-88.

Location: Gateway Canyons Resort, 43224 Highway 141, Gateway, CO 81522. Getting there is a great road trip in the "red rock" country of western Colorado, up against the Utah border. About a five-hour drive west of Denver or 3-4 hours north of the Four Corners National Monument.

Admission: $$

Hours: Daily, 10 a.m. to 5 p.m.

Phone: (970) 931-2895

Web: www.GatewayAutoMuseum.com

SHELBY AMERICAN COLLECTION
Boulder, CO

The **Shelby American Collection** holds over 30 custom Shelby Cobras, Daytona Coupes, GT 350s, GT40s, and other high-powered vehicles. There's also a wide variety of Shelby-related auto memorabilia, including crew uniforms and artwork, along with various auto body parts and chassis. Unlike many car museums, the hoods on many of the autos are raised so gearheads can marvel at their powerful engines. There are also a variety of rare prototype and development parts.

One special car is a flaming-red **1956 Ferrari 410 Sport Scaglietti Spider** that was raced by Carroll Shelby himself to a half-dozen victories in the 1950s. A rare **1957 AC Bristol BEX 254** was the inspiration for the Cobras that came later. The first racing Cobra, a **1962 Cobra CSX 2002 289 Sebring Roadster,** is also on display. Check out the unusual **1963 Ford Falcon Delivery Van,** which made a brief appearance in the movie *The Killers* starring future president Ronald Reagan.

Number of vehicles: 30+

Highlights: GT40 Mk IV driven by Mario Andretti at the 1967 24 Hours of Le Mans; Cobra Daytona Coupe CSX 2299, which won at Le Mans in 1964 with Bob Bondurant and Dan Gurney taking turns behind the wheel.

Location: 5020 Chaparral Court, Boulder, CO 80308

Admission: $ **Hours:** Sat, 10 a.m. to 4 p.m.

Phone: (303) 516-9565

Web: www.ShelbyAmericanCollection.org

Side Trip: The Shining

From Boulder, take a picturesque 38-mile drive north to the village of Estes Park, the gateway to Rocky Mountain National Park, and stay at the venerable Stanley Hotel. The inn was built by Stanley Steamer co-founder F. O. Stanley in 1909, when he moved to the mountains for his health. Guests were squired up the steep road in a Stanley Steamer 12-Passenger Mountain Wagon, one of which is on display at the **Dougherty Museum** in Longmont, Colorado. The Stanley gained infamy in the 1970s, when it was the inspiration for the Stephen King novel *The Shining* and later the film of the same name. A TV mini-series based on the novel was filmed at the Stanley in 1997. And just up the road there is a pet cemetery, which may have inspired another King novel. The Stanley Hotel, 333 Wonderview Avenue, Estes Park, CO 80517. (970-577-4000) www.StanleyHotel. com.

MONTANA

MONTANA AUTO MUSEUM
Deer Lodge, MT

Chevy Row contains over a half dozen 1955 through 1957 Bel Airs.

A part of the **Powell County Museum** complex, over 150 vehicles are displayed in a unique setting – an old prison. There's a wide range of vehicles, from 1903 to muscle cars of the 1960s and '70s. You can even drive away in some of the vehicles, because they are on consignment. *USA Today* chose the Montana Auto Museum as one of the top ten in the nation.

The Brass Era is well represented by several autos, including a **1913 Cole Model 60** seven- passenger touring car. Farther along, the **1929 Ford Model Station Wagon** was the company's first attempt at that body style; the **1932 Franklin Airman** was a luxury air-cooled car.

Chevy lovers will enjoy the extensive collection of 1955-'57 Chevys. The need for speed is not left out, with a **1964 Pontiac GTO**, the first year of what is considered by many to be the first "muscle car." "Corvette Drive" consists of eight of these beauties, including a 1964 tilt-top, going toe-to-toe with several dozen muscle cars. This is rural Montana, so trucks are also well represented, including a **1928 REO Speedwagon**. Oddities include a **1967 Amphicar Model 770**, **1974 Citi Car** (the electric car of the future!), and a **1973 VW Dune Buggy** used in *Mad Max*.

Cases are stacked full of old brass lamps, tools, spark plugs (many in their original boxes), service manuals, and old sales brochures, while vintage advertising lines the walls. An interesting exhibit highlights the Yellowstone Trail. This little-remembered route went from Plymouth Rock in Massachusetts to Puget Sound in Washington. It was formed in 1912, a year before the better-known Lincoln Highway.

Number of vehicles: 150+

Highlights: 1914 Trumbull Cyclecar; 1915 Seagrave fire truck; 1958 Porsche 356A Coupe.

Location: 1106 Main Street, Deer Lodge, MT 59722. One mile off I-90 between Missoula and Butte.

Admission: $$ Ticket price includes the Old Prison and several other historical museums. You can easily spend a day here.

Hours: Spring: February through mid-May, daily 10 a.m. to 4 p.m. **Summer:** mid-May through September, daily 8 a.m. to 6 p.m.; **Fall:** October through mid-December, daily 10 a.m. to 4 p.m.; **Winter:** closes mid-December through January 31;

Phone: (406) 846-3111   **Web:** pcmaf.org/wordpress

NEVADA

Auto Collections at the **LINQ**
Las Vegas, NV

Billed as "The World's Largest Classic Car Showroom," this attraction is part museum and part vintage car sales showroom. While some of the vehicles are historic and part of the permanent collection, many of the others are for sale. It's not all "Concours d' Elegance"-level cars that aren't meant to be driven, making some of the prices approachable for the average buyer.

The collection rotates regularly, so it's hard to know what will be there on a particular visit. You can count on seeing TV talk-show host Johnny Carson's **1939 Chrysler Royale Sedan,** though. It's the car he learned to drive in while growing up in Nebraska; years later, he tracked it down and bought it. You can even watch home movies showing Carson posing by the car before his senior prom. There's also the **1962 Lincoln Continental Limousine** that squired President Kennedy around New York the week before he was assassinated in Dallas.

A sampling of cars for sale on my visit included: **1955 Ford Thunderbird** ($19,500, needs work); **1958 Lincoln Continental Mark III** ($35,000, one of the largest cars ever built); and a **1964 Impala SS Sport Coupe** ($34,500). If you just won the lottery, there's also a **1957 Maserati 3500GT Frua Spyder** for a cool $3 million.

Number of vehicles: 50+

Highlights: Johnny Carson's 1939 Chrysler Royale Sedan; JFK's 1962 Lincoln Continental Limousine; 1974 Hong-Qi CA-770 Red Flag Limousine (Chinese made).

Location: LINQ Casino, 3535 Las Vegas Boulevard. South, Las Vegas, NV 89109. Right on "The Strip," at the rear of the LINQ Casino.

Admission: Print out free pass on their website.

Hours: Monday through Saturday, 10 a.m. to 5 p.m.

Phone: (702) 794-3174   **Web:** AutoCollections.com

NATIONAL AUTOMOBILE MUSEUM: THE HARRAH COLLECTION
Reno, NV

With "National" in its name, this museum had better deliver – and it does. It focuses on pre-1950 vehicles, with an emphasis on cars collected by the renowned William Fisk "Bill" Harrah. The sleek, black **1938 Phantom Corsair** is one of the coolest cars you'll see anywhere. Because it was a one-off, this is the only place you will.

Located in glitzy Reno, there are many celebrity-owned vehicles, including John Wayne's **1953 Chevrolet Corvette Convertible Series,** of which only 300 were built (not sure how the Duke even crammed himself into it), and Frank Sinatra's **1961 Karmann Ghia L.6.4 Hardtop**.

There are also a few cars that have become film stars in their own right: a **1912 Rambler 73-4CC Cross Country** appeared on the dock before the ill-fated voyage in *Titanic;* a **1949 Mercury Series 9CM Six-Passenger Coupe** was driven by James Dean in *Rebel Without a Cause*; and a **1960 Flying Caduceus Experimental Streamliner** (the first turbo-jet car to run on the Bonneville Salt Flats) appeared in *The World's Fastest Indian*.

There are many other collections here, including vintage clothing, license plates, and gas pumps. There are also mock street scenes from the 1900s, 1930s, 1950s, and the modern era.

NAAM member.

Number of vehicles: 200+

Highlights: Lana Turner's 1941 Chrysler Newport; 1936 Mercedes-Benz Type 500k Special Roadster; and a 1937 Airomobile Experimental Sedan, an odd fishtailed car that it never made it to full production.

Location: 10 S. Lake Street, Reno, NV 89501

Admission: $$ **Hours:** Monday through Saturday, 9:30 a.m. to 5:30 p.m.; Sunday, 10 a.m. to 4 p.m.

Phone: (775) 333-9300   **Web:** www.AutoMuseum.org

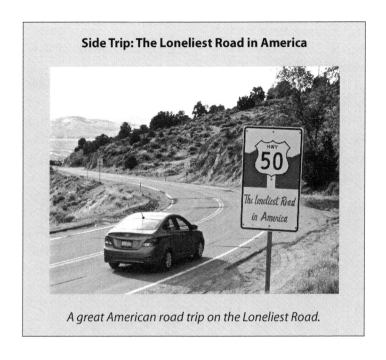

Side Trip: The Loneliest Road in America

A great American road trip on the Loneliest Road.

In 1986 *Life* magazine declared a 287-mile stretch of Highway 50 that crosses the barren Great Basin Desert in Nevada as "The Loneliest Road in America." When first proposed in 1913, it was part of the Lincoln Highway, connecting New York City and San Francisco, that became the first transcontinental highway in America. Mundane numbering of roads didn't occur until the 1920s.

With its arid landscape-of-the-moon setting, the view of central Nevada is awe-inspiring; there aren't many places left where you can stretch your eyes like this. A vintage car seems just right for taking in the sights on the Loneliest Road; because parts of Highway 50 parallel the old Pony Express Route, it only seems natural that a 1964 1/2 Mustang would be the most appropriate car to take the drive.

In Eureka, there's a weathered metal plaque in front of the courthouse stating "GENERAL MOTORS SECTION OF THE LINCOLN HIGHWAY – EUREKA UNIT – LENGTH 22 MILES." The antique sign represents a $100,000 contribution GM made to complete the construction of this segment in 1919.

While announcing the donation, GM's President W. C. Durant declared that he hoped the federal government would eventually step in to "construct such highly necessary routes."

Just beyond the western end of the Loneliest Road there's a bonus for car buffs. The **National Automobile Museum: The Harrah Collection** (see prior listing) in Reno displays over 200 vehicles.

SHELBY MUSEUM
Las Vegas, NV

Shelbys old and new on display.

Carroll Shelby is a racing legend whose influence is still felt all over the automotive world. At Shelby American in Las Vegas, his legacy lives on as the company continues to turn out custom automobiles. If you don't have $30,000 sitting around to upgrade to a custom Shelby GT, do the next best thing and watch them being made. Along the way, you can see some of the cars that Shelby created over the years.

The tour starts with a long history of Carroll Shelby and the chance to "ooh" and "aah" over some of his early creations. Until the summer of 2016, this ogling included his personal 1962 Shelby Cobra CSX 2000. Known as "The One," it's the first Shelby ever built. However, in August the Carroll Hall Shelby Trust put it up for sale in Monterey where it went for a cool $13.75 million, a new record for an American car.

The tour continues to the edge of the shop floor, where – from a distance and behind a low wall – you can briefly watch the customizers in action. (You don't really see much more than you can from the showroom.) If the tour times don't fit your schedule, just stop by during opening hours, walk around the gallery of cars, seek out Shelby-themed souvenirs in the mammoth gift shop, and watch the shop floor through the windows.

Some of the cars on the tour can be purchased, so if you had a big weekend in Vegas … well, you never know. Maybe that 750-horsepower GT500 Super Snake you admired will end up in your driveway after all.

Number of vehicles: 20+

Highlight: Watching the tradition continue with new Shelbys being built.

Location: 6405 Ensworth Street, Las Vegas, NV 89119

Admission: Free

Hours: Guided tours are offered Monday through Friday, 10:30 a.m. and 1:30 p.m.; Sat, 10:30 a.m. However, you can stop in at any time and skip the tour.

Phone: (702) 942-7325

Web: www.ShelbyAmerican.com/Tours.asp

UTAH

BROWNING-KIMBALL CLASSIC CAR MUSEUM
Ogden, UT

This museum is part of a larger complex called **Union Station**, located in the historic 1924 Spanish Colonial Revival train station. There are three other museums: the Utah State Railroad Museum, the John M. Browning Firearms Museum, and the Utah State Cowboy and Western Heritage Museum. One reasonably priced admission ticket provides access to all four museums. The modest car collection includes a dozen pre-World War II rarities from 1901 through 1937. Also on display are vintage Utah license plates, scale model cars and fire engines, and two antique gas pumps.

Number of vehicles: 12

Highlights: 1901 Oldsmobile; 1911 Knox; 1930 Cadillac.

Location: 2501 Wall Avenue, Ogden, UT 84401. About 40 miles north of Salt Lake City.

Admission: $

Hours: Monday through Saturday, 10 a.m. to 5 p.m.

Phone: (801) 393-9890

Web: www.TheUnionStation.org

Side Trip: A Pinch of the Salt Flats

Growing up, I remember seeing pictures in the newspaper of rocket-propelled cars driven by guys like Craig Breedlove setting land speed records on the parched Bonneville Salt Flats in the Utah desert. Attempts at new records still take place there during Speed Week in mid-August, the World of Speed in mid-September, and at other times throughout the year. Spectators can watch these events or get permits to drive the course in their own vehicles. The Flats also make an appearance in the movie *The World's Fastest Indian*. Starring Anthony Hopkins, it's the real-life story of Kiwi Burt Munro's attempt to set a speed record with an Indian motorcycle. The Bonneville Salt Flats Speedway is located about 110 miles west of Salt Lake City, Utah. For more information, go to www.SaltFlats.com.

7

Southwest

Cadillac Ranch in the Texas Panhandle has long been a popular stopping point for travelers on Route 66, but Amarillo also offers other quirky outdoor vehicle sculptures – **Combine City** and the **VW Slug Bug Ranch.** Nearby is one of two recreational vehicle museums in this book, the **Jack Sisemore Traveland RV Museum.** For a less populated state, New Mexico packs a punch car-wise, with the **Unser Racing Museum** and the **War Eagles Air Museum** among its various treasures. In Tucson, Arizona a sandy road leads to the **Franklin Automobile Museum,** an unusual place to find a display of these upstate New York cars.

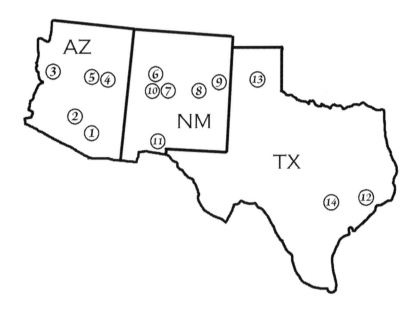

THE SOUTH WEST

ARIZONA

    1) Franklin Automobile Museum
      Muffler Man

    2) Martin Auto Museum
      Penske Racing Museum

    3) Route 66 Electric Vehicle Museum

4) Wigwam Motel

5) Winslow

NEW MEXICO

6) J and R Vintage Autos

7) Lewis Antique Auto & Toy Museum

8) Route 66 Auto Museum

9) Russell's Truck & Travel Plaza

10) Unser Racing Museum

11) War Eagles Air Museum

TEXAS

12) Art Car Museum

13) Cadillac Ranch
   Combine City
   Jack Sisemore Traveland RV Museum
   VW Slug Bug Ranch

14) Dick's Classic Garage Car Museum

ARIZONA

Franklin Automobile Museum
Tucson, AZ

Turn left at the cactus for the Franklin Museum.

If you can find the unassuming **Franklin Automobile Museum**, congratulations are in order. It's tucked away in a residential neighborhood north of downtown Tucson that opted not to have their streets paved. So plan on driving on some sandy roads for a few blocks to get here, which is really part of the fun when viewing such a fine assemblage of pre-World War II autos.

This large collection of Franklin automobiles grew out of the passion of one man, car restorer Thomas Hubbard. He purchased his first Franklin in 1950 and never stopped. Although he is no longer with us, Hubbard's foundation continues to acquire cars for the museum. It recently bought a **1905 Franklin Model A Runabout** with a rare rear-entry *tonneau*.

Franklins were produced in Syracuse, New York from 1902 through 1934. All of its cars were air-cooled; only about 3,500 survive. Because air-cooling removed the need for a bulky radiator, Franklin cars took on some unusual front-end shapes including barrel hoods, shovels, and horse collars.

There are three rooms' worth of well-marked autos here. See if you can find the handy (and surprisingly small) golf bag on the **1929 Franklin Convertible Coupe**. Since early cars required constant maintenance, the **1918 Franklin Model B Touring** came with tool kits, the originals are cleverly hidden inside the front doors, with extra spark plugs to boot.

A **1929/1930/1931 Franklin Model 153** is unique because it was company founder Herbert Franklin's personal vehicle. The reason it has so many model years attributed to it was that he brought it into the shop annually to update it to the current model year. There is also a research library of Franklin-related material. NAAM member.

Number of vehicles: 25+

Highlights: 1905 Franklin Model A Runabout and a one-off 1931 Franklin Model 153 Sport Phaeton.

Location: 3420 N. Vine Avenue, Tucson, AZ 85719. (Mailing address is 1405 E. Kleindale Road, Tucson, AZ 85719.)

Admission: $$

Hours: Mid-October through Memorial Day: Wednesday through Saturday, 10 a.m. to 4 p.m.

Phone: (520) 326-8038

Web: www.FranklinMuseum.org

Side Trip: Do You Know the Muffler Man?

Anyone who loves road trips across America is aware of the Muffler Man statues that sprinkle the heartland. These distinctive, 20-foot-tall fiberglass figures were mostly erected in the 1960s to lure visitors to various shops and attractions. They were cleverly designed so the statue could hold an object related to the business they were promoting.

Because many of them ended up holding mufflers to promote service stations, they've come to be known as the "Muffler Men." There's one in Tucson, just two miles southwest of the Franklin Museum. It's been presiding over the corner of N. Stone Avenue and E. Glenn Street since 1964 and may be the original Muffler Man statue. Although this one's dressed up as Paul Bunyan holding an axe, it's still auto-related, as it stands in the parking lot of Don's Hot Rod Shop. 2811 N. Stone Avenue, Tucson, AZ 85705.

Detour: If you're really into quirky sights, and a music fan to boot, head 1.6 miles east on Glenn Street until you arrive at the intersection of Glenn & Campbell for a nifty photo op of the crisscrossed street signs. The singer's name only has one "n" but it's close enough.

MARTIN AUTO MUSEUM
Phoenix, AZ

Founder Mel Martin achieved success in the towing business before creating this museum "dedicated to the preservation of collectible and rare automobiles for educational purposes." On its website, the museum offers lesson plans and curriculum guidelines to teach kids from pre-kindergarten to 12th grade about the history of automobiles, 1950s dream cars, transportation safety, and more. Since the museum's goal is to educate, the vehicles are not just pretty faces. Many have their hoods open so visitors can peer inside at the engines. The collection amazes with its breadth and quality spanning decades of driving history, from the Brass Era through 1970s muscle cars.

The Martin's **1965 Shelby Cobra 427** is unique. It sat for years in Carroll Shelby's showroom with no engine. When Martin purchased the car at auction, he commissioned Shelby to build an engine for it; it now has only six miles on it. This Cobra looks like it really wants to tear it up on the track, so maybe one day it'll get a chance to do so.

There are a few cars from film and TV here, including Col. Klink's army-green **1951 Mercedes Phaeton** from *Hogan's Heroes*. Only two of them were made. (Yes, a 1951 car stood in for one that would have been driven in the 1940s, but the body style hadn't changed all that much so it worked.) A **1954 Cadillac/Oldsmobile 98 Starfire Convertible** is a mish-mash of an Olds chassis and body in front and a Cadillac body in the rear that was built for the Art Carney movie *The Late Show*. The walls are covered with photos and memorabilia; a few antique gas pumps are scattered about, along with a carousel and display cases devoted to toy cars. NAAM member.

Number of vehicles: 60+

Highlights: 1928 Chevrolet "Woody" Wagon; 1930 LaSalle Dual-Cowl Phaeton (twice driven in the trans-America Great Race); 1930 Duesenberg Boattail Speedster (once owned by a Chicago gangster, now worth over $2.5 million); 1965 Shelby Cobra 427.

Location: 17641 N. Black Canyon Highway, Phoenix, AZ 85023

Admission: $

Hours: Thursday through Saturday, 10 a.m. to 5 p.m.

Phone: (602) 298-2377   **Web:** www.MartinAutoMuseum.com

Phoenix, AZ

Racing legend Roger Penske's Museum is built for speed.

Roger Penske is a giant in the auto racing world. Among his accomplishments is the most wins at the Indy 500. If all you know about the name is the infamous "Penske file" from *Seinfeld*, here's a chance to learn more about the man's storied career. The **Penske Racing Museum** showcases a wide array of racing cars and memorabilia, including several Indy 500 champion vehicles. Among the cars that rode into the Winner's Circle are the **Penske PC-6** driven by Rick Mears in 1979 and the **March 84C** Mears pushed to victory again in 1984. Driver Mark Donohue died in 1975 at the age of 38; the **1973 Porsche IRIC RSR** he drove for a win in the first IROC race in 1973 is on display along with a replica of his 1972 Indy-winning McLaren. NASCAR is not left out, with a **2004 Dodge Intrepid** twice driven to victory by Ryan Newman.

The museum is in the middle of the Scottsdale 101 Auto Collection, which features, among others, dealers for Lamborghini, Aston Martin, and Bugatti. If you've got a quarter-million dollars burning a hole in your pocket, this would be the place to part with it.

Number of vehicles: 30

Highlights: Two Indy Pace Cars, a 1972 Hurst/Olds Cutlass and a 2006 Chevrolet Corvette Z06; 1985 Penske March 85C (the "Spin and Win" car in which Danny Sullivan won the Indy 500 in dramatic fashion, after spinning out in front of Mario Andretti.)

Location: 7125 E. Chauncey Lane, Phoenix, AZ 85054. The mailing address is Phoenix, but it's located in North Scottsdale, about 15 miles northeast of downtown Phoenix off of Route 101.

Admission: Free

Hours: Monday through Saturday, 8 a.m. to 4 p.m.; Sunday, noon to 5 p.m.

Phone: (480) 538-4444   **Web:** www.PenskeRacingMuseum.com

Route 66 Electric Vehicle Museum
Kingman, AZ

This collection is the brainchild of Roderick Wilde and the Historic Electric Vehicle Foundation, who have created the first auto museum devoted solely to electric-powered vehicles. Electric vehicles have been around for over a century and once outnumbered gasoline propelled cars, and some people think that could happen again.

Wilde's personal **1930 Detroit Electric** is on display, as well as electric micro-cars and even high-performance racers. Yes, you can race in electric vehicles; Wilde was the first driver to break 100 mph in a standing quarter-mile race. A new addition that went "on the road again" to get here is singer Willie Nelson's Rolls-Royce-styled golf cart. Appropriately enough, the museum is housed in the circa 1910 Powerhouse, which provided electricity before the construction of nearby Hoover Dam.

Number of vehicles: 12+

Location: 120 W. Andy Devine Avenue, Kingman, AZ 86401. It's in the same building as the Kingman Visitor Center and the Route 66 Museum.

Admission: $ Admission includes Route 66 Museum.

Hours: Daily, 9 a.m. to 4:30 p.m.

Phone: (928) 753-3185

Web: www.hevf.org/route-66-ev-museum

Pit Stop: Teepees & Vintage Cars

If you've ever dreamed of spending the night in a concrete teepee surrounded by vintage cars (and who hasn't?), you'll enjoy the Wigwam Motel in Holbrook, Arizona. At one time there were seven Wigwam Motels stretching from Kentucky to San Bernardino, California. This property is one of two survivors and is conveniently located on Route 66. It's a must-stop for road trippers on the Mother Road. Rooms are relatively cheap for this retro-1950s experience. To make a reservation go to www.galerie-kokopelli.com/wigwam.

Side Trip: Standin' on a Corner in Winslow, Arizona

Jackson Browne and Eagles co-founder Glenn Frey wrote a song that forever put a dusty old Arizona town along Route 66 on the map of rock-and-roll destinations. *Take it Easy,* on which Frey also sang lead vocals, included a line about "standin' on a corner in Winslow, Arizona" while a girl swings by in a flatbed Ford.

Winslow has embraced this burst of fame by creating "Standin' on the Corner Park" at the intersection of Route 66 and North Kinsley Avenue. You can't miss it – there's a giant highway shield of Route 66 painted on the road. Parked curbside is a bright red, 1960 Ford flatbed truck for a unique photo op.

Winslow is a pretty interesting town to visit. You can stay in the historic La Posada Hotel, a former Santa Fe Railroad hotel from 1929. East of town there are a few relics from Route 66's glory days of welcoming travelers, even a spot where the road literally ends.

Address: Intersection of 2nd Avenue (Old Route 66 eastbound) and North Kinsley Avenue. Winslow is 58 miles east of Flagstaff. You'll take I-40 to get to Winslow, so make sure to exit the interstate to get downtown. Open 24/7 and there is no admission. For more information, go to standinonthecorner.com.

NEW MEXICO

J AND R VINTAGE AUTOS
Rio Rancho, NM

Robert "Gab" Joiner, who started from humble beginnings to become a successful contractor, founded this collection. He, his wife Evonna, and family members have been active in the annual Great Race of vintage cars across America. The cars they've driven in this automotive marathon (all of them convertibles) are on display and include a **1917 Marmon Chummy Roadster** (in which they won the 1995 Great Race), a **1931 REO Speedwagon,** and a **1932 Hupmobile**.

A **1979 Ford Thunderbird** doesn't quite fit in with the rest of the collection, but it was the largest Thunderbird ever produced, so it's interesting from that angle to see where Ford went wrong with this car. Joiner is also a truck enthusiast, so there are quite a few in the museum, including a **1922 White Truck** and a **1959 Ford Custom Cab F-100** that belonged to his dad. Off to the side of the parking lot, be sure to visit the "graveyard" of old trucks. These may never make it into the restoration shop, but there are some real treasures out there soaking up the New Mexico sun.

Many of the vehicles have red stars on their information placards, indicating they are for sale. Check first before visiting if there's a particular auto you want to see. The gift shop focuses on car books and die-cast models. *Note:* Mr. Joiner passed away in 2015, but his family promises to carry on his legacy with the museum.

Number of vehicles: 65 (about half are for sale)

Highlights: 1950 Ford Custom Deluxe Crestliner (only 8,750 built); 1959 Studebaker Pickup Truck.

Location: 3650A Highway 528 Rio Rancho, NM. 87144. About 20 miles north of Albuquerque.

Admission: $

Hours: Monday through Saturday, 10 a.m. to 5 p.m.

Phone: (505) 867-2881   **Web:** www.JRVintageAutos.com

LEWIS ANTIQUE AUTO & TOY MUSEUM
Moriarty, NM

You can go on an all-day scavenger hunt here.

Picture a massive junkyard in the blazing hot sun of the New Mexico desert; that'll give you an idea of the Lewis Antique Auto & Toy Museum right on old Route 66. As you approach it, you'll realize pretty quickly that this is not your typical museum.

With his grizzled countenance, piercing eyes and cowboy hat, owner Archie Lewis looks like the long-lost brother of Willie Nelson. He's been collecting for decades and doesn't seem like he'll ever stop. But this is no junkyard. Lewis makes it clear that he doesn't sell spare parts, so the vehicles are more or less intact. (Well, sometimes <u>very</u> less. A few look like they were towed here directly from the scene of an accident decades ago.)

Pride of place goes to the cars protected from the elements and stored in the massive warehouse. Here you'll find antique toys, plus rows of original-condition and semi-restored **Ford Model Ts, Model As, Thunderbirds,** and more. It's a bit musty and dusty, but a true walk down memory lane. It's the opposite of seeing all the cars in pristine showroom condition. Plus, with over 1,000 toys on display, odds are you'll find a favorite toy from your childhood.

Outside, it's not just cars. There are also school buses, tractors, trucks, fire trucks, and more. A large collection of diminutive Crosleys look more like bumper cars from an amusement park than something you'd take on the open road. The museum is a great place to stop if you're into automotive archaeology or photography. You'll get some incredible photos under the same cobalt blue skies and crisp clouds where *Breaking Bad* was filmed.

Number of vehicles: 600+

Highlights: Assorted Crosleys, school buses, and just about anything else you can think of.

Location: 905 US 66 East, Moriarty, NM 87035. Right off I-40 at exit 197, about 40 miles east of Albuquerque.

Admission: $ **Hours:** Daily, 10 a.m. to 5 p.m., but best to call ahead to confirm someone is there.

Phone: (505) 832-6131   **Web:** None

ROUTE 66 AUTO MUSEUM
Santa Rosa, NM

Located on historic Route 66, this is more of a vintage car showroom than a museum, because most of the cars are for sale. That said, it's worth the nominal admission fee to walk around and see the vehicles and maybe dream of owning one. The walls are lined with Route 66 memorabilia, car-themed movie posters, vintage auto advertisements, and display cases full of model cars. Menu stands from old drive-in restaurants take you back in time. Gearheads will appreciate the eight vintage engines on display. Predictably, the gift shop carries Route 66 memorabilia and, unpredictably, rattlesnake skins.

Number of vehicles: 30+

Highlights: Most of the cars are for sale, but the permanent collection includes a 1963 Chevrolet Corvette Split Back and two 1965 Ford Mustangs.

Location: 2866 Historic Route 66, Santa Rosa, NM 88435

Admission: $

Hours: April through October: Monday through Saturday, 7:30 a.m. to 6 p.m.; Sunday, 10 a.m. to 5 p.m.
November through March: Monday through Saturday, 8 a.m. to 5 p.m.; Sunday, 8 a.m. to 5 p.m.

Phone: (575) 472-1966

Russell's Truck & Travel Plaza
Glen Rio, NM

When you're just looking for a hot meal after a long day on the road, it's quite a surprise to come across Russell's. This is a working truck stop complete with a diner, gift shop, shower facilities, and a chapel. Tucked in behind the restaurant is a free car museum devoted to Route 66 and 1950s nostalgia items. In such a compact space, it crams in more stuff per square foot than just about any museum anywhere.

At the entrance is a tribute to "The Intimidator," Dale Earnhardt Sr., consisting of photos, car models, and even cereal boxes that featured him. The large room holds about two dozen cars that look like they're in original showroom condition. They range from a **1940 Ford Deluxe Convertible** through a **1964 Ford Galaxie 500** which was truck stop owner Mark Russell's ride in high school. There's also a **1955 Chevy Cameo Pickup Truck**.

The walls are lined with cases full of toy cars, Texaco trucks, autographed movie star photos, TVs playing vintage car commercials, Elvis collectibles, soda paraphernalia, and more. In keeping with the retro theme, the restrooms are marked "Elvis" and "Marilyn."

Number of vehicles: 20+   **Highlights:** 1953 Oldsmobile Super 88 Convertible (only 64 were produced); 1955 Corvette Roadster (#15 of 700 produced); 1959 Ford Galaxie Skyliner with retractable hardtop.

Location: Exit 369 on I-40, 3 miles west of the New Mexico/Texas state line.

Admission: Free   **Hours:** Daily, 7:30 a.m. to 9 p.m.

Phone: (575) 576-8700   **Web:** www.RussellsTTC.com

Unser Racing Museum
Albuquerque, NM

The Unser family is one of the most legendary in auto racing history, providing 14 top racers so far. The most famous are brothers Bobby and Al Unser, followed by Al's son Al Jr. Between them, the trio has won the Indy 500 nine times. It's hard to beat the "wow" factor when entering the museum, with a bright yellow 1986 Indy 500 car spinning on a turntable beneath sparkling spotlights. It was the backup vehicle when Al Unser won his fourth Indy 500 in 1987.

The round building is set up like a wheel, with the turntable in the center and each exhibit hall radiating from it like spokes. The cushy flooring is made up of recycled tires. Video displays placed next to the vehicles show them in racing action. You'll also see four generations of cars that competed in the Indianapolis 500 or climbed Pike's Peak, pace cars, and antique cars. Interactive exhibits include computer games for kids and an actual racing gearbox that demonstrates how it works. There's also a row of engines for a close-up look at what powers these racers.

Don't miss the second building out back, which highlights about 35 vehicles from Al Senior's vintage car collection. The trophy room includes hundreds of awards won by the Unsers, as well as racing uniforms, championship jackets, scuffed race-worn helmets, and artwork. In the parking lot there is a Jersey barrier that Al Senior crashed into at the 1989 Indy 500. NAAM member.

Number of vehicles: 60+

Highlights: 1923 Sterling Truck; Pike's Peak Championship Car #58, built by Jerry Unser Sr. (spot the walnut shells that were imbedded in the tires to improve traction); 1970 Oldsmobile 442 Indy Pace Car won by Al Sr.

Location: 1776 Montaño Road NW, Los Ranchos de Albuquerque, NM 87107

Admission: $$

Hours: Daily, 10 a.m. to 4 p.m.

Phone: (505) 341-1776   **Web:** www.UnserRacingMuseum.com

WAR EAGLES AIR MUSEUM
Santa Teresa, NM

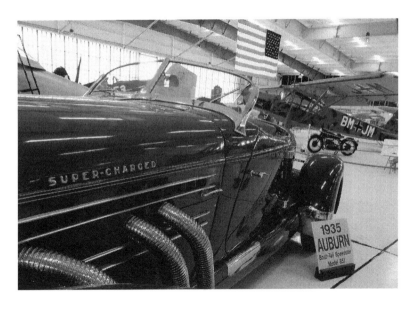

The sleek 1935 Auburn Speedster
looks like it could outrace some airplanes.

The **War Eagles Air Museum** is devoted to vintage aircraft, but also offers quality automobiles. Sitting in a giant hangar are dozens of airplanes and cars, so it's not unusual to see a **1937 Chevrolet Sedan** parked under the wing of a Lockheed P-38 Lightning fighter plane. A burgundy **1935 Auburn Boattail Speedster Model 851** stands out, with its curving sweeping lines designed by automotive legend Gordon Buehrig. It looks very cool sitting next to a World War II-era P-51 Mustang. Nearby is a pristine **1959 Rolls-Royce Silver Cloud II**. In an allusion to a famous TV commercial from the 1980s, there's a jar of Grey Poupon mustard visible through the windshield.

A **1967 Ford Thunderbird** drew our attention, because it was the same model and color that my father-in-law drove. A tiny **1972 Honda 600 GT Coupe** was a giant-killer in many ways. The 600 was at the vanguard of Honda's eventual ascendency in the American auto market and is a rare find in a museum. Don't miss the collection of vintage gas pumps. On the aviation side, check out the DC-3 that you can step inside.

Number of vehicles: 50

Highlights: 1908 Overland, 1938 Packard Super 8 Convertible, 1967 Maserati Mistral Spyder.

Location: 8012 Airport Road, Santa Theresa, NM 88008. 20 miles northwest of downtown El Paso, TX.

Admission: $

Hours: Tuesday through Sunday, 10 a.m. to 4 p.m.

Phone: (575) 589-2000

Web: www.war-eagles-air-museum.com

TEXAS

Dick's Classic Garage Car Museum
San Marcos, TX

A Tucker is just one of the many highlights at Dick's.

Dick Burdick started collecting cars in 1979 with a **1927 Ford Model T.** The "car that started it all" sits in the lobby greeting visitors. The highlight of the collection is the lowest-mileage **1948 Tucker** in the world. This maroon beauty was the last one to roll off the assembly line and sports only a half-mile on the odometer! A monitor next to it plays *Tucker: The Man and His Dream* on a continuous loop. The real sweet spot of the collection consists of cars from 1929 through 1959.

There are four Duesenbergs, among them a **1929 Duesenberg Model J by Bohman & Schwartz.** It sold for $18,000 when new, but would likely fetch over a million dollars at auction today. Continuing the museum's high-end lineage, their **1931**

Chrysler CG Imperial Dual Cowl Phaeton won best of show at the Hilton Head *Concours d'Elegance*, along with many other awards coast-to-coast. A fire engine-red **1957 Cadillac Series 62 Convertible** sports giant rubber-tipped chrome torpedoes on the front bumper called "Dagmars," after a similarly endowed actress of the time. The only surviving Lone Star auto, a **1919 Lone Star 4-30,** seems like a tribute to Texas. While the Lone Star Truck and Tractor Association was a San Antonio-based company, the cars themselves were manufactured in Virginia by the Piedmont Motor Car Company.

A **1950 Nash Ambassador Super** came with a fold-down front seat that combined with the rear seat to form a bed. Nash also offered a custom-fit mattress as an option, creating a "motel on wheels." The collection includes toy cars, hood ornaments, engines, and more. The place is really hopping the third Saturday of every month, when there is a vintage car cruise-in from 5 p.m. to 8 p.m., complete with live rockabilly style music and free admission to the museum. NAAM member.

Number of vehicles: 80+

Highlights: 1921 Stanley Steamer; 1931 Cadillac 355 Roadster; 1939 Chrysler C-24 Custom Imperial Parade Phaeton that transported King George IV and Queen Elizabeth during their visit to the 1939 World's Fair in New York; 1948 Tucker #1050.

Location: 120 Stagecoach Trail, San Marcos, TX. Just off I-35, 35 miles southwest of Austin.

Admission: $$ **Hours:** Monday through Saturday, 10 to 5 p.m.; Sunday, noon to 5 p.m.

Phone: (512) 878-2406

Web: www.DicksClassicGarage.com

Jack Sisemore Traveland RV Museum
Amarillo, TX

Jack Sisemore's brewing up some strong coffee.

This museum is an outgrowth of Jack Sisemore Traveland, a large dealer of recreational vehicles in the Texas Panhandle and the oldest Winnebago dealer in the state. Sisemore started out in the early 1960s with a service station, which he purchased with money borrowed from his grandmother. When he started taking trips in RVs, he realized he should get into the business and eventually became very successful. As a hobby he began collecting vintage RVs, which he showcases in the free museum along with an impressive collection of motorcycles.

The museum is well-curated by Jack and his son Trent, with vintage campers set up in tableaux with period furnishings, games, and picnic supplies. One of the neatest things is that visitors can step inside the campers and really feel what it was like to set out on a mid-century "adventure." The oldest vehicle is a **1936 Alma Trailer** with a wooden interior. A new addition is a **1941 Westcraft** that came complete with a hand-cranked Victrola.

Also check out the period avocado-and-harvest-gold interior in the **1972 Winnebago,** along with avocado-colored appliances that may bring back childhood memories of watching *The Brady Bunch*. A **1975 Itasca** boasts serial #1 and is the first one ever built. It has only 6,000 miles on it, since it sat long-term in the Winnebago Welcome Center in Forest City, Iowa. Film buffs will recognize the **1948 Flxible Clipper Bus** that was driven by Jeff Daniels in the Robin Williams movie *RV*. Go inside. You'll notice that, since it was a film vehicle, the cabinets are dummies and don't function.

Jack Sisemore is also a legend on the Grand National dirt-track racing circuit, so there's a fine collection of motorcycles stacked among the RVs. (Another RV museum is the **Recreational Vehicle and Manufactured Home Hall of Fame** in Elkhart, Indiana. See separate listing.)

Number of vehicles: 15

Highlights: 1937 Elkhart Traveler in original condition; 1953 Fleetwood Trailer (first year they were built); 1970 Avion Pickup Camper.

Location: 4341 Canyon Drive, Amarillo, TX 79110. Only 10 miles east of **Cadillac Ranch**, see separate sidebar below. The museum is five miles south of where old Route 66 runs through downtown Amarillo.

Admission: Free

Hours: Monday through Friday, 9 a.m. to 5 p.m.; Saturday, 9 a.m. to 4 p.m.

Phone: (806) 358-4891 **Web:** www.RVMuseum.net

Side Trip: Amarillo's Outdoor Vehicle Sculptures

The windswept plains of Amarillo, Texas are world-renowned for being the home of **Cadillac Ranch**, a series of tail-finned Cadillacs driven grille-first into the ground like they crashed from outer space. But there are several other vehicle-themed sculptures to visit in Amarillo; all of them can easily be visited in a two-hour loop.

Cadillac Ranch is an iconic spot in the Texas Panhandle.

Cadillac Ranch – The granddaddy of them all, this outdoor car sculpture inspired the others. A San Francisco-based art group called Ant Farm installed it in 1974. Ten Cadillacs, from a 1949 Club Sedan through a 1963 Sedan de Ville, are tilted into the ground just so, creating an irresistible lure for budding graffiti artists.

Periodically the cars are whitewashed, then the spray-painting starts all over again. Located on the southern side of I-40 on the western outskirts of Amarillo, Texas.

Combine City – If imitation is the sincerest form of flattery, then Cadillac Ranch has several admirers in the area.

Started in 2002 by the wonderfully named Orville Ladehoff, Combine City is a series of 14 combines planted in the ground as a tribute to the farmers of West Texas. It's located just southeast of Amarillo, on the northern side of Claude Highway/FM 1151/Business Loop 40 near the intersection of South Whitaker Road in Canyon, Texas. Don't bring your itchy spray-paint trigger fingers to this one; the combines are set up behind barbed wire. www. CombineCity.com

VW Slug Bug Ranch – The automotive tributes continue with this array of Volkswagen Beetles stuck into the ground. To say that the colorfully painted cars are mere shells of their former selves is an understatement, with some of them barely intact. There's also an abandoned service station adjacent to it that adds to the stark Texas Panhandle atmosphere. It's just south of I-40 at exit 96 for Conway, Texas, 30 miles east of Amarillo.

Side Trip: Houston, We Have an Odd Car Museum

The **Art Car Museum** in Houston, Texas is definitely "out there." Their mission is to turn cars into artwork – and in some cases, vice versa. Past exhibits have included cars covered in seashells, built out of wood, and even a Volkswagen Beetle decorated with garden gnomes. As I said, it's an unusual place that really pushes the envelope of what a car can look like. Admission to the Art Car Museum is free. Since 1988, Houston has hosted a yearly art car parade that has grown to wacky 250 vehicles, with over 250,000 spectators lining the parade route. Each spring, it's the highlight of the three-day Houston Art Car Parade Weekend. www.ArtCarMuseum.com.

8

West Coast & Alaska

It's hard to think of California without dreaming about cars, and the Golden State does not disappoint with over a dozen automotive attractions. Start out at the revamped **Petersen Automotive Museum** for a look at California car culture. Oregon reveals its rugged roots at the **Pacific Northwest Truck Museum** and **Northwest Vintage Car & Motorcycle Museum.** Tacoma, Washington boasts a high number of classic cars per capita with both the **LeMay-America's Car Museum** and the **LeMay Family Collection.** Each is a legacy of one man's obsession with collecting automobiles. In Alaska, you can venture to the Arctic Circle while visiting the **Fountainhead Antique Auto Museum.**

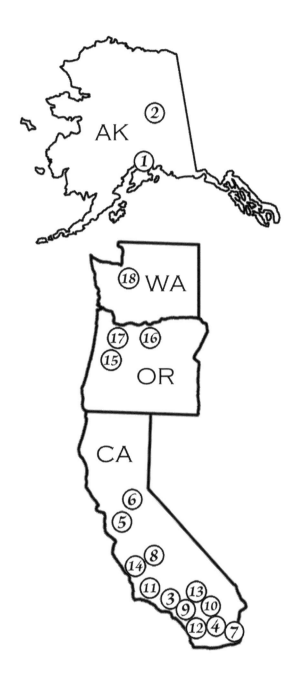

West Coast & Alaska

ALASKA

   1) Alaska State Trooper Museum

   2) Fountainhead Antique Auto Museum

CALIFORNIA

   3) Automobile Driving Museum
      Metropolitan Pit Stop
      Nethercutt Museum and Collection
      Petersen Automotive Museum

   4) Automotive Research Library

   5) Blackhawk Automotive Museum

   6) California Automobile Museum

   7) Cloud Museum

   8) James Dean crash site

   9) Marconi Automotive Museum

   10) Motte Historical Museum

   11) Mullin Automotive Museum
       Murphy Auto Museum

12) San Diego Automotive Museum

13) Wally Parks NHRA Motorsports Museum

14) Woodlands Auto Display

OREGON

15) Northwest Vintage Car & Motorcycle Museum
Pacific Northwest Truck Museum

16) Western Antique Aeroplane & Automobile Museum

17) World of Speed

WASHINGTON

18) Griot's Garage
LeMay – America's Car Museum
LeMay Family Collection

CALIFORNIA

AUTOMOBILE DRIVING MUSEUM
El Segundo, CA

Taking visitors out for a Sunday drive.

Located only five minutes from Los Angeles International Airport, the **Automobile Driving Museum** boasts that it is the car museum "where you'll get taken for a ride." Every Sunday they roll four or five cars off of the museum floor and take visitors for a spin around the block. On any given Sunday you can ride in a **1947 Studebaker**, a **1909 Model T**, a **1975 AMC Pacer** (yes, the oft-maligned Pacer is now considered a classic), or almost any car in the vast collection. Check the website, which posts the schedule of cars to be taken for Sunday drives.

All the cars have detailed informational placards describing their history, including the original factory price. One of the favorites of museum co-founder Stanley Zimmerman is a **1951 Nash,** whose seats turned into a bed. He recalls, "Of course, dads wouldn't let you go out on dates with their daughters when you pulled up in that car."

Number of vehicles: 130+

Highlights: Riding in the cars on Sundays; 1886 Benz Motorwagen; 1916 Twin Six convertible Packard, considered the world's first production V-12; 1955 Packard Caribbean Convertible given by Howard Hughes to his second wife, actress Jean Peters.

Location: 610 Lairport Street, El Segundo, CA 90245. Just off Route 1, two blocks south of Los Angeles International Airport.

Admission: Free, but donations are accepted.

Hours: Tuesday through Sunday, 10 a.m. to 4 p.m. Automobile rides are offered on Sunday only, with the last ride at 3:30 p.m.

Phone: (310) 909-0950

Web: www.AutomobileDrivingMuseum.org

Cars in Film

When visiting the Los Angeles area, you may stumble upon a movie or TV shoot. When they are filming a period piece, there are usually some vintage cars on display to set the tone. If you ever watch a movie and are curious which cars are in it, head to the Internet Movie Cars Database at www.IMCDB.org. The listings are incredibly detailed, to the point that 45 different cars are identified from *The Godfather* alone.

Automotive Research Library
La Mesa, CA

Sponsored by the Horseless Carriage Foundation, this is an incredible reference library of automotive magazines and materials, more than 300,000 of which have been scanned and are available online. You can get lost for hours reading back issues, ranging from the 1895 *Horseless Age* to 1960s copies of *Motor Age* and much more. Learn how to service your 1960 Valiant or read an ad in a 1935 issue of *The Motor World* for the "new" Ford V8. A nominal membership fee is required for full access, but you can conduct research in person for free. Many old manuals and reference materials are also available for sale. NAAM member.

Number of vehicles: None, this is a research library.

Highlights: Old issues of automotive magazines and literature dating as far back as the 1890s.

Location: 8186 Center Street, Suite F, La Mesa, CA 91942. About 15 miles northeast of downtown San Diego.

Admission: Free

Hours: Tuesday through Friday, 10 a.m. to 4 p.m.; Saturday by appointment only.

Phone: (619) 464-0301

Web: www.hcfi.org

BLACKHAWK AUTOMOTIVE MUSEUM
Danville, CA

The autos are so artfully displayed here that it's hard to tell if it's a car museum or an art gallery. This makes sense in a place that considers its cars to be rolling sculptures. To give you an idea of the quality of the collection, many arrive after being exhibited at the Pebble Beach *Concours d'Elegance*. Displays have included a **1911 Mercedes Labourdette Skiff**, a **1937 Figoni et Falaschi Delahaye 135,** and a **1968 Bizzarrini 5300 S.I. Spyder**. There's also a large collection of gas pumps and a gallery of classic jukeboxes from the early 1910s through the 1950s. A popular monthly event is "Coffee & Cars," a Sunday morning gathering for car aficionados.

A permanent display, "The Spirit of the Old West," tells the story of the western frontier from before, during, and after the expansion westward. Included are artifacts from the period, a large diorama depicting key historic moments, and other elements from frontier days. NAAM member.

Number of vehicles: 50+ (Many of them are on loan, so exhibits change periodically.)

Location: 3700 Blackhawk Plaza Circle, Danville, CA 94506

Admission: $$

Hours: Wednesday through Sunday 10 a.m. to 5 p.m.

Phone: (925) 736-2280

Web: www.BlackhawkMuseum.org

CALIFORNIA AUTOMOBILE MUSEUM
Sacramento, CA

Relics of the early years of motoring.

Drawing from its own collection and loans, this museum has more than 150 cars on display, from 1885 to recent models. Given that the museum's members are referred to as "Gearheads," it's not surprising that the exhibit starts by teaching the mechanics of automobiles. Car engines and chassis are exposed with their parts color-coded to show how they work.

The winding path through the museum allows views of both the front and back of most vehicles. Tableaus and murals are arranged chronologically to make visitors feel as if they're back in the early age of motoring. Some cars are marked "Photo Opportunity," so you can sit behind the wheel and snap a pic.

Among the more unusual cars is a French **1924 Delage DI,** with a curved wooden tail that wouldn't look out of place on a vintage Chris-Craft boat. One of my favorites is a **1936 Hudson Essex Terraplane Six**. Besides the cool name ("terraplane" is meant to evoke speed on land), it boasts a rare Griffin hood ornament that was only available for that model year. Another piece of automotive history is the **1941 Lincoln Town Car** once owned by Henry Ford's wife, Clara.

When Jerry Brown was governor in the 1970s, he famously tried to cut costs by selecting his official state vehicle, a **1974 Plymouth,** from the motor pool. It sits next to his one-time girlfriend Linda Ronstadt's black **1982 Porsche 911SC**, demonstrating their vastly different tastes in automobiles.

An unusual feature of the California Auto Museum is that some of the cars are for sale. They're taken on consignment and displayed off to the side. On any given visit, you might find a **1926 Ford Model T Touring** ($14,500), a **1965 Mustang** ($18,500) or, for those with deep pockets, a **1958 Porsche 356** ($139,000). After you get all fired up viewing vintage autos, it's tempting to make an offer.

In a cool twist, the museum also offers classes on driving and working on a Model A Ford. Hundreds of vintage issues of car magazines are for sale in the gift shop at reasonable prices. NAAM member.

Number of vehicles: 150+ (displays are rotated frequently)

Highlights: 1910 Peerless Model 27 Touring; 1936 Graham Supercharger Trunk Sedan; 1940 Lincoln Zephyr; 1949 DeSoto Carry-All Sedan (the rear seat folded down to expand the space in the trunk).

Location: 2200 Front Street, Sacramento, CA 95818. It's tucked away in an old warehouse near the tourist area of Old Sacramento.

Admission: $ **Hours:** Daily, 10 a.m. to 5 p.m. On the third Thursday of each month, they're open until 9 p.m.

Phone: (916) 442-6802   **Web:** www.CalAutoMuseum.org

CLOUD MUSEUM
Bard, CA

If you're into barn finds and old Fords, this is the place. More than 100 **Ford Model T** and **Model A** autos are lined up like soldiers inside crusty old buildings and outside in the arid climate. It's the creation of collector Johnny Cloud, who is often available to regale visitors with stories about his collection. The whole place is a giant photo opportunity, making it popular with photographers. It's the exact opposite of seeing cars restored to gleaming showroom condition. For a taste of what's in store, Google the address and take a gander at the satellite photo of all the cars out on the edge of the desert. It's pretty wild.

There's also an extensive collection of old mining and farming equipment, including Fordson tractors (Fordson was a division of Ford Motor Company). Those not into cars can examine exhibits on early American life, including rooms furnished with old kitchen items and antique furniture.

Number of vehicles: 75+

Highlights: One of the largest collections of Model Ts in the world; 1914 Model T Roadster; 1922 Chevrolet Model T Truck (yes, Chevy also made a Model T).

Location: 1398 York Road, Bard, CA 92283. About 12 miles north of downtown Yuma, in the far southwest corner of Arizona.

Admission: $ **Hours:** Daily, 8 a.m. to 4 p.m. It's best to call ahead since hours are variable, particularly during the hot summer months.

Phone: (928) 919-5508

Web: CloudMuseum.DynamiteDave.com

Photo courtesy Marconi Automotive Museum

This museum started with the contribution of namesake Dick Marconi's automotive collection. It is also a charity for at-risk youth, so funds earned from admission, special events, and donations are distributed to benefit local children.

One look at the museum's red logo with its emblazoned horse's head tells you that its specialty is Ferraris. But that's not all: You'll also see Formula One race cars and not one, but two, **1989 Lamborghini Countachs** sitting side-by-side. A rare **1991 Cizeta-Moroder V16T** was spawned by electronic musician Giorgio Moroder's short-lived foray into high-end car production. Among all the fire-engine-red Ferraris, it's easy to miss an actual fire engine lurking in a corner, a **1937 Ahrens-Fox**. American muscle is included with a trio of **1965, 1967, and 1969 Shelby Cobras** plus a **1971 Dodge Challenger**. Motorcycle fans can choose from a variety of models: Ducati, Honda, Harley-Davidson, Buell, and BMW.

The walls are plastered with auto memorabilia, plus an actual dragster and several racing cars, including a **1968 Lotus 15B** and a **1988 McLaren F1**. Now that's some fancy wall art!

Number of vehicles: 100

Highlights: 1950 Ferrari 195S; 1991 Ferrari F40; 1995 Ferrari F50; 1996 Ferrari FX; 1996 Jaguar XJ220-S

Location: 1302 Industrial Drive, Tustin, CA 92780. In the Los Angeles area, just southeast of Anaheim.

Admission: $

Hours: Monday through Friday, 9 a.m. to 4:30 p.m.

Phone: (714) 258-3001   **Web:** www.MarconiMuseum.org

MOTTE HISTORICAL MUSEUM
Menifee, CA

The Motte family has a long agricultural history, farming in the Perris Valley since the 1880s. They set up this museum to highlight their car collection, along with the pioneering spirit of the families who settled here. John Motte started his acquisitions in 1951 with a **1926 Chevrolet Touring Sedan** that he purchased for $15. Another special vehicle is the **1936 Plymouth Deluxe Business Coupe,** in which Leon Motte dated the future Mrs. Motte. The latest-model car in the collection is a **1969 Lincoln Continental Mark III,** which the Mottes purchased new from the dealer. Also here are a few motorcycles, such as a **1910 Harley** and a **1928 Indian Scout**. The museum is housed in a 9,000-square-foot barn built in 1985 with salvaged materials, giving it a vintage look appropriate for the vehicles stored inside. NAAM member.

Number of vehicles: 20+

Highlights: 1928 Packard 4-43 Club Sedan; 1931 Cadillac Cabriolet; 1937 Packard V-12 Club Sedan that the patient Mottes spent the better part of 37 years restoring.

Location: 28380 Highway 74, Menifee, CA 92585. It's 65 miles southeast of downtown Los Angeles.

Admission: Free

Hours: Wednesday through Saturday, 10 a.m. to 4 p.m.; first and third Sunday of each month, 10 a.m. to 4 p.m.

Phone: (951) 928-3210   **Web:** www.MotteMuseum.com

Mullin Automotive Museum
Oxnard, CA

This is the private collection of business tycoon Peter Mullin, who has a passion for French Art Deco-era automobiles, particularly Bugattis. An auto you definitely won't see anywhere else is the **1925 Bugatti Type 22 Brescia** (known as "The Lady in the Lake") that was recovered after lying on the bottom of Italy's Lake Maggiore for 75 years.

There are also automotive artifacts including original tools, doors, furniture, and fixtures from the original Bugatti factory. The **Mullin Automotive Museum** also has sculpture from the Art Deco era, along with a collection of rare turn-of-the century furniture, silverware, and a banjo crafted by Carlo Bugatti.

Number of vehicles: 65

Highlights: The "Lady in the Lake" 1925 Bugatti Type 22 Brescia; the 1939 Bugatti Type 64 (Jean Bugatti's *tour de force* was only a chassis when Bugatti was killed that year in a road test of another vehicle. The museum has built it to Bugatti's original vision.)

Location: 1421 Emerson Avenue, Oxnard, CA 93033

Admission: $$ **Hours:** 10 a.m. to 3 p.m. on scheduled Open Days, usually twice a month. On Open Days, docent-led tours are generally held at 10:30 a.m., noon, and 1:30 p.m. Private visits are available when the museum is closed. See the website for details.

Phone: (805) 385-5400

Web: www.MullinAutomotiveMuseum.com

MURPHY AUTO MUSEUM
Oxnard, CA

Ranging from a **1910 Durocar** to a **2008 Mustang Shelby GT500KR**, the Murphy Auto Museum offers a century's worth of mostly American vehicles. The Durocar, a rare piece of early California automotive history, was built in Los Angeles and has never been driven out of the state. The museum presents a mix of cars seen elsewhere, such as a **1926 Ford Model T Roadster,** along with vehicles not often found in museums.

Some of the more unusual cars include a **1935 Brewster Buick**, customized by the Brewster Coach Company on a Buick chassis; a **1960 Imperial Le Baron** (Imperial was a separate division of Chrysler at the time); and a **1963 Studebaker Wagonaire Daytona**, which looks ready for a family road trip. Check out the award-winning **1956 Lincoln Capri Hardtop Coupe,** with its contemporary eyebrow headlights. Pickup trucks are often overlooked at car museums, which makes the **1955 Studebaker E Pickup** stand out even more.

The museum's clothing collection is displayed on mannequins dressed in appropriate period garb and posed by the autos. If you're into trains, you'll enjoy one of the largest HO Scale model railroad layouts in the country. NAAM member.

Number of vehicles: 60

Highlights: 1930 Willys Knight 70B sedan; 1956 Packard Caribbean hardtop (only around 250 were produced); 1959 Cadillac Series 62 (the peak year for tail fins); 1964 ½ Ford Mustang.

Location: 2230 Statham Boulevard, Oxnard, CA 93033. Along the California coast, about 60 miles northwest of Los Angeles.

Admission: $

Hours: Year-round: Saturday, 9 a.m. to 4 p.m.; Sunday, 10 a.m. to 4 p.m. Additional hours April through December: Wednesday, 6 p.m. to 10 p.m.; Friday, 10 a.m. to 4 p.m.

Phone: (805) 487-4333

Web: www.MurphyAutoMuseum.org

NETHERCUTT MUSEUM AND COLLECTION
Sylmar, CA

There are really two attractions here, the **Nethercutt Collection** and the **Nethercutt Museum**. For the Collection, you'll need to take a guided tour, available at limited set times three days a week. The Museum, which houses the overflow of cars, is open six days a week for self-guided tours; it's your best option if you have limited time or the Collection tours are all full.

The Nethercutt Museum and Collection grew out of the Merle Norman Cosmetics fortune. It features more than 250 American vehicles ranging in vintage from 1898 to 1997, plus rare mechanical musical instruments and antique furniture. There are so many highlights that it's hard to list just a handful.

The Collection sprawls over four floors of a lavish building that evokes an opulent 1920s automotive showroom. The tour starts in the Lower Salon, which houses 25 automobiles from the early 1900s to the early post-World War II era. Next up is the Grand Salon, with its gleaming black marble floors and soaring columns. Here you'll find an additional 30 autos from the 1910s through the 1930s. Lined up side by side are high-end models from Duesenberg, Cadillac, Isotta Fraschini, Delahaye, Minerva, and more. The remainder of the building is occupied by a collection of radiator hood ornaments and antique French furniture.

The Museum, across the street from the Collection, houses cars from the Brass Era through the 1970s. The rarities include a French-built **1909 Gobron-Brillié 70/90/Tourer** with two opposing pistons per cylinder, a complicated idea that didn't catch on; a **1923 Voisin Model C-5 Sporting Victoria**, formerly owned by 1920s screen star Rudolph Valentino; and perhaps the slickest car, a bright red **1967 Ferrari 365 California Spyder**, one of only 14 built.

In addition, railroad buffs will enjoy walking through a 1937 Canadian Pacific Royal Hudson Locomotive and a 1912 Pullman Private Car that are open Tuesday through Saturday.

Number of vehicles: 200+

Highlights: 1923 Hispano-Suiza H6B Cabriolet DeVille; 1937 Talbot-Lago Type 150-C SS/Sport Coupe; 1956 Mercedes Benz 300SL Gullwing Coupe.

Location: 15200 Bledsoe Street, Sylmar, CA 91342. Just north of Los Angeles.

Admission: Free   **Hours: Nethercutt Museum:** Tuesday through Sunday, 9 a.m. to 4:30 p.m. This is the self-guided portion, so no reservation is necessary. **Nethercutt Collection:** Free two-hour guided tours are offered Thursday, Friday and Saturday. Children under 10 are not permitted. Tours are by advance reservations only, so call well ahead for tickets and to confirm times.

Phone: (818) 364-6464   **Web:** www.NethercuttCollection.org

PETERSEN AUTOMOTIVE MUSEUM
Los Angeles, CA

Founded by Robert Petersen of Petersen Publishing, which included *Hot Rod* and *Motor Trend* among its magazine titles, this museum has quite the automotive pedigree. However, there are really two parts to the **Petersen Museum**: the posh museum upstairs that sprawls over three floors, with the shimmery cars displayed as if they were 10-carat diamonds in a jewelry store, and the famous vault of rare cars in the basement. The above-ground floors are dedicated to three themes: History, Industry, and Artistry. There are always a few temporary exhibits focusing on unique bits of car culture, so check ahead to see what will be there. In 2015, the Petersen underwent a multi-million-dollar renovation to reconfigure the interior and add a funky, spaceship-like stainless steel skin to the exterior.

It wouldn't be a Los Angeles car museum if it didn't have cars that appeared on TV or in the movies. So the Hollywood Gallery includes the Batmobile, Walter White's **2004 Pontiac Aztek** from *Breaking Bad*, and many more, including vehicles from several James Bond films. The Disney/Pixar *Cars* Mechanical Institute educates children on how cars work and gets their attention with a life-sized Lightning McQueen. The Hot Rod Gallery focuses on cars that were featured in *Hot Rod* magazine, including CadZZilla, formerly owned by ZZ Top's Billy Gibbons.

Hardcore car buffs shouldn't miss a tour of the Vault, which, as the guide pointed out, is a fancy name for a basement. The block-long subterranean parking garage holds the overflow, and some of the crown jewels, of the Petersen collection. With its concrete floor, it's not lavish, but the variety and quality of vehicles on display are impressive. The Vault tour costs extra.

Cars are periodically rotated from the underground vault to the main display areas upstairs, so the same cars won't always be exhibited. Perhaps you'll see the 1962 seafoam-green Thunderbird from *Thelma & Louise* parked next to a rather nondescript green 1951 Hudson: It's the car that Steve McQueen drove to the store when he didn't want to be recognized.

The red Ferrari from *Magnum, P.I.* is here too. At 6-foot-4, Tom Selleck had a tough time squeezing into it, so the top was kept off, even if it had just rained. The actor visited the Vault a few years ago. When he saw his old nemesis sitting there, he laughed and declared, "It was the most uncomfortable car." Elvis Presley's infamous lime-green Pantera sits nearby. One day the mercurial Presley couldn't start, it so he plugged it with three rounds from his .38 pistol. Look closely for the bullet holes. NAAM member.

Number of vehicles: 150+ on display with another 150+ in storage.

Highlights: Michael Keaton's Batmobile; 1948 Tucker #30; too many others to list; Vault tour.

Location: 6060 Wilshire Boulevard, Los Angeles, CA 90036. Across from the Los Angeles County Museum of Art, on the west end of the "Miracle Mile."

Admission: $$ (Vault tour extra.)

Hours: Daily, 10 a.m. to 6 p.m.

Phone: (323) 930-2277

Web: www.Petersen.org

Side Trip: Take a Pit Stop

Just nine miles north of the Petersen, you'll find a quirky business and museum devoted to a quirky car. Operating since 1975, the **Metropolitan Pit Stop** bills itself as "the leading authority on Metropolitan parts and restoration." The building is easy to find; just look for the one with a Metropolitan car "smashed" into its façade. Inside is a small museum that features several cars, including a **1961 Metropolitan** and an early production **1953 NKI Custom.** Each is 100% original. The most bizarre-looking vehicle is a **1955 Astra-Gnome,** which was exhibited at a 1956 car show in New York. It was supposed to represent how cars would look in the far-distant future of the year 2000. However, its advanced space-age styling has not yet taken root here on planet Earth. Metropolitan Pit Stop. 5324 Laurel Canyon Boulevard, Valley Village, CA 91607. www. MetPitStop.com

---

SAN DIEGO AUTOMOTIVE MUSEUM
San Diego, CA

If this car could talk... Louis Mattar's indestructible 1947 Cadillac.

This museum is located in vast Balboa Park along with more than 20 other museums and attractions, including the world-famous San Diego Zoo. The permanent collection is not huge, but there are also temporary exhibits throughout the year. Recent offerings included a tribute to "Lead Sleds," which are modified cars of the pre-Bondo era, and the "British Invasion."

One of the quirkiest cars you'll find anywhere is Louis Mattar's "Fabulous $75,000 Car." It's a heavily tricked-out **1947 Cadillac** in which Mattar set a *nonstop* endurance driving record of 6,320 miles in 1952. Mattar and two associates drove round-trip across the United States, filling up from moving fuel trucks along the way. The car was equipped with a then-revolutionary mobile telephone, along with a shower, a drinking fountain and, of course, a toilet.

The axles were drilled to inflate the tires while turning, and the car changed its oil on-the-run automatically. It's truly bizarre. Watch the video to see how the men ingeniously changed a tire while the car was still moving.

One celebrity car here is Frank Sinatra's **1967 Austin Petrol Hire Car.** It's the same style as the ubiquitous black taxis that navigate London streets. I'm not sure why New Jersey's Ol' Blue Eyes was squired around in this, but he owned it for four years. The motorcycle collection includes dozens of bikes, including one owned by actor Steve McQueen and several early Indian models. NAAM member.

Number of vehicles: 80+

Highlights: 1909 International Harvester "Model A Auto-Wagon" (the farm equipment maker briefly produced autos); 1931 Lagonda Low Chassis 2L (British sporting car); 1951 Kaiser Deluxe; 1953 Jaguar XK 120 (restored by volunteers at the museum).

Location: 2080 Pan American Plaza, San Diego, CA 92101. Between the Air & Space Museum and the Hall of Champions in Balboa Park. (***Note:*** For fans of the *Rocky* movies, a full-size copy of the Rocky Balboa statue is in the Hall of Champions, just steps away from the museum. Sculptor A. Thomas Schomberg, who created the Rocky statue that is a popular tourist attraction next to the "Rocky Steps" outside the Philadelphia Museum of Art, originally made three of them.)

Admission: $

Hours: Daily, 10 a.m. to 5 p.m.

Phone: (619) 231-2886

Web: SDAutoMuseum.org

Note: Just three miles north of the San Diego Automotive Museum, look for the **J.A. Cooley Museum**, a little gem owned by its octogenarian namesake. Along with antique toys, Victrolas, trains, and clocks, it houses a collection of 20 cars, including an 1895 Benz Velo and a 1933 Franklin Olympic. Call before your visit. 4233 Park Boulevard, San Diego, CA (619-296-3112)

WALLY PARKS NHRA MOTORSPORTS MUSEUM
Pomona, CA

Wally Parks founded the National Hot Rod Association (NHRA) and helped popularize drag racing. He also helped start this museum. The 28,500-square-foot, Art Deco building hosts an impressive array of drag racing cars and memorabilia. The floor is chock-full of vehicles, while the walls are lined with vintage racing helmets, jackets, championship trophies, race photos, and more.

From April through December, stop by on the first Wednesday of the month for Twilight Cruise Night, when local car aficionados show up in a wide array of hot rods and muscle cars. (This event may be suspended in September because of the Los Angeles County Fair.) NAAM member.

Number of vehicles: 75+

Highlights: Ed Iskenderian's 1925 Model T Roadster; Mickey Thompson's Challenger (first American car to hit 400 mph).

Location: 1101 W. McKinley Avenue, Building 3A, Pomona CA, 91768. On the Fairplex grounds, 35 miles east of downtown Los Angeles.

Admission: $$

Hours: Wednesday through Sunday, 10 a.m. to 5 p.m. Extended hours during the NHRA Winternationals and NHRA Finals. Hours change during the annual Los Angeles County Fair.

Phone: (909) 622-2133

Web: www.museum.nhra.com

WOODLAND AUTO DISPLAY AT ESTRELLA WARBIRDS MUSEUM
Paso Robles, CA

Checking under the hood is encouraged.

This ever-expanding collection featuring midget, racing, exotics, muscle cars, and classics is on the grounds of the **Estrella Warbirds Museum**, so auto and aviation fans get a two-for-one experience here.

A **1932 Ford**, converted into a jalopy in 1960, highlights local racing history and a time when it was easy for DIY builders to convert an old barn find. A bright red **1937 Vukovich Midget "Old Ironsides"** was raced by the legendary Bill Vukovich, Sr. He was behind the wheel when he won the American Automobile Association National Midget Championship in 1950. He went on to win the Indy 500 in 1953 and 1954, before being killed in a crash during the 1955 race.

The road-racing success of the limited-production **1951 Allard K2 Roadster** (here in British Racing Green) was an inspiration for Carroll Shelby's Cobra. A championship **1962 Sprint Car** was built by Don Brown, a member of the **National Sprint Car Hall of Fame** (see separate listing). The **1993 Western Auto Chevy Lumina** was built for Darrell Waltrip, one of America's top racers. On the slower side, peek inside the **1929 REO Speed Wagon Camper**. With its sofa bed, kitchen, and stove, it's a forerunner of today's motor homes.

Glass-front cabinets here are stocked with toy cars, and the walls of the museum are lined with vintage racing photos and automotive memorabilia. One wall is covered with a vintage mural of a former local landmark, Wilson's Drive-In. There is also an assortment of military vehicles on the Estrella Warbirds side of the museum, including a **1912 Ford Model T** restored as a World War I ambulance and a **1943 Ford GTB "Burma Jeep"** that saw action in the Pacific Theater.

Number of vehicles: 50+

Highlights: 1929 Marmon 3-Window Coupe; 1966 Edmunds Super Modified (chassis #1, seen on the cover of *Hot Rod*); 1978 Grant King Sprint Car.

Location: 4251 Dry Creek Road, Paso Robles, CA 93446

Admission: $$

Hours: Thursday through Sunday: 10 a.m. to 4 p.m.; open Monday only on major Federal holidays, 10 a.m. to 4 p.m.

Phone: (805) 227-0440

Web: EWarbirds.org

Side Trip: James Dean's Crash Site

On September 30, 1955, popular actor and aspiring race car driver **James Dean** was motoring along State Road 466 (now 46) in his 1955 Porsche Spyder 550, with mechanic Rolf Weutherich at his side. They were heading to Salinas for a series of weekend races. As they approached the intersection of Route 41, a driver made a left turn in front of them. Dean was unable to stop, and the resulting fiery crash killed him; Weutherich and the other driver survived.

A green-and-white road sign stating "James Dean Memorial Junction" marks the spot. Even with the passage of time, the parched California countryside looks little changed from 1955. About a mile west of the intersection is a metal sculpture tribute to Dean, outside the roadside Jack Ranch Café.

Afterward, drive about 30 miles east on Route 46 to Blackwell's Corner General Store at the intersection of Routes 46 and 33. You can't miss the giant James Dean poster outside, marking the shop where Dean made his last stop before continuing his fateful drive. The crash site is about 40 miles east of Paso Robles in central California.

OREGON

NORTHWEST VINTAGE CAR & MOTORCYCLE MUSEUM
Brooks, OR

Sitting behind an old-fashioned Texaco filling station, this museum places the emphasis on vintage cars, trucks, and motorcycles. Rather than a large permanent collection, it has a rotating selection of vehicles loaned by museum members. Some permanent items that have been donated include a **1909 Cadillac,** a **1919 Willys Overland,** and several **1920s Model T Speedsters.**

One of the museum's interesting education missions is its Speedster program. The museum works with high school students to build and restore Ford Model T speedsters and other vintage vehicles. It also has period memorabilia and auto models, operating cross-sectioned motors, tools, vintage auto ephemera, and a Model T replica assembly line. In addition, the museum hosts several car and motorcycle shows every year; check the website to find out when. NAAM member.

Number of vehicles: 15 cars and 15 motorcycles, plus a few scooters.

Highlights: 1928 Whippet; 1949 and 1951 Hudsons.

Location: 3995 Brooklake Road NE, Brooks, OR 97305. *Note:* Located within the Antique Powerland Complex, which includes more than a dozen museums, including the **Pacific Northwest Truck Museum** (see following listing).

Admission: $ to get into the Antique Powerland Complex, then the museum is free.   **Hours:** Weekends from early June through late September: Saturday, 9:30 a.m. to 4 p.m., and Sunday, 12:30 p.m. to 4 p.m.

Phone: (503) 245-5444   **Web:** NWCarAndCycle.com

Buddy, can you spare a wrench?

The Pacific Northwest Truck Museum is a real find for truck enthusiasts. It highlights trucks that were either built or used in this rugged and forested region of the nation. Vehicles range from local delivery vans to long-haul rigs. It's pretty cool to walk inside a building and see so many 18-wheelers on display. The museum was founded in 1989 by trucking executives and drivers to honor their legacy, with support from Kenneth Self, the late CEO of Freightliner and a rabid truck enthusiast.

An **1899 Grain Wagon** pulled by two horses harkens back to the term "teamster" for a truck driver; it originally meant someone driving a team of horses. A **1942 Diamond T Model 201 Panel Truck** is rare for an unusual reason: Only five were built before the factory's manufacturing lines were requisitioned for wartime production. A crowd-pleaser is the colossal **1959 Oshkosh Snowplow,** which was used at Fairchild Air Force Base in Spokane to clear the runway for B-52 bombers during the Cold War. A **1985 T-600A Prototype by Kenworth** was the first truck to sport an aerodynamic front nose, called an "anteater."

A unique collection of license plates from the 1930s and '40s reveals a seamier side of life. Because of an increase in cattle rustling, beef dealers were issued their own plates that said "Oregon Meat Dealers License." Anyone caught transporting beef without these plates was assumed to have procured the meat by nefarious means. Worth the trip for gearheads is a wall covered with the world's largest collection of monkey wrenches in the world: 1,006 of them lined up (see the sidebar "Monkey Business," below, for more information). Check the museum's website for info on its annual summer truck show in late August.

Note: To see more of the trucks from the collection, head to the **Jubitz Travel Center and Truck Stop**, where a few are always on display. It's located off exit 307 of I-5 at 10210 North Vancouver Way, Portland, OR 97217.

Number of vehicles: 100+

Highlights: 1918 GMC Truck (one of 450 built to be used in World War I); 1920 Doane chain-drive truck; 1938 Ford (its first cab-over-engine truck); 1962 Freightliner Fireliner fire truck, one of only six built at the Portland, Oregon factory.

Location: 3995 Brooklake Road NE, Brooks, OR 97305. Located within the **Antique Powerland Complex**, which includes the **Northwest Vintage Car & Motorcycle Museum** (see prior listing).

Admission: $ for the Antique Powerland Complex, then the museum is free.

Hours: Hours are limited, so plan accordingly. Early April through late September: Saturday and Sunday, 10 a.m. to 4:30 p.m.

Phone: (503) 463-8701

Web: www.PacificNWTruckMuseum.org

Monkey Business

One of the highlights of the Pacific Northwest Truck Museum is the world's largest collection of one-of-a-kind monkey wrenches. Displayed on a wall are 1,006 of the tools (no, I didn't count them), with no two the same. They were collected and donated by Oregonians Phil Holsheimer, Jr. and his wife, Georgie. But why were so many unique wrenches floating around out there? Back in the day, machine shops hand-forged their own tools rather than buying them, with each craftsman adding his own touch to the finished product.

WESTERN ANTIQUE AEROPLANE & AUTOMOBILE MUSEUM (WAAAM)
Hood River, OR

Located in 2.5 acres of hangar space in the shadow of Mount Hood, the varied collection of WAAAM appeals to automobile, motorcycle, and aviation enthusiasts alike. Its claim to fame is being a "living museum," so most of its antique cars can be driven and its planes still flown.

Automobiles: Vehicles range from a **1909 Franklin Model D** to a pocket-sized **1972 Honda N600 2-door Sedan** (zero to 60 in only 19 seconds!), with an emphasis on the 1920s, '30s and '40s.

A crowd favorite is the **1941 Lincoln Zephyr**; with its forward-leaning curves, it looks as if it could star in *Who Framed Roger Rabbit?* On select summer days, WAAAM offers a Model T driving school where you actually drive a legendary Tin Lizzie. How cool is that?

Aeroplanes: Airplane aficionados will find, among other treats, a 1917 Curtiss JN4D Jenny, used as a trainer during World War I and later as a barnstormer; and a striking yellow 1937 Aeronca LC. The 75 aircraft are taken out for flights as often as possible, hence the museum's location next to an airfield.

Military: From a World War II-era Willys MB Jeep through a 1974 AM General M151 MUTT.

Motorcycles: The collection has almost 30 motorcycles. They are included with the other vehicles, so they often get overlooked. A fun game for kids is to try and find them in a sort of motorcycle scavenger hunt. Some fan faves are a fleet-looking 1927 Harley-Davidson JD and a nearly toy-sized 1954 Cushman Eagle that would look right at home on the streets of Rome.

Number of vehicles: 130+ (plus 75 aircraft)

Highlights: 1914 Detroit Electric; 1923 Locomobile Model 48 Sportif; 1929 Franklin.

Location: 1600 Air Museum Road, Hood River, OR 97031. Located 65 miles east of downtown Portland between exits 62 and 63 off I-84, adjacent to the Hood River Airport.

Admission: $$

Hours: Daily, 9 a.m. to 5 p.m.

Phone: (541) 308-1600

Web: www.WAAAMuseum.org

WORLD OF SPEED
Wilsonville, OR

Newly opened in 2015, the World of Speed highlights many facets of motorsports, including NASCAR, Indy car, drag racing, land speed racing, sports cars, motorcycles, and their drivers, with a particular focus on the Pacific Northwest.

Special exhibits include:

Daytona Banking: Display features a track angled at 31 degrees, just like the original tri-oval track at Daytona. Cars "racing" on it include Dale Earnhardt Jr.'s **2000 Chevrolet Impala** and Cale Yarborough's **1979 Oldsmobile 442**.

Zero to 1000 MPH: Highlights the history of setting the land speed record by both autos and motorcycles and includes Mickey Thompson's original Assault 1.

Wall of Sound: Explores the connection between fast cars and the emergence of rock-and-roll music, with exhibits of record albums and guitars celebrating America's fascination with driving.

Three driving simulators allow visitors to get behind the wheel: a 1962 Lotus Formula, a 1995 Lola Indy Car, and a 1998 NASCAR Ford Taurus. There are also many racing artifacts, including race suits, helmets, historic racing programs, car magazines and more, as well as exhibits related to motorcycle racing.

One of the primary missions of the museum is to introduce young people to the world of motorsports and career opportunities in this field. Accordingly, a car-themed summer camp is offered for children in grades 3 through 12. NAAM member.

Number of vehicles: 90+

Highlights: 1963 Plymouth Belvedere Stage II Max Wedge; 1958 Don "Duck" Collins Champ car; 1979 Gaines Markley Winston NHRA Top Fuel World Championship car driven by Rob Bruins.

Location: 27490 SW 95th Avenue, Wilsonville, OR 97070

Admission: $$

Hours: Tuesday through Sunday, 10 a.m. to 5 p.m.

Phone: (503) 563-6437   **Web:** WorldOfSpeed.org

WASHINGTON

LeMay-America's Car Museum
Tacoma, WA

When chrome was king—a 1958 Pontiac Bonneville.

Tacoma has not just one, but two, huge auto museums that have the name LeMay in them. Although both are based on cars from the collection of the LeMay family, they are operated separately and offer different visitor experiences.

As the **LeMay Family Collection** (see following listing), also in Tacoma, outgrew its location, the **LeMay-America's Car Museum** (ACM) was created with a sizable gift of cars from the LeMay family. It's a bit confusing, but the museums are separate entities at different locations, with different people running them.

The LeMay–ACM, with its slinky silver roof, was purposely built to be an auto museum when it opened in 2012. Its mission is "to celebrate America's love affair with the automobile." The building is set up like a parking garage, with multiple floors connected by ramps. Each ramp is set aside for a different thematic display, including ones about custom coachworks, NASCAR, alternative fuel cars, and Route 66.

In the coachworks section are a variety of coach-built cars, including a luxury **1917 Crane Simplex** purchased by John D. Rockefeller for $26,000 as a birthday gift for his father. On the alternative fuels ramp, you'll see a **1912 Standard "Electrique,"** a **1919 Stanley Steamer,** and a **1981 Commuta-Car**, which looks like a silver door wedge (it's about the same size, too). You can also take a photo for free in a **1923 Buick**. The **1963 Avanti #1001** "Rescue Project" is the ongoing complete restoration of the first production Avanti sold in North America. The car is on display periodically, as a work in progress.

Take kids to the Family Zone, where they can race toy cars down wooden ramps or view the skeleton of a color-coded vehicle. They may also want to see the customized "Flintmobile" driven by actor John Goodman in *The Flintstones*. The gift shop appeals to both adults and kids and is packed with car-related toys, books, clothing, memorabilia, and car-care products. Check the schedule for monthly cruise-ins from April through October. NAAM member.

Number of vehicles: 300+

Highlights: 1913 Oakland 35; 1926 Rolls-Royce Silver Ghost, built in Springfield, MA; one of the first "woodies," a 1950 Oldsmobile Futuramic 88 Station Wagon.

Location: 702 East D Street, Tacoma, WA 98421. Right off I-5 next to the Tacoma Dome, 30 minutes south of Seattle.

Admission: $$

Hours: Daily, 10 a.m. to 5 p.m.

Phone: (253) 779-8490

Web: www.LemayMuseum.org

Pit Stop

Griot's Garage is a mecca for car-care enthusiasts, many of whom have been shopping online or from its catalog for years but still make the pilgrimage to the Tacoma flagship store. The pristine shop includes a mega-garage where enthusiasts can bring in their autos for a free class on car detailing. Another room highlights rotating collections of themed vintage automobiles. It's hard to walk out of here without wanting to buy a '57 Chevy just so you can wax it. 3333 South 38th Street, Tacoma, WA 98409 (888-246-2646) www.griotsgarage.com.

LeMay Family Collection
Tacoma, WA

The cars are stacked to the gills at the LeMay Family Collection.

The **LeMay Family Collection** grew out of the automotive obsession of one man, Harold LeMay. He grew up as a farm boy, served in World War II, then returned to Tacoma to start what became one of the largest privately owned rubbish-hauling companies in the country. When his collection topped 3,000 vehicles, it was listed in the Guinness Book of Records as the world's "Largest Antique and Vintage Vehicle Collection." The museum sprawls across the former home of the Marymount Military Academy, with cars and memorabilia tucked into every possible corner, including the former showers and indoor rifle range.

Tours of several of the buildings are led by knowledgeable volunteers who are passionate about cars. One of the things that make the LeMay Family Collection unique is its wide range of vehicles on display. Tucked in between the showstoppers are ordinary cars from yesteryear; it's almost like walking across a supermarket parking lot around the year 1972. The collection doesn't stop at cars; there are also fire trucks, wreckers, tractors, and buses on display.

In the White Building, vehicles are stacked in so tightly that some are on a three-tiered rack. Despite the inconvenience of displaying them, they are exchanged frequently with hundreds of cars in off-site storage so those can be seen, too.

A Soviet-built **1974 Gaz Chaika Limousine** sits next to a U.S.-made **1955 Packard** on which it was modeled, highlighting the progress (or lack thereof) of the Soviet automotive industry. The Chaika was so out of style that it's probably the only 1970s car that sported tail fins. The **1948 Tucker** has a special story: It's the one car that always got away from Harold LeMay. In a closing of the circle, his family purchased it after his death.

TV/film cars include a 1**969 Charger "General Lee"** from *The Dukes of Hazzard;* the **1948 DeSoto Suburban Sedan** that was the Cunningham family car on *Happy Days*; and a **1986 Cadillac Brougham** that was used as a presidential limo in *The American President* and *In the Line of Fire.*

A special event occurs on the last Saturday in August, when shuttle buses take visitors a few miles to the LeMay family home; there, another 200+ vehicles are on display. Believe it or not, the family is still adding to the collection. NAAM member.

To see more autos that were owned by LeMay, visit the **LeMay-America's Car Museum** (see prior listing) that was created with a sizable gift of cars from the LeMay family.

Number of vehicles: 500+

Highlights: 1948 Tucker (#7 of 51); 1959 Opel P-1 that set a record for 376 mpg (that's miles per gallon, not mph); 1976 Chevrolet Vega Cosworth; 1938 Graham Custom 97. ***Note:*** For more about the Opel, go to www.376mpg.com.

Location: 325 152nd Street, Tacoma, WA 98445. About eight miles south of **LeMay–America's Car Museum.**

Admission: $$

Hours: Tuesday through Saturday, 10 a.m. to 5 p.m. Regularly scheduled tours of about two hours run throughout the day.

Phone: (253) 272-2336

Web: www.LeMayMarymount.org

ALASKA

Fountainhead Antique Auto Museum
Fairbanks, AK

This museum in central Alaska earns the title for the most remote attraction in this book. Located on the grounds of the Wedgewood Resort, it highlights early American cars from the 1890s through the 1930s, with a special emphasis on makers you won't come across often, including a trio from upstate New York: Buckmobile, Franklin, and the very limited-production Rochester. Several autos in the collection are one of a kind, including a **1921 Heine-Velox Victoria Touring** (at $25,000, it was the most expensive car in the world that year) and a Connecticut-built **1898 Hay Motor Vehicle Stanhope Phaeton.** This four-cylinder prototype was never put into production.

Among the row of "Thirties Classics" are a **1931 Cord Cabriolet L-29,** one of the first production front-wheel-drive models made in America, and a **1932 Cadillac Imperial Limousine,** which boasts a V-16 under its long hood. Detailed placards explain the cars' history, and most of them still run.

The museum also highlights the toughness it takes to go motoring in the 49th state. The walls are plastered with photos of the automobile's early years in Alaska. For those visitors not into driving, there are period fashion displays that tie in with the era of the autos. You can even try on some vintage garb and take a photo behind the wheel of a **1911 Everitt Four-30 Touring.** NAAM member.

Side Trip: If you make it this far, Fairbanks is only 200 miles from the Arctic Circle via the Dalton Highway. Take a road trip north and get a certificate at the Arctic Circle visitor center to prove you made it.

Number of vehicles: 70+

Highlights: 1898 Hay Motor Vehicle; 1906 Pope-Toledo Type XII; 1917 Owen-Magnetic (an early hybrid car); extremely rare 1933 Auburn Model 12-161A Custom Boattail Speedster.

Location: 212 Wedgewood Drive, Fairbanks, AK 99701

Admission: $$

Hours: Summer: Sunday through Thursday, 11 a.m. to 9 p.m.; Friday and Saturday, 11 a.m. to 6 p.m. Winter: Sunday only, noon to 6 p.m. Summer hours are usually Memorial Day through sometime after Labor Day; check the website for updates.

Phone: (907) 450-2100

Web: www.FountainheadMuseum.com

Alaska State Trooper Museum

Anyone who's been caught speeding recognizes this sight.

Because of Alaska's rugged, and a bit offbeat, reputation the state has become ratings bait for reality TV shows. Fans of the National Geographic Channel TV show *Alaska State Troopers* will enjoy learning about their real-life exploits at an Anchorage museum dedicated to them. The official name, the Fraternal Order of Alaska State Troopers Law Enforcement Museum, belies its compact size. Displays give a sense of how difficult it is to police such a sprawling state that endures a harsh climate much of the year. Car buffs will appreciate the restored **1952 Hudson Hornet**. This former trooper vehicle was a speed demon in its day. 245 West 5th Avenue, Anchorage, AK. www.AlaskaTrooperMuseum.com.

INDEX

(Index by states is on page 329.)

Index by States

ABOUT THE AUTHOR

Award-winning travel writer Michael Milne has loved driving since he operated his first pedal car in Ohio. He covers car museums and road trips for *Hemmings Motor News*, *AAA Magazine*, and other media outlets. With his wife, Larissa, he also co-authors the weekly "Field-Tested Travel Tips" column in the *Philadelphia Inquirer.* They spent two years on an epic American road trip, viewing thousands of vintage cars from coast-to-coast, to research this book.

They are also the authors of *Philadelphia Liberty Trail: Trace the Path of America's Heritage,* which takes a revolutionary approach to the city's historic district. Global nomads since 2011, Larissa and Michael write about their adventures at www.ChangesInLongitude.com.

Note: Every attempt is made to keep the information in this book up to date. If you find something that's changed, or an attraction that you feel should be included in the next edition, please contact me at Michael@ChangesInLongitude.com.

If you enjoyed this book, please leave a review of it on Amazon. I greatly appreciate it.

Acknowledgments:

Thank you to:

Paula Fuchsberg
Jerry Milne
Rod Willis
Jeff Thorneycroft
Michael McNessor
Ann Hemken

Thank you to all the guides who patiently and enthusiastically walked me through their museums.

Crew Chiefs whose encouragement helped make this book possible:

John Discepoli
Wayne Weaver
Marc d'Entremont

Book layout by Alistair Lowde